Prospecting Your Way to Sales Success

How to Find New Business by
Phone, Fax, Internet, and Other New Media

Bill Good

Scribner

SCRIBNER and design are trademarks of Jossey-Bass, Inc.,
used under license by Simon & Schuster, the publisher of this work.

DESIGNED BY PAUL DIPPOLITO

Set in Caledonia

Manufactured in the United States of America

10   9   8   7   6   5   4

Library of Congress Cataloging-in-Publication Data
Good, Bill.
Prospecting your way to sales success : how to find new busi-
ness by phone, fax, internet, and other new media / Bill Good.
p. cm.
Originally published: 1986.
1. Selling. 2. Telephone selling. I. Title.
HF5438.25.G65   1997
658.85—dc21   97-18085
CIP

ISBN 0-684-84203-3

Contents

Acknowledgments   6
Introduction   7

1   Prospecting: The Old School vs. the New School   15
2   Pick the Cherries, Not the Pits: The New Way to Prospect   23
3   The Variables   43
4   The Campaign Development Checklist   49
5   Filling the Bathtub: List Development and Improvement   55
6   How to Keep the Bathtub Full: More on List Development   74
7   List Management   92
8   The Campaign Objective   116
9   The Campaign Style   122
10 The Offer   128
11 To Script or Not to Script: What You Say   132
12 Script Rewriting: How to Have Professionally Written
    Scripts If You're Not a Professional Writer   143
13 More Lead Generation Scripts   167
14 Lead Processing Scripts and Voice Mail   197
15 Lead Processing Letters   209
16 Direct-Mail Letters: How to Have Good Letters Even If
    You're Not a Good Letter Writer   220
17 Getting Letters Out the Door   236
18 How You Sound   241
19 How to Make More Calls   250
20 Breakout: Putting It All Together   274
21 For Managers Only: How to Work Magic with Your
    Sales Force   289

    Index   309

Acknowledgments

Looking back, there were many who helped.

My Mom and Dad, my Mom for the joy of learning, my Dad for the joy of life.

Herb Hazelman, my band director at Greensboro Senior High. Before excellence was a fad, he demanded it. And in the process of teaching music, he taught so much more.

Mrs. Weaver and Mrs. Winchester, two ninth grade teachers who made a difference, and who still do.

My wife Joava. After months of preparation, I was ready to start my business, but had less than a thousand dollars to live on. Too risky. So I told her I was going to wait. She took me on a walk around the block. She asked, "What's the worst that could happen?" I replied, "We'd go broke, the creditors would get the furniture and car, and we would have to go on welfare?" "Do you think you could ever work again?" she wanted to know. "Sure," I said. "A good salesman can always work." "So what are you going to do?" "I'm going to go for it." Without that nudge, I might not have done it. Life since would not have been as much fun.

Howard Shenson, president of Howard L. Shenson, Inc. When I met Howard in 1977, he was "big time" in the seminars business. I was trying to figure out how to get started. I called and asked him for help. He gave a lot. And if I have made a success at it, he pointed the way.

Barry Weiner, president of Homeowners Marketing Service. When I didn't have the money to promote my first seminar, he let me slip a brochure in his own customer mailing and didn't charge me for it.

The late L. Ron Hubbard. Beneath the controversy, such wisdom. Anyone who is serious at all about improving their communication and organizational skills will study the works of this giant.

And of course, my staff at Telephone Marketing, Inc.

E-mail or write to the following:

E-mail: JZRAI9A@Prodigy.com

Fax: (801) 572-1496

Mail: Bill Good, Bill Good Marketing, Inc., 406 West South Jordan Parkway, South Jordan, UT 84095

Introduction

This book is about one thing and one thing only: SALES PROSPECT-ING. In it I'll show you how to find more and better prospects. For you this means only two things: more sales and more MONEY.

So, the goal of this book is to help you make more sales and more money by improving the quantity and quality of your prospects. Whatever your level of selling skill, if you have more and better prospects, you will make more sales and more MONEY.

We will use several tools in our search for prospects.

We'll use the telephone. Properly used, it's faster and more effective than wearing out shoe leather.

We'll use the mail. There are a variety of ways to use direct-mail letters. You can use them to replace the telephone altogether or to supplement the phone.

We'll use some "new media." A rapidly growing portion of my own sales prospecting uses e-mail. Today, there are millions of people on the move. They are in one city today, another one tomorrow. Forget about trying to call them or sending any mail. But they do pick up their e-mail every morning. So you have to know how to use it.

We'll also talk about faxes. Instead of waiting a few days to mail a prospect requested information, you can deliver it right now. And why not?

As you know, there is a problem with the phone. Most salespeople would rather do almost anything than prospect by phone, and indeed some get to the point where they believe the phone weighs five hundred pounds or may even be one of the new models that only accept incoming calls. If this describes you, you've got the right book, because I'm going to show you how to enjoy prospecting more. (OK, you may be among those who will never like prospecting. But if you follow my methods, I promise you will SUFFER LESS.)

Who Should Read This Book?

Notice I said "Who should read this book?" I naturally think everyone should buy one. But once you've bought it, don't read it unless you're "qualified." And by that I mean:

- You don't like prospecting and would prefer a visit to the dentist or at least would prefer to do something else. If you like it, chances are you're good at it. And unless you want to get better at it, after you've bought the book, just pass it along to a friend.

- You need more prospects. If you have all the prospective customers you need, you obviously don't have to study up on how to get more.

- You can find "enough" prospects' names with addresses and phone numbers.

To see if you're qualified to read this book, we need to spend a little time on the question: Can you get enough names? That is, are there enough prospective customers out there for your product or service?

Can You Get Enough Names?

The answer to the question is, ultimately, a matter of numbers. How many is "enough"? The rule of thumb I work with is "several hundred." Depending on your market, to begin a profitable prospecting campaign, you need to be able to identify several hundred potential buyers.

Let's take an example of when there are *not* enough. Let's say you are an account executive for a creative advertising house specializing in print ads for motion pictures. You might have as few as twenty-five to thirty prospects, all motion picture studios. That's twenty-five or thirty in the whole United States! So you can't afford to waste a single one. You have an extremely limited market, and some prospecting approach would have to be followed other than the one I will outline in this book. My methods do *allow* for waste and mistakes.

If you have an extremely limited market, your method for prospecting it will most likely have to be based on some version of the "old boy" network. Your success will depend on who you know and how well you know them.

By way of contrast, let's take a look at some markets that clearly lend themselves to a telephone-prospecting campaign:

- Computer sales: There are new companies popping up all over the place. New companies need new computers. How do you find these new businesses? How do you contact them? Well, you'll learn about that.

- Credit collection account sales: Let's say you work for a company that pursues people who don't pay their bills. The techniques you will learn here won't necessarily help you track down the deadbeats, but they will help you track down the business that needs to buy your services.

- Residential real estate: Sixteen percent of the American population moves each year, according to a 1996 study by The Employee Relocation Council. If you are in residential real estate, you need to find the people who are thinking about a move and develop a relationship *before* they decide to put the house on the market. When they're ready to move, you will have a good shot at the listing. Clearly this market is big enough to support a prospecting campaign.

- Commercial real estate: With all the change, expansion, and contraction of new businesses being formed and old businesses being bought, sold, and going bankrupt, there is a constant need for commercial offices and buildings. In any of the major metropolitan markets, the telephone is usually the prospecting method of choice. However, you will learn a vital role for direct mail as well.

- Securities industry: My company, Bill Good Marketing, Inc., has trained tens of thousands of stockbrokers, financial consultants, investment management consultants, and financial planners since 1980, and any hour of the day, someone I have trained can pick up the phone and find two to four *good prospects* in that single hour! We have perfected direct-mail techniques for this industry and others as well.

- Insurance: One out of nine adults in the United States will buy life insurance this year. In virtually every state, anyone with a driver's license is required by law to have automobile insurance.

- Dentistry: Some years ago, I read an article that said 45 percent of the population does not have a regular dentist. I applied the principles I'll be teaching you to that market and created a low-key prospecting campaign that generated eighty-two new patients in the first month for our "test dentist." His previous record was thirty-five new patients in a single month.

- Home repair, home improvement, and automobile sales: These quite obviously lend themselves to a prospecting campaign. What about all those car salesmen you see waiting in line at the dealership for a prospect to come in the front door? If I were running those dealerships, there wouldn't be a line of salespeople. They would all be on the phones, with only one person waiting.

- Banking: This is a natural in today's deregulated business climate.

- Office equipment and supplies: Obviously.

- Books, educational materials, and instruction of any kind can be prospected for by phone. As a matter of fact, I have a $40 University of

North Carolina Alumni Association Directory sitting on my bookshelf as the result of a talented, pleasant saleswoman.

Go through any issue of a daily newspaper and you'll see the tremendous application prospecting can have for finding customers. Here are some applications I got by going through one issue of one paper:

Season tickets to sporting events

Furniture

Telephone campaigns to credit card holders at department stores

Temporary employment agencies

Executive placement agencies

Classified ad sales

Display ad sales for newspapers

Book sales

New members for churches

Prepaid funeral services

Newspaper subscriptions

Family portraits

Chimney cleaning

Photocopiers

If your product or service fits or resembles any of these categories, read on!

Who Shouldn't Read This Book

This book is not for superstars or those who aspire to superstar status. A superstar is a "natural" salesperson. Occasionally, such people write books, and a typical book jacket will read: "Roland Macho was, at age thirteen, the youngest million-dollar salesman ever. By fifteen, he had purchased his own insurance agency and was well on his way to his second million. Now he shares his secrets with you."

Or, "By age eight, Joanne Macha had sold more lemonade at her stand at the corner of 8th and Grand than has ever been sold in the history of the world. By age eleven, she had 11,467 people in her direct-marketing group, and is listed in the *Guinness Book of Records* as the most successful child since Mozart. You, too, can learn the secrets of MILLION DOLLAR selling by reading her book."

These people are superstars, and this book is not for them. Nor is it for people who are on a fast track to achieve superstar status. The typical superstar can sell "ice to Eskimos" and, frankly, can do things that you and I could never do, and possibly would not do even if we could.

Three Steps to Success

Notice I include myself in that category of nonsuperstars. As a salesman, I'm good. I can sell most any decent product. But I am not one of those who can sell something to someone who doesn't want it. I concentrate on finding people who need what I've got and then get them excited about it. If you follow this approach, closing the sale is no big deal.

My own abilities to practice what I will preach have brought me and my company from nowhere to the front page of the *Wall Street Journal;* to guest appearances on the most highly rated business radio talk show in the country; to training accounts with many of the country's major financial services firms, insurance companies, and real estate firms; to speaking engagements in England, Brazil, Canada, and Puerto Rico, as well as thousands in the United States; to prime-time TV appearances; to a monthly column in *Research Magazine,* the major trade magazine in the securities industry; and to a keynote address before the Securities Industry Association in Philadelphia.

To succeed in sales, as I have, you need only to do three things:

1. Find a product or service you like, know, and believe in and which people need and want.

2. Develop a way to find those who want it and can afford it NOW!

3. Have a well-designed sales presentation, and two or three different closes.

In this book, we'll be concentrating on Step Number 2: developing a way to find those who want it and can afford it NOW! As you get into the book, you'll see that we'll really just be talking commonsense methods. You'll wonder why no one ever taught them to you before.

The origin of these ideas goes back to my first selling job, selling dictionaries door-to-door for Southwest Publishing Company one summer while I was in college. Not only was I not a superstar, but I found the entire process of sales so frightening that I used to get sick every morning at the very thought of being rejected.

I can recall hours spent and gallons of gas wasted while I drove around looking for the perfect house—the one that contained a buyer, someone who would welcome my approach, who needed my dictionary, and who could afford the $10 to buy it.

Admittedly, the idea that I could identify a guaranteed buyer by looking at the outside of a house was flaky at best, But the germ of the idea—that there ought to be a way to find *good* prospects—was right. Frankly, this book is proof that my misguided search actually paid off. Of course, I never did learn how to identify the perfect house merely by looking at it. But I guessed then, and I know now, that there had to be a better way to find business than talking to everyone on the block.

I figured that there were indeed people somewhere who needed what I had to offer. The trick was simply to find them. The answer, ultimately, was simple. Not necessarily easy. Just simple.

What You Will Learn

To improve your sales and commissions by improving the quantity and quality of your prospects, you'll need to know some things you don't know now. Among other things, I'll show you:

- How to become the "rejector," not the "rejectee." We'll end the pain of prospecting at a single stroke.

- How to develop lists of qualified prospects who are likely to be interested in your product or service and want it NOW.

- How to deal with voice mail and screeners. If your blood pressure rises at the thought of being put on hold by just one more screener, you're in for a treat.

- How to design a prospecting call that can help you find out if a particular prospect is right for your business.

- How to make more calls than you ever dreamed possible. Since the birth of business, sales trainers have preached that "sales is a numbers game." I'm going to show you how to make the hidden truth in the numbers game work for you, not against you.

- How to run different kinds of campaigns. Instead of being a one-trick pony, you'll have lots of different approaches to any market. And you'll know how to find the one that's best for you.

- Very important, you will learn how to keep track of hundreds of prospects before they become clients.

Free Material to Download

Part of what you get by buying this book are the passwords to the *Prospecting Your Way to Sales Success* section of my home page. There, you can download various scripts, letters, checklists, and cheatsheets. Since I have designed the web page for people who buy *and read* this book, I have buried the various passwords throughout the text. You'll just have to buy and read the book to find them. Fair enough?

A Warning

The methods I will outline are simple, but they do require some old-fashioned hard work.

Not pressure.

Not force.

Just hard work.

So if you are browsing through the introduction of this book before buying it, and if it looks like something you might benefit from, then go ahead. It will make your life in sales easier and more enjoyable. And you'll certainly enjoy more good prospects than you have ever dreamed possible.

So did you want one book or two?

Cash, check, or charge?

1

Prospecting

The Old School vs.
the New School

"Don't throw good money after bad."

—Bill Good, age nine

My family frequently went to dinner at the S&W Cafeteria in Greensboro, North Carolina. They had some kind of wishing well in the lobby. My brother Ed was throwing handfuls of coins in it. I said, "Ed, quit it! Don't throw good money after bad." As near as I can figure, some fellow who worked for an ad agency overheard my comment. He ran some kind of local ad with a picture of a kid throwing money in a wishing well and used my statement as a slogan. Whatever he was selling never caught on. But within a matter of months, my statement became known worldwide.

Many of the famous statements you have grown up with were actually said first by me. From ages nine to eleven, I was, frankly, precocious. Many of my comments on life were picked up by others and even made into advertising or political slogans. I never received credit or money. By age eleven, I realized that others were profiting from my comments, and so I shut up for a long time. With the publication of this book, however, I decided to accept the recognition due the authorship of these statements. You will find many of them in *Bartlett's Familiar Quotations.* Look in the author section under "Anon."

You came into sales to sell, but it's not working out that way. Perhaps you wanted to be a financial adviser and help people make their fortune (as well as your own, of course). You didn't think most of your time would be spent making phone calls in an endless search for people with money. And worse, you had no idea that people wouldn't welcome your call. After all, you have ideas that should help people get a better return on their money than they now enjoy.

Or perhaps you're in real estate. You wanted to help people find new homes, not spend hours sitting at an open house that no one attends, or walking door-to-door to meet the neighbors. And just last week, a dog scared you half to death as it lunged at you from under a shrub.

Or you sell life insurance. You know that if you can help one or two families each week protect their assets and provide for their families, you can make a very good living in the process.

You found out in a hurry, of course, that most people really don't want to talk to a life insurance agent. But not even in your most pessimistic brooding about your future did you realize it could be as bad as it really is.

The problem is really driven home to you at your wife's company Christmas party. She had warned you not to talk business, but in the back of your mind, you had an idea that people would at least want to know about some of the new life insurance products on the market.

Drink in hand, you bided your time, then, as expected, someone asked what you do for a living.

"I'm a life insurance agent," you said.

You might as well have said, "I'm a mentally disordered sex offender currently under psychiatric care." The room couldn't have emptied out any faster.

Now, you certainly didn't come into sales to frighten or offend people.

The Problem with Sales Is Prospecting!

Where did all the prospects go? Are there just too many salespeople, or did something happen to scare them off?

Worse, the longer you've been in sales, the more you hate prospecting. Why? They turn you down, reject you. And because they reject you and because prospects are so hard to come by, you try harder and harder. And the harder you try, the more scared they get.

It's interesting that the major problem in sales is not really a problem with sales. It's a *prospecting* problem. And that problem is scarcity. Most salespeople act as if there are too few good prospects.

The reason you are reading this book is that *you don't have enough prospects.* If you had all you could handle, you certainly wouldn't be looking at a book on prospecting. Yes, I am very well aware that 99 percent of the salespeople in this country believe that rejection is THE PROBLEM. But that's not it. If you *really believed* that there were enough prospects for you, would you care if some jerk hung up on you? But since you and most other salespeople believe—consciously or subconsciously—that prospects are scarce, then rejection threatens survival. And that hurts.

So rejection is not the problem in sales. Nor is it closing, a lack of product or service knowledge, too high a price, the "competition," or poor company advertising. The problem is *scarcity of prospects.* But we live in a country of 266 million people. How can prospects be scarce?

Julius Caesar said, "The fault, dear Brutus, is not in our stars, but in ourselves, that we are underlings."

I say, "The reason for a scarcity of prospects lies not in the market but in our method." And that method is one I call the Old School.

The Old School Style of Selling

Every sales trainer I ever had, plus all that I've read, has focused on overcoming objections and on closing. J. Douglas Edwards, perhaps the best of what I call the Old School trainers, preached that "half of your sales will be made after the prospect has said no six times." Mona Ling, a prominent trainer in the insurance industry, promotes "tested answers" to life insurance objections. A flyer promoting a set of cassette tapes came across my desk recently featuring a photo of the trainer and the back end of his car. His vanity license plate said, "CLOSER."

This concentration on closing and overcoming objections has defined a lifestyle for countless millions of salespeople. In order to understand fully the fact that this is not another book in that tradition, I do think we should spend a few minutes highlighting the Old School. Then you will understand what my system *isn't.*

Old School Teachings

If you have been around sales more than one day, I am certain you have heard one or more versions of the three principles summarized below. I personally have no idea where I first heard them and doubt if anyone should be given credit, or blame, as the case may be. At any rate, here are the philosophical foundations of the Old School.

- All buyers are liars.
- Don't believe the prospect until he or she has said no three, six, twelve, or twenty-seven times.
- Every no gets you that much closer to a yes.

As you can well imagine, if you believe these principles, they will affect the way you live your life. If you sell insurance, when the prospect says no, you will press ahead anyway thinking you are that much closer to a yes. If you are a financial adviser or planner and the prospect tells you he or she doesn't have any money now, you won't believe him or her but will charge forward anyway, ruining the prospect's evening and your own when the prospect tells you which anatomical portion should receive your solicitation.

Most Old School salespeople, consciously or otherwise, believe and act as if there is a war between buyer and seller, and that your job as seller is to win! "We Shall Overcome" was not just the theme song of the civil rights movement. It's a song the "sales movement" has been singing for generations. It's one reason your call usually isn't welcome. Too many generations of prospects have been overcome.

Applying Old School Principles

If you work in insurance, real estate, most financial services (except, of course, where my company does the training!), appliances, automobiles, or just about anything else, you have most likely been trained in the Old School—*if you have had any training at all.* If you have had no formal training, you've still gotten the Old School message. Like a powerful undertow, whenever you put a toe in the sales water, it's tugging on you.

Let's assume, for the sake of argument, that you are a salesperson in a financial services company. Perhaps you sell stocks and bonds. As I am sure you will recognize, the yarn I'm going to spin for you is all too typical. If you don't recognize yourself as the key player, I'm sure you know someone to whom this applies directly.

So let's assume you are fairly new in the business, and your branch manager or sales manager has made it perfectly clear that you are expected to cold call—that is, phone someone to whom you've never spoken before—at least five hours a day and probably a couple of evenings each week. On your part, you would much rather wait for someone to call you or at least be provided with twenty or thirty direct-mail leads each week.

But—as you learn to your dismay—it doesn't work that way. So you decide to take the plunge one evening when no one is in the office. You sit down at your phone and start calling. Before long, you get Dr. Jones on the phone.

Now, you happen to have heard that Dr. Jones has a $300,000 annual income, lives in a $600,000 home, and that he and his spouse, Dr. Smith-Jones, drive his-and-hers Mercedes. This couple would, of course, be highly desirable customers.

Here's how the usual conversation goes:

> YOU: (*Ring, ring.*)
> DR. JONES: Hello.

YOU:	May I speak with Dr. Jones, please?
DR. JONES:	Speaking.
YOU:	Dr. Jones, this is Fred Smithers with Beam of Light Financial Services.
DR. JONES (*interrupting*):	Excuse me, but I am really not interested.

Before continuing with this now classic conversation, let's review your Old School training.

First of all, you will undoubtedly have been trained to persist. In sales school, you probably heard countless anecdotes about how various superstar salespeople have persisted and triumphantly returned with the prized order. Plus, your sales manager or your peers will have surely relayed some or all of these Old School gems of wisdom:

- "No is just a stepping stone on the way to yes."

- "The more nos you get, the closer you are to a yes."

- "No is simply a misunderstanding on the part of the prospect and is just a way of saying that he or she requires additional information."

With these philosophical pearls jangling loose in your purse or pocket, let's pick up on your conversation with Dr. Jones, who was saying:

DR. JONES:	I am really not interested.
YOU:	Of course you're not interested. If you had been interested, you would have called me, right?
DR. JONES (*angrily*):	I guess I would, but I didn't. So what does that tell you?
YOU:	I understand you are not interested, Doctor. But let me just ask you this: What are you interested in?
DR. JONES:	I'm not interested in you. I'm not interested in Beam of Light Financial Services. But I'm very interested in my dinner, and besides, I'm busy.
YOU:	I understand you're busy. I find that most of my clients are busy and it's for that reason that . . .
DR. JONES:	(*Click. Dial tone.*)
YOU:	Sigh. (*Addressing room at large*) I wonder what I did wrong?

From the Old School point of view, you certainly must have done something wrong. Weakness? Wimpy tone in voice? Failure to persist? Insufficient goal orientation? Bad phone breath? Sadly, you recall the words of Old School trainer J. Douglas Edwards, who said that half of your sales would be made after the prospect has said no six times. So sitting there with a long face and with a fly buzzing obnoxiously about the pizza crust on the table, you reflect on the magic number *six*.

"If only I could have gotten Dr. Jones to say no six times," you say to the fly, "I might have gotten his account. But," you say to the coffee cup with bits of creamer curdling on the surface, "Rome wasn't built in a day."

And so you grind through another eight or twelve calls, and not one sale or appointment do you get. At the end of an hour, you feel as if you have been passed back and forth through a paper shredder. You're tired and discouraged.

Walking toward the door, you make a face at Dr. Jones's prospect card, which you have taped to your phone to remind yourself to call him tomorrow and grind a few more nos out of him.

As you lock up, a terrible thought strikes. There was that videotape you saw in training. What was it the trainer said? Was it, "Don't believe the prospect until he has said no twenty-seven times?" It couldn't have been!

Poor you. You couldn't even get Dr. Jones to say it six times.

What a Way to Make a Living!

Now I submit to you that the Old School *is* one hell of a way to make a living. If you happen to be brand new to sales and think I exaggerate that people are trained this way, just pick up any other sales book or attend any sales meeting anywhere. (Definite exception: sales organizations that have had my training.)

If you would like to conduct your own tests of Old School methods, by all means verify the following:

1. It's very hard on the salesperson. If you don't already hate prospecting, you probably will—if you stick to Old School methods.

2. It is very hard on prospects. Why do you think the room empties out when a life insurance agent introduces himself? It's not the product. People buy it every day. It's the sales method. After decades of nail-pulling sales methods, people have finally come to believe that a session with a life insurance agent will be unpleasant. And so it is.

But, lest you think that this school of sales is entirely without redeeming social value, it did serve its purpose. Undoubtedly it came of age in an era in which the old-time peddler could not make more than one call a day. And in the old days, if you didn't sell on that one call, you didn't eat.

Today we live in an entirely different era in sales. Instead of being limited to one call a day, you can cover more territory by phone in an hour than the old-time salesperson could in a week, or even a month. In seconds, you can blast out an e-mail broadcast to prequalified clients and prospects. While you are wrapping up a sale or setting up an appointment, your personal computer can be cracking out twelve letters a minute. And who knows how many people can check your latest price quote on your company's web page?

It's a different world. Yet the old methods, unfortunately, still persist.

This book, however, is most definitely not about this Old School style of selling.

It's about what I'll call the New School.

The New School

The system of prospecting I'm going to outline relies upon two very basic assumptions:

1. There are enough prospects in your market area who are *interested and qualified today* to make it worthwhile to look for them and to ignore the rest.

By "interested," I mean INTERESTED. Ask a child, "Are you interested in ice cream?" The child's yes is the one I'm talking about. Ask the child, "Are you interested in going into the backyard and weeding the garden?" That no is the one Old School salespeople grind away on in their misguided efforts to convince the child there is some remote benefit in weeding the garden.

By "qualified," I mean "has capability to buy NOW." In different industries, *being qualified* will, of course, mean different things.

As I pointed out in the Introduction, you need several hundred prospect names. I guarantee you that unless you have an extremely limited market, you can develop a simple way to look for those who are interested and qualified NOW. No problem.

As you will see, we can approach this market in a variety of ways. We can use the telephone, direct mail, fax, e-mail, or almost any combination of the above. But whatever the method, I'll show you how to *find* prospects who are INTERESTED and QUALIFIED.

2. Not all "buyers are liars." In fact, we'll assume the opposite, that buyers tend to be truth tellers.

The idea that "buyers are liars" is the fundamental assumption on which the Old School is based. The Old School believes that if someone tells you they're not interested, what they really mean is "I need additional information." Or, when buyers tell you, "I don't have any money," what they really mean is "I don't have any money for that idea, but if you come up with another idea, of course I could raise the money."

I call this "translating English into English." And it assumes the prospect doesn't know his or her own mind or is spinning a lie.

Frankly, if you treat people as if they are lying or don't know their own mind, you shouldn't be surprised if they don't respond well to your sales message. Undoubtedly, there are many people out there who will lie to you, who will create a smoke screen to tell you they're not interested when they are, and who will rely on other subterfuge to mislead you. Yes, their lies and smoke screens can be penetrated by Old School selling. But my question to you is: Do you want a customer list full of liars?

You can build a selling system on one of two assumptions. First, you can assume, along with the prophets of the Old School, that many buyers are indeed liars. If you make that assumption, you must follow it with all of the various techniques to overcome opposition. You must be prepared to suffer endless rejection, and you must continue the endless process of translating English into English. Or, second, you can shed the Old School and join the New School and make life almost infinitely easier.

The implications for your daily activity of what I just told you are quite profound.

Remember Dr. Jones, who got the call from Beam of Light Financial Services? Here's how a practitioner of the New School would have handled it.

YOU:	May I speak with Dr. Jones, please?
DR. JONES:	Speaking.
YOU:	Dr. Jones, this is Fred Smithers with Beam of Light Financial Services.
DR. JONES *(interrupting)*:	Excuse me, but I am really not interested.
YOU:	Thankyouverymuch for your time. Have a great day. *(Click. Dial tone.)*

Thankyouverymuch, uttered as a single word, becomes the modern equivalent of *Hiyo Silver* and you disappear into the electronic haze of the telephone system in search of a prospect.

So, let's leave the Old School and its tired, old methods and go in search of the New School, a better way to prospect.

You have been spending a lot of time and money on the Old School. Now it's time to follow my advice: "Don't throw good money after bad," OK?

CHAPTER 2

Pick the Cherries Not the Pits:

The New Way to Prospect

"Actions speak louder than words."

—Bill Good, age eleven

This statement had such an innocent start. My mother had promised to give me my allowance a day early so I could go to the movies. I kept reminding her, and she kept saying, "Just as soon as I finish getting ready for the party." And then, "I promise I will give it to you as soon as I get back from the store." Finally, in desperation, I said, "Mom! Actions speak louder than words. I want my money!" She was so taken with my formulation of this concept that she not only gave me my money, but mentioned what I had said at the bridge club that night. One of her guests worked at one of the big textile mills in Greensboro. They were involved in a contract dispute with a local union. They ran a big ad in the *Greensboro Daily News* telling the union to put up or shut up (also one of mine). The statement became known worldwide, and no one gave me credit.

Many of the examples in this chapter seem to apply to prospecting via an outgoing phone call. However, as you will see, there are lots of ways to find a good prospect. Whether you are using the phone to make the initial contact, using the phone to follow up an incoming ad call, or going door-to-door, you will find the principles discussed in this chapter apply 100 percent.

Now that I've given the Old School a blow to the head, I had better offer something in its place. And that's what I am going to do in this chapter. Indeed, the remainder of this book is designed to replace that tired, worn-out way of prospecting.

Prospecting

Frequently in my training seminars I ask all the trainees in the room to close their eyes. I then say, "Create a picture in your mind of a prospector." When I see they have done that, I then ask them to open their eyes and tell me what they saw. Most people report seeing an old man with a mule, a pick on his shoulder, and a big pack on the back of the mule. Well, we're going to talk about prospecting in exactly the same sense as the old gold prospector.

A decent dictionary definition of the term "prospecting" is: "the act of searching for something of value." And that is exactly what the old gold prospector did.

Once gold was discovered in California, people came by the millions. They came to California because gold had been found there. They didn't stop in Fort Lauderdale or detour through Rio de Janeiro or Easter Island. They were heading for gold-rush country! When they got there, they looked for certain geological signs that told them gold might be found in one spot rather than another. Among the things they looked for were deposits of black sand, a heavy, iron-based sand. If there was any gold around, it would be mixed in with that sand. After the old prospector staked his claim, he would shovel the sand into his gold pan, and from that point on his primary interest was getting rid of the dirt. Gold prospecting *was and still is primarily the act of discarding that which is not gold.* The prospector gets rid of such things as dirt, grit, gravel, mud, and twigs. And assuming there is gold in his sample to begin with, the more "nongold" he discards, the more gold he finds.

So, if the New School has historical roots, they are in the California goldfields, and not with the old-time peddler. In New School prospecting, the first thing you do is: *disqualify nonbuyers.* The Old School sales trainer counsels various techniques that enable the salesperson to hang on to anyone who will speak with him or her. But the New School prospector says, "If it don't glitter, it's dirt and out it goes."

So from the New School point of view, let's rerun the phone call you made to Dr. Jones:

YOU:	*(Ring, ring.)*
DR. JONES:	Hello.
YOU:	May I speak with Dr. Jones, please?
DR. JONES:	Speaking.
YOU:	Dr. Jones, this is Fred Smithers with Beam of Light Financial Services.
DR. JONES *(interrupting)*:	Excuse me, but I am really not interested.
YOU:	Sorry to have bothered you. Thankyouverymuch for your time. *(Click. Dial tone.)*

That was easy, wasn't it?

Since you didn't try to twist Dr. Jones's arm, you at least didn't make an enemy. And he certainly didn't have time to insult you and then grind it in by hanging up on you.

Simple, right?

Right.

The First Principle of New School Prospecting

Here is a question for you to consider: What effect do you think you would have on people if, instead of attempting to *keep* everyone you talk to, you try and get rid of them? How will they react? While you're pondering your answers, let me tell you something that happened to me.

One benefit to owning my kind of business is I can live where I want. In 1980, I moved from Los Angeles to Sandy, Utah, which is just south of Salt Lake City. Not long after we had arrived and settled in, I got an idea. One thing you'll learn as we progress through this book is that I've had lots of ideas. Some of them are very good, which is why I'm not poor. But some of the ideas have been real turkeys. Probably the reason my company is alive and well is that I kept the good ideas and packed the others off to the great turkey farm in the file cabinet.

At any rate, this particular idea dealt with how to promote our "Public Seminar," which, at the time, focused on telephone prospecting only. Offered by Bill Good Marketing, Inc., it was to be a seminar on telephone prospecting to which salespeople in every industry are invited. Some of our programs are geared to the specific needs of a single company or industry, but the public seminar is one virtually anyone could profit from.

The idea went like this: I wonder if I can send out a cassette tape of my sales presentation, get various sales managers to play it for their crew, and get some of them so excited that they would show up at a seminar. By doing that, I would at least not have to make that same presentation over and over and over.

It sounded like a good idea to me, so I made up about twenty copies of a cassette tape, prepared some written material, and then one morning sat down with the *Salt Lake Tribune,* cut out some ads that contained phone numbers, and started calling. (I've always liked calling people who pay money to publish their phone numbers. They tend to answer the phone on or before the third ring.)

One of the first people I called was the local representative of a very well known sales training course. I figured it would be quite a score to sell them a prospecting course.

The conversation went like this:

ME:	Mr. Jones, this is Bill Good with Bill Good Marketing. We specialize in training salespeople to find new business by phone. Tell me, is the telephone at all important to you as a marketing tool?
MR. JONES:	Well, yes. It is.
ME:	Very good. We're having a seminar on February 9 in the Salt Lake Hilton. We have prepared a free cassette tape that will tell you all about it. Would you like to receive a copy of this tape?
MR. JONES:	Well . . . you can send it out if you want. We would probably listen to it.
ME:	Well, Mr. Jones, it sounds to me like you have everything under control there. Since this tape costs us $1.52 to get out the door, if you don't mind I'll just pass at this time. So, thankyouverymuch. *(Click. Dial tone.)*

Now, there probably isn't one of you reading this book who would have just tossed Mr. Jones out of the gold pan as I did. Where there's life, there's hope, right? (I made this statement at age eleven when a friend said that her mom was hopeless. I said, "Where there's life, there's hope." Someone overheard it and mentioned it to our preacher, who used it in a sermon. The rest, as I said later, is history.)

So why did I hang up on him?

I hung up on him because he was *not interested enough!* I knew I could probably have sold this man a seminar ticket, or perhaps several. But I also knew that to do it, I would have had to first send him the tape, then call him back six times before he would play it for his salespeople. And then I would have had to call him back another three times to find out how many people would be coming to the seminar.

I also knew that I could take the same amount of time I would have spent with him, call rapidly down my list, and find someone who was *very interested* in attending one of my programs.

Yes, I know it's possible to sell people who are initially not interested. But your time is much better spent by letting those who are not interested go and looking for someone who is. There is no shortage of good prospects!!!

When you find someone who is interested in your product, the relationship goes so much more smoothly that it makes sales a joy, rather than the agony of tooth extraction that many sales trainers have made it.

So the first principle of the New School is:

☞ *When the prospect says, "I'm not interested," believe him or her. Politely hang up. Go find someone who is interested.*

The Thoughts Behind the Words

I want to introduce you to another concept that plays a key role in this prospecting system. According to me, "Actions speak louder than words."

Obviously, verbal communication means words. But there should also be some physical action. By combining action with words, you enormously increase the power of the communication. So let's take a look at the communication I delivered to Mr. Jones. When I withdrew my offer to send the tape (action) and told him I felt he had everything under control, I delivered another communication as well.

Didn't I tell him that unless he was really interested, I wasn't?

Didn't I also tell him I had all the business I could handle?

Suppose I had taken the flicker of interest he showed and just jumped down his throat. What would my actions have said about my product? Wouldn't my actions have said, "This is hard to sell. So just show me a glimmer of interest, and we're going to the mat."

What did I say when I told him that I was not going to send him the tape because it cost $1.52? Didn't I tell him—by my actions—that he was worth less than $1.52? And finally, what did I say when I just hung up, politely, of course? Didn't I say, "Listen, Mr. Jones. There are a lot of people out there who would love to know about this program. So while you're sitting there thinking about it, I'll go find them and you'll miss out"?

In short, I delivered a big package of communication to Mr. Jones in just a few words. That's how to put power in your words. Use just a few words and communicate the rest of the thought with an action.

After all, actions do speak louder than words.

The Second Principle of New School Prospecting

The story of Mr. Jones is obviously incomplete as it now stands and, of course, it has a happy ending. Here is what actually happened.

When I'm testing a marketing idea, I do what we call Stage I testing. In Stage I, I normally write a script, get an idea for a prospect list or two (I'll explain more about this in Chapters 12 and 13), and then make calls myself to see if it works. I work out any bugs I find and then, when I can make it work, I turn it over to someone else in my organization for Stage II.

In Stage II, someone I have trained makes a lot of phone calls to see if my initial results continue to hold. In this case, I turned the test over to Jill Olsen, then my assistant and now the senior executive of marketing at Bill Good Marketing, Inc.

At this point in our testing, we weren't too concerned with finding out which prospect list was best, so Jill just grabbed the Chamber of Commerce Directory. She started calling and before long she managed to encounter the same Mr. Jones I had spoken with on the first day of my test. The conversation went like this:

JILL:	Mr. Jones, this is Jill Olsen with Bill Good Marketing.
MR. JONES *(interrupting)*:	Are you the folks trying to give away that tape?
JILL *(no clue where that remark comes from)*:	Yes, we are.
MR. JONES:	I want one.

Needless to say, this time he got a tape. And sent two people to the course.

So we can conclude:

☞ *You can call a list of prospects more than once if you don't rough them up the first time.*

How Many Times Can You Recycle a List?

As you'll see in the chapters on list development, a "good list" is quite obviously an important part of the New School system. Wouldn't it be wonderful if you didn't have to keep developing new lists of potential customers, but could use some of the old ones over and over? And what if they got better, not worse?

In other words, if you can call back a list once, maybe you can call it back several times. How many times can you call a list? To answer that question, let's talk for a moment about our friend, the gold prospector.

Now this old codger went up into northern California, found himself a claim on a pretty stream, and dug a couple of ounces of gold right away. At the end of the first day, you can suppose that he had a tough question to answer: What shall I do tomorrow? Well, if you were the gold prospector, you would answer, "I think I'll stay right here." Two ounces of gold a day is definitely profitable. Well, how long will you stay there? Until all the gold is gone? Hardly.

Let's say that you have been there for six months. You are only taking out half an ounce a day. Should you stay or go look for a better claim? Well, it depends on the alternatives, doesn't it? You may hear that upstream they're taking out two ounces a day. Your risk is: Stay for a sure half ounce a day or risk losing that and go for the big strike. Which do you do? It depends on how much risk you want to take, doesn't it? Let's say you stay another month. Now your claim is producing only an ounce a week. At this level, it costs you more in supplies than you are making in gold. So naturally you head upstream.

It's the same with a prospect list. Let's say you call or mail a list and get a profitable response. Prospect the same list again!

The second principle of the New School says:

☞ *Call a profitable list again in forty-five to ninety days.*

How often you call back depends on the type of product you sell. In the securities market, where money comes and goes and moves all over the place, you can prospect the same list again every forty-five to sixty days. In residential real estate, try sixty to ninety days. It's about the same for insurance. For automobiles, sixty to ninety days. For expendable supply items, thirty to forty-five days. For commercial real estate, check back every three to four months. For seminars, try every couple of months.

To rephrase the second principle of the New School:

☞ *Stick with the same claim as long as it's profitable.*

The Third Principle of New School Prospecting

Believe it or not, you can actually improve the response you get from a prospecting list. And you can improve it by calling it over and over and over again.

The principles you employ to improve a list come basically from mass marketing. We have simply taken them and applied them to the limited market within which most salespeople operate. These list improvement techniques are:

1. Repetition.

It has been said that the three main laws that determine the value of a piece of property are: location, location, and location. Well, the three main laws that determine recognition or familiarity are: repetition, repetition, and repetition.

Major firms use the Principle of Repetition over and over again. On any TV miniseries, you'll see the same ad four to six times per night. Some companies—American Express, McDonald's, Coca-Cola—run with an ad for years. If large corporations will spend hundreds of millions of dollars repeating the same ad, don't you think it might make sense for a salesperson with a limited market of only fifteen hundred prospects or so to do the same thing?

Whether you are calling, mailing, or using some combination of the two, get *repetition* working for you.

Here is a rule of thumb for you: It takes at least six times for a person to hear your name before he or she will remember it. If you contact your prospecting list once, don't be surprised if it doesn't work too well. After you have warmed it up, perhaps by mailing and calling, and have demonstrated through your actions that you are pleasantly persistent and that you will be there tomorrow, you will see people begin to recognize you, respond to you, and even call you to request information or place orders.

2. Make it safe to communicate.

In my opinion, many salespeople deserve the fear the American population puts into them. They have specialized in high-pressure tactics, have pestered and hounded people, and therefore justly deserve their reputation.

Perhaps those with the worst reputation of all are life insurance salespeople. If any one of you now reading this book is a life insurance salesperson, you know that if you leave a house without a signed contract, you are considered something less than a macho (or macha) salesperson, if not a downright wimp, or worse, an order-taker.

Those of you who have been on the receiving end of a visit from a life insurance agent know just as well that the time came when you had to buy or had to eject the person from your home.

So, if you are a life insurance agent, I have good news for you. You, too, can convince a group of people it's safe to communicate with you. How? Simple. When the prospect says, "I'm not interested," you say "Thankyouverymuch." *Click. Dial tone.*

After a while, people will come to believe that it is safe to talk to you. They will understand that you won't jam something down their throats. At that point, you will find you are no longer making cold calls. You are talking to people who trust you. And after all, who wants to be condemned to making cold calls forever?

3. Create interest.

Most salespeople suffer from verbal diarrhea. They think that if they can cover everything about the product, the prospect will hear something he or she likes and decide to buy.

In fact, the opposite is true: You create interest by what you withhold, not by what you disclose.

If in your opening remarks you offer a benefit and not a description of your product, and if at the first sign of no interest you hang up, you will leave the prospect on the other end of the phone wondering what it is all about.

If you do it again and again and again, you will also have communicated who you are, that you persist to stay in business, and that you have a product in high demand. Otherwise, you would be acting like other salespeople and jamming it down your prospects' throats.

4. Encourage word of mouth.

The easiest way to encourage word of mouth is to select a list on which word of mouth can happen. As a rule, I am truly not interested in getting started on a list if there is no connection among the prospects on it so that word of mouth can occur. In 1978, I advertised a seminar in the *Los Angeles Times.* Some seventy people showed up, among them a broker from E.F. Hutton and some agents from Farmers Insurance.

After the seminar, I followed up. I sold in-house seminars to Hutton and Farmers. I got the lists of Hutton branch managers and Farmers district managers. And I started calling and writing. From 1978 to 1980, my trainers and I trained approximately five thousand Farmers agents. In 1980, I did over eighty prospecting seminars for Hutton. From Hutton to Dean Witter, PaineWebber, etc., etc.

How? I got lists on which word of mouth was possible and made damned certain it happened and that it was good! (This same principle can wipe you out if you don't deliver a good product or service.)

Whatever industry you are in, get a list on which word of mouth can occur. In Chapter 5, I'll go over how to develop such lists.

This brings us to our third principle of the New School:

☞ *Select a limited market and through the four techniques of list improvement, seek to dominate the market totally.*

To state the principle another way: At any one time, a prospect is located, not created. Over time, through repetition, by making it safe to communicate, by creating interest, and by encouraging word of mouth, good prospects can be created.

The Old School Revisited

I trust you see, by now, that there is a certain truth to the Old School that I have retained. If someone says, "I'm not interested," the New School says, "Thankyouverymuchhaveagreatday." But we call back.

In the New School, we take only one no at a time. The Old School will take as many as it can get on one call. But the New School gives you the right to go back, and over time, you will come to own a given market.

So let's move on and talk more of good prospects and where and how to find them.

Cherry Picking and the Fourth Principle of New School Prospecting

We'll call our New School method "cherry picking," which brings us to our fourth principle. It's a long one. But understand it well.

☞ *On any list, there are a few hot prospects, some cherries, some green cherries, some very mildly interested leads (I call 'em info leads), a few jerks, and lots of pits.*

The hot prospects are ready to begin a selling cycle.

The cherries are interested but not hot yet, though they might be soon. We'll work with them.

The green cherries need low-key contact between now and when they're ripe.

Info leads need a couple of pieces of literature and a requalification.

And leave the pits on the list.

Oh yes, the jerks . . . well, you'll see what I have in mind.

As we get into some degree of detail, let's remember what this is all about.

As prospectors, we're searching for something of value.

What is it?

It's someone ready to start the sales process. In short, it's a *hot prospect.*

The other prospects we'll encounter aren't hot . . . yet. So we have to fan the flame a bit. How do we do that? Well, that's what we'll cover next.

OK, Bill, What Am I Going to Find When I Go Prospecting?

You will encounter various kinds of prospects on what I will call the Prospect Food Chain. Unlike the biological chain, our life-forms can move up to higher forms as well as down to lower forms or even drop off the scale entirely.

As you prospect, it is essential that you know what you've found and what to do with it. You should know the definitions to follow exactly, because if you don't, you will misclassify your prospects, and we're then not talking about stuff falling through the cracks. It will be whooshing through the floorboards.

By the way, on my web site, you can download a Prospect Definitions Cheatsheet in various MS Word formats. Print it out, laminate it, and post it at eye level. That www address is: http://www.billgood.com. Naturally, you will need your password, which is: thankyouverymuch.

By the way, the documents I am making available on my web site are intended for people who read the book. I'm well aware that you can give the password away, and there's not a darn thing I can do about it except sue you for copyright violation if I can figure out who you are. Use freely all the materials I have provided. But if someone asks for the password, just say, "Thankyouverymuch. Go buy the book." Deal?

OK. Now let's take a look at the various kinds of prospects on our Prospect Food Chain, where they come from, and what to do with them. Each type of prospect defined below receives different follow-up actions. I call these actions the *track*.

To change our analogy for a moment, imagine a toy racetrack with little cars running down defined tracks. The prospects you find are the cars; the channels that lead to the finish lines are the *tracks*. Got it?

As you study these tracks, you may become overwhelmed at the idea of using all the letters I am mentioning. Not to worry. I have written a draft of each of them for you and and made my draft available on my home page. Download it, edit it, and you're ready to go.

Hot Prospect

DEFINED: Anyone interested enough to begin the selling process right now.

SOURCE: Almost any prospecting campaign, including referrals, can kick up hot prospects. Most hot prospects, however, will come by cultivating prospects lower on the food chain.

TRACK: Set up an appointment or start the selling process over the phone. If you think you have to send a hot prospect some information, you don't have the concept yet. *By definition,* the hot prospect is ready to start NOW. If you have to send information, *by definition* you have a cherry, as defined below.

RULES:

1. Set the appointment as close to right now as possible.

2. If set more than two or three business days away, confirm by phone the day before.

3. If set four or more days away, confirm in writing by fax or letter. Confirm by phone.

A = Cherry

Defined: Anyone who is interested NOW, has a need, is the decision maker or on the team, and is qualified for money NOW.

Clarified: How do we find out if someone is interested? Simple: We ask. And how do we find out if they have any money? Again, we ask.

Will they lie to you? Yes, some of them will lie. But we are going to assume that people tell the truth. So even if we know they have money when they say they don't, we'll believe them.

Let's give a cherry a grade of A. We will use this designation later on to set up an A-B-C callback file system to help us keep track of all the prospects we are going to find using this system. (I'll discuss this in detail in Chapter 7.) For now, let's just assume that A means "active" or "cherry" or whatever. An A prospect is any prospect interested and qualified NOW.

When qualifying, we normally qualify for interest first; then, if appropriate, for power to make a decision; and finally, for money. Here are some examples of qualifying questions:

In the securities industry:

INTEREST: Mr. Jones, would you like to see some information on this tax-free municipal bond fund?

MONEY: By the way, I am accepting accounts now for $10,000 and above. If you like the idea, would that amount be a problem for you at this particular time?

In commercial real estate, income residential property:

INTEREST: Have you given any thought to increasing your real estate holdings?

MONEY: If you did find a building you liked, could you handle a down payment of at least $50,000?

In life insurance:

INTEREST: If I could show you how to increase the amount of coverage you now have without spending any more money, would you want to hear about it?

MONEY: If you need to write a check for a couple thousand dollars to start the new policy, could you handle that?

For a computer store:

INTEREST: Would you like to take a look at some information on the new network server we just got in?

AUTHORITY: If you like what you see, would you alone be able to make a decision or would others be involved?

MONEY: Lease payments probably wouldn't run more than $400 a month. If you like the idea, could you handle that?

TRACK:
1. Send requested information today or tomorrow at the latest.

2. Schedule for a callback in seven days (if info sent by mail) or two days (if sent by e-mail or fax).

RULES:
1. When sending printed material, always mark up the material. Use highlighters, sticky notes, and personal notes. This is called the Mutilation Principle. You will get the full explanation in Chapter 15.

2. As a cross check on interest level, always ask for daytime phone number if calling residents in the evening, or direct extension number if calling businesses during the day.

3. Expect that one or two out of five cherries will be hot when recontacted; one or two will be false cherries (won't answer the phone or return call); one or two will be reclassified as green.

B = Green Cherries

DEFINED: A prospect who indicates interest, but with money and/or ability to decide at a known later date. We'll call that later date the *opportunity date.*

CLARIFIED: When Bill Good Marketing, Inc., trains financial advisers and planners, we teach that when a prospect says, "I don't have any money," the adviser should respond, "Do you expect to have some funds available to invest or reinvest in the next six months?"

If we can find out when money will be available, we have an authentic green cherry, or "greenie." In life insurance, a green cherry would be someone who is interested and will give you a date at which he or she will have money and/or be able to make a decision. In residential real estate, a greenie would be a homeowner who tells you to call back in July because she will have heard by then if she will be transferred. (Call back in June!)

We give green cherries a grade of B.

Track:

1. Send requested information. Follow the Mutilation Principle.

2. Ten days later: send letter introducing your firm and giving benefits (not features) of your product.

3. Ten days later: send information about you and give still more benefits (not features) about your product.

4. Send a letter or make a low-key call every month until the money is due or until a decision can be made. (For sample letters, visit our web site at billgood.com.)

5. Call back two to four weeks before the opportunity date. Determine if prospect is now hot, red, green with later date, or downgraded to info lead (see next section).

Rules:

1. By sending three letters quickly, you have a good chance of being remembered later.

2. By stressing benefits, not features, you will build interest.

3. If you don't stay in touch by phone and mail between the initial contact and the opportunity date, you will become just so much mental history.

C = Info Lead

Defined: A prospect who expresses mild interest but cannot be pinned down as to when funds will be available or when a decision can be made. When an attempt is made to qualify for funds or decision-making opportunity, a typical response is "Just send me the information."

Clarified: Let's say you're me. You're prospecting for one of my seminars. You contact a sales training manager, say, at a hotel.

YOU: Could we send you some information on this seminar?

MGR.: Sure, why not?

YOU.: Great. If you like this idea, would you and perhaps one other person from the Roach Hotel like to attend?

MGR.: Probably not right now.

YOU: Is there a point in the future we could reestablish contact?

MGR.: Probably not right now.

YOU: You do want the information, correct?

MGR.: It's something we would consider.

YOU: OK, I'll send you some information about who we are and what we do. I'll check back with you maybe in a month or so. Meantime, I'll enclose my card so you can call me with any questions, fair enough?

Is this person interested? Yes.
How do we know? She said she was.
Hot? Definitely not.
Cherry? Hardly.
Green? Couldn't get a date?
Throw her away? Nope.
What kind of lead? Info: interested, but not enough to decide now and no later date.

TRACK:

1. Send requested information.

2. Send info about company.

3. Send letter about you.

4. Call and requalify as hot, red, or green.

RULES:

1. The requalification call is critical. If you don't make it, you can wind up with lots of people on your list who are really not interested or qualified.

2. When requalified, if the prospect does not upgrade to hot, red, or green, an info lead must specifically request to remain on your mailing list.

> YOU: Would you like us to continue sending you information on our line of nose rings?
>
> PROSPECT: Probably not.
>
> YOU: No problem. We'll be happy to take your name off our list.

D = Pitch and Miss

DEFINED: A prospect you have made a presentation to and missed. You pitched . . . and missed.

CLARIFIED: By pitch and miss, I don't mean someone you sent some information to as a cherry who then will not take your phone call. That person is actually a *false cherry*, a pit wearing a vinyl cherry skin.

I mean a prospect you have made a full-blown presentation to, probably including profiling, preparing a written proposal, even asking for the order. You did all of that, and you didn't get the sale. The competition beat you. Oh, woe!

I will tell you this without any hesitation at all: If this prospect is someone you regret not doing business with, keep the name. Put them on the pitch and miss track below. And over a period of time, you will get a substantial percentage.

At my company, *approximately half our business comes from people who previously turned us down.* This ain't theory, folks!

Track:

1. Send a pitch and miss letter (see Chapter 15).

2. Send a letter every month about something the prospect is interested in (Chapter 16).

3. Place a low-key phone call to the prospect every ninety days. In a low-key manner, try to upgrade the prospect to hot, red, green.

Rules:

1. If you want to do business with someone, and you swung and missed, keep that person on your prospect list until:

    a. You die

    b. The prospect dies

    c. Prospect buys

    d. Prospect becomes a jerk

2. The minute you don't want to do business with that person, remove him or her from your list.

Pits (and the Fifth Principle of New School Prospecting)

Defined: Anyone who is uninterested, unqualified, and/or unable to make a decision.

Clarified: If you are like most salespeople, you have an intimate knowledge of pits, because you spend the bulk of your prospecting time doing what I call pit polishing.

As an activity, pit polishing is singularly unrewarding, consisting as it does of talking to, grinding on, and applying Old School skills to people who are uninterested and unqualified. It is virtually impossible to create interest on a single phone call or appointment. Pit polishing is the single biggest destroyer of salespeople that exists.

So here is the fifth principle of New School prospecting. Study it well.

☞ *Pits are seeds. They sometimes grow into cherry trees. That's why we leave them on the list as long as the list is profitable.*

TRACK: Leave pits on the list.

RULES:

1. After talking to a pit, don't write "pit" beside the name. By doing so, you prejudice your list when time comes to call it again. After all, who wants to call a list with "pit" written by most of the names? And initially, most of the names on any list are pits, aren't they?

2. Don't write down anything by a name unless it's good. It'll save you a lot of time if you only write down the good news.

3. As a very broad rule, don't take pits off the list. Let me give you an example. In doing some test marketing for a dentist recently, I decided to see if this principle held. So I asked my researcher to call back a list of people who, less than two months earlier, had told us they were "happy with their present dentist." Guess what? They acted like they had never received a call from us, and we put lots of cherries in our basket from the list we had called earlier. This is in perfect agreement with the "cherries and pits theory." Now, weren't they telling us the truth the first time when they said they were happy? Undoubtedly. *But they came originally from a list that produced a profitable number of cherries.* Like picking cherries from a tree, pick the ripe prospects when they're ripe. Then go back and get some more. After a time, perhaps when you have called the list six times or sixteen or sixty-six, the list will no longer be profitable. Or it may be unprofitable after the first. Then throw the whole thing out.

Remember, prospecting, as a branch of marketing, deals with groups. Keep everyone but jerks on the list as long as the *list* is profitable. We'll get into how to determine "profitability"—or "how good does a good list have to be?"—in Chapter 5.

Jerks

DEFINED: Not just your usually grouchy prospect. These are NOT just run-of-the-mill pits. Jerks yell, curse, and generally act like the body parts they are. There won't be any question when you find one.

CLARIFIED: Regrettably, every list is inhabited by what we have scientifically identified as jerks. These are the people you call who make you feel bad. Here's how we think such conversations should go:

YOU:	*(Ring, ring.)*
DR. JONES:	Hello.
YOU:	Is this Dr. Jones?
DR. JONES:	Yes, it is.

> YOU: Dr. Jones, this is Jane Smithers with Beam of Light Financial Services.
>
> DR. JONES: Are you trying to sell me something? Why, you have your nerve, calling me at home. Who is your manager?
>
> YOU *(banging phone on table three times):*   Did you hear that sound?
>
> DR. JONES *(alarmed):*   Yes. Is there something wrong with the phone?
>
> YOU: No. That was just opportunity knocking. *(Click. Dial tone.)*

If you find that a little strong, try this:

> DR. JONES: Are you trying to sell me something? Why, you have your nerve, calling me at home. Who is your manager?
>
> YOU: Oh, no. I'm not selling anything. I was just calling to tell you that you are the beneficiary of a very large . . . *(Click. Dial tone.)*

OK, OK. I got carried away here. I'm really not recommending you do this. Jerks are very few and far between. Yes, I personally have hung up on them from time to time. Maybe four or five times over the past eighteen years or so. So don't confuse the point here with the drama of its expression.

The point is that, under the system I am teaching you in this book, *you are the rejector, not the rejectee.* If in doubt as to whether a particular prospect is a pit or a jerk, always remember that good manners is good business.

Still . . .

TRACK: Trash can.

RULES:

1. If using a paper list, scratch off the list.

2. If the name is in a database, *leave it in the database* but mark it in some way so that he or she never gets mail or appears on a calling list. By leaving the jerk in your database but marked so that it never gets mail or calls, you can exclude the jerk as a duplicate if you ever get his or her name on some other list.

The Cherry Picker's Attitude

Since the beginning of time, sales trainers have preached to their sales crews the importance of a positive attitude. Frankly, a positive attitude isn't really necessary to be a cherry picker. If anything, you really don't need one at all. What you do need is a "don't care" attitude. Imagine you are sitting on an assembly line. Every minute an item drops out of a chute for you to inspect. It's either a hot prospect, cherry, green cherry, info lead, pitch and miss, pit, or jerk. Your job is to quickly test it and then, depending on what it is, drop it into another chute. Do you care if it's a cherry or not? Of course not. As long as you know what it is.

This don't-care attitude is crucial to cherry picking. Here's why.

People like doing business with professionals. A professional doesn't get all emotionally involved in whether he or she will succeed or not. The professional just knows that if right actions are taken, anticipated results will follow. No big deal.

Further, professionals have arrived at a point in their careers where they have all the prospects they need. If they had any more, they wouldn't know what to do with them. This *fact of abundance* communicates to the prospect, who realizes that it is he or she, the prospect, who must qualify to do business with the professional. And that, according to my theory, is why the don't-care attitude is so important.

In other words, the art of assuming the correct attitude is the art of acting like a professional before you may actually be one.

The Cherry Picker's Method

The remainder of this book will be a detailed expansion of the method outlined below. I give it to you here in summary form so you can begin practicing its concepts as you go about your work.

1. Find a good list. (We'll have lots to say about this!)

2. Contact the list, by mail or phone, in a low-key, nonoffensive manner. Pluck off the hot prospects, the cherries, green cherries, and info leads. *Leave the pits on the lists.* (Pits are seeds, remember?) Don't even bother to write down "not in," "not interested," and so on. You'll be calling them back at a different time anyway and then they may well be "in" and "interested."

3. Call the list again in forty-five to ninety days. Once again, remove from it people who are hot, red, green, or info leads. Follow up with each according to the correct track.

4. Continue calling or mailing to the list *as long as your response from it compares favorably with the response available from other lists.*

The Cherry Picker's Way of Life

Cherry picking is a very pleasant way of life for a salesperson.

If someone is not interested, you're not.

If they're unpleasant, don't deal with them. Go look for people you would like to do business with.

And when someone isn't interested, just utter the cry of the cherry picker—thankyouverymuch—and disappear into the electronic haze of the telephone system. Some have even said that "Thankyouverymuch" is the modern equivalent of "Hiyo Silver."

Not all your cherries will pan out. Or as the old prospector might say, "Everything that glitters ain't gold. But if there's no glitter, for sure, it ain't gold."

Chapter 3

The Variables

Campaigns

It's time to dig in.

The process of prospecting, as I have developed it, is *campaign driven.* So first, let's define campaign: a series of steps or actions, taken in a given market, that produces predictable results. For example: You send out flyers in newsletters promoting free nose piercing for your line of jeweled nose rings. Every time you send out 10,000 flyers, you get between 150 and 200 phone calls.

You have a campaign! It involves a series of steps that can be repeated in a given market with predictable results. Whether you are making a profit in the nose ring business or not is not the issue. A campaign has to produce only *predictable* results to meet our definition of a campaign.

Let's assume that most of the calls you're getting are outraged parents telling you which orifice can receive your nose rings. OK. Let's change something, say, the publication. Instead of sending your local flyers out in the regional edition of the *Christian Science Monitor,* you switch to a heavy metal magazine. Now you get two hundred calls and these are all from kids wanting nose rings.

What changed the result?

You changed a variable.

Variables Defined

So now let's define variable: A *variable* is anything over which you have control that can change the outcome of a direct-response campaign. In our nose ring campaign, a variable is your list—in this case, the people who read the publication you're using to distribute your flyers.

Well, the kind of prospecting campaigns I have developed are made up of variables, things you can control. By controlling your variables, you can control your outcome. By controlling your outcome, you can control your commissions.

In this chapter, I'm going to give you a quick overview of what the key variables are. When you understand them, you will understand the pieces that make up the campaigns we will be discussing. The first five variables I'm going to tell you about refer to the design or creation of the campaign. The last two refer to its execution.

A complete campaign is simply one in which all variables are present and accounted for. Subsequent chapters will expand each of these variables so that you will know exactly how to develop them. Here goes:

THE LIST: I always, always, always begin developing a campaign by deciding on which list to use. While it's almost impossible to quantify the exact degree of importance that any one variable plays in the whole mix, in my opinion the List is by far the most important. Paradoxically, it probably receives the least amount of care and attention. I have run into companies spending literally millions of dollars in their marketing efforts who just bought some commercially available lists without ever testing them. On the individual level, I have seen countless salespeople grab the first list they can find and start calling. Since they keep no records, they have no clue as to whether they have a good list or a bad list, or whether it's Tuesday, for that matter.

The List, as a variable, is too important to be treated in this manner.

THE CAMPAIGN OBJECTIVE: There is a whole range of possible objectives for a campaign. I define *objective* as the degree of hotness a lead must attain before it is turned over to a salesperson. This opens up a big can of worms, as we'll see. I will cover objectives very thoroughly in Chapter 8. For now, just know that the objective of a prospecting campaign is always a lead—the name of a person either more or less ready to begin the selling process.

THE STYLE: *Style* is defined as the medium or combination of media used to produce the lead. Are you going to send a letter and follow it with a phone call? Are you going to call first? Are you going to walk door-to-door? How are you going to achieve your campaign objective? In making that decision, you have decided upon *the style*.

THE OFFER: The *offer* is defined as an end that you stress in your campaign that someone might enjoy as a result of buying your product or service. Although the offer never appears by itself anywhere, I have included it as a separate variable because it must be thought out so that it can then be included in your script and/or direct-mail piece. It is the offer that primarily determines the responsiveness of a list. Great lists plus lousy offer equal lousy response. Medium or even poor lists plus great offer can equal acceptable response.

THE MESSAGE: This is what you actually say in your calls and letters. It's the words. It's the script. It's the text of your letters. There are definite rules for constructing these vitally important pieces of a campaign. We'll go over these rules. Break them at your peril.

THE SOUND: How you sound. Once you have developed your scripts and letters, it's time to go prospecting. If I had to pick one of these variables as second in importance to the list, I would choose sound, the way you sound on the telephone. I cannot tell you the number of times people have told me that a campaign doesn't work, yet when I did it myself or gave it to someone with proven telephone skills, it worked quite well. The difference: the sound.

THE NUMBERS: You have heard it said that sales is a numbers game. Well, it is. And in Chapter 19 you will learn some wrinkles that you didn't expect. Normally, when I am debugging a campaign, my first question is, How many calls are you making an hour? If I hear five, or some other ridiculously low number, I *know* that I could have a highly successful campaign on my hands, but the players are not cranking enough numbers into it. The numbers of a campaign are the easiest thing to control.

The Second Most Important Question You'll Ever Ask About Prospecting

Before getting to this, I want to remind you that we've already asked and answered the very most important question: How long does it take to find out if a person is a prospect or not? The answer: Less than a minute. With two or three quick questions, you can find out: Does this person have any interest? Can this person make a decision? Can this person afford your product?

OK, so here's the second most important question: How long does it take to find out if a particular campaign itself is a cherry or a pit? The answer: A lot less time than you think.

The subject we're introducing, then, is *campaign evaluation.* If you do not evaluate your campaign, you will be stuck at some point with a loser, and you will miss a winner, and you will be a hurtin' dog. Over its life, there is only one way to evaluate a campaign: profitability. Response rate, as long as it's greater than zero, doesn't necessarily matter if your campaign is profitable. I have run campaigns that produced an enormous response but failed miserably because the people responding were non-buyers lured in by some free offer I made.

I've also run campaigns with a tiny response rate, even 25 percent or so, that have been wildly profitable because a very high percentage of the response bought an expensive product. So, at a very minimum, you need to keep track of your expenses, your responses, your buyers, and the total revenue, and then calculate whether or not your campaign makes any money.

In the shorter run, though, don't be shy about making quick, even snap evaluations, and kicking out failing campaigns. Just kick your losers to the curb and look for better ones. Remember, you need to see a campaign through to its end to verify that it's a winner, but you can spot and discard obvious losers much earlier on.

It's in adjusting a campaign that this concept of variables is so valuable. Here's the rule: If, early in the testing of a campaign, it does not seem to be working, change one variable. (If you change a whole bunch, you'll never know which of the changes was good . . . or bad.) Then back to testing. If your campaign starts to look good (we'll define "good" shortly), don't change anything; just keep prospecting. In the meantime, let the leads you're generating move down the pipeline. Keep good records so you can figure out if *enough* of the leads you're generating are buying your product or service to make the campaign *profitable*. So, suppose you send out a thousand letters, get a couple of replies, and end up with no sales. What should you do? Well, remember the definition of variable? It's anything over which you have control. You can control response by changing a variable—perhaps your list. Now, run it again. This time you get ten responses and a couple of solid appointments that look good.

Perhaps it will only take one sale to guarantee success. If you get it, maybe this is a home run. If you don't get it, maybe you'd better generate ten more leads and see what happens. At some point in monitoring your results, you will come to the conclusion that you have either a winner or a loser.

If it's a winner, roll it out.

If it's a loser, change another variable. Or, if you have changed several already, it's time to ditch this campaign and start all over.

All of which leads us to . . .

The Four Basic Mistakes

Over the years, I have seen far too many salespeople fail, many, if not most, needlessly. By paying very close attention to the four mistakes that follow, you can ensure that you don't follow in their failing footsteps.

1. Failure to keep adequate records so that campaigns can be evaluated.

I promise you, I guarantee you, I assure you that if you do not evaluate campaigns, you will throw out lots of babies with their dirty bathwater. Or worse, you'll end up with just the dirty bathwater. If you do not keep records of your campaigns and periodically review those records, you will wind up, at the end of the month, quarter, year, or career, with far less than you should. You will have retained failing campaigns and thrown out winners.

2. Get a bad idea and stick to it.

One of the reasons rookie salespeople go toes up is that they get a bad campaign and they stick to it. They are not failing because they fail to work hard. All too frequently, they work like Roman galley slaves. But what they're doing is just not effective. Sometimes, when confronted with numbers that demonstrate the campaign is failing, they still want to stick to the blasted thing. Why? Maybe it's the "winning isn't everything, it's the only thing" attitude. They don't want to fail. Throwing out a failing campaign is seen as failure rather than as common sense.

You need to understand that there's nothing wrong with failure in direct-response marketing. Expect it more than success. But you may need only one good campaign to ensure that you'll retire a rich person. Perhaps you go through twenty or thirty or forty or even fifty campaigns to find the one. Are you a failure? No. Just smart by throwing out or changing something that doesn't work. Are you a success? Maybe not yet, but if you keep trying one campaign after another, you will be. Wildly so.

3. Get a good idea and change it.

This is an insidious mistake. I've committed it many times myself and have tried to buffer my own tendency to do it by having people around me who have enough sense to say, "But, Bill, we did it differently last time and it worked great. Don't change it!"

One of my staff members was recently investigating why a particular direct-mail letter that we had used successfully did not seem to be working. It was a letter we called "Monster Rabbit University." You can check it out at our web site, if you would like to see a classic.

As she went back through our records, this staff member found that I had made some changes in an effort to improve it. When the changes didn't work, instead of reverting to the original letter, we decided that the campaign no longer worked. We then canceled the campaign. In doing so, we committed Basic Mistake Number 3. When we dug out the original version of the campaign and reran it, it worked like a champ, just as it always had.

The big danger in Mistake Number 3, then, is assuming that a once successful campaign doesn't work when you run an altered version of it.

4. Get a good idea and don't do it enough.

There are lots of salespeople out there who had a good idea but didn't really roll it out. Perhaps you sent out a mailing and made a ton of money, and then didn't do it for a while, if ever again. It's not uncommon to hear people say, "It worked so well I quit doing it." (Not my statement!) When you get the good profitable idea, go to the bank, mortgage your house, sell your second car, cancel your kids' allowance. Roll it out. And stay with it.

Summary

In this chapter you have learned:

What a campaign is made up of.

How to modify a campaign to make it work.

How to modify a working campaign to make it *not* work—by changing one or more variables.

Your ability to control your variables determines your success in direct marketing.

4

The Campaign Development Checklist

In this chapter, we're going to introduce a key tool for developing campaigns. I have called it simply the Campaign Development Checklist. Not only will it guide you step-by-step through the development of a campaign, it will also guide us, you and me, through the rest of this book.

Developing a campaign is a step-by-step process. You need to think it through and then do it.

My Campaign Development Checklist guides you through this process, and it will guide me as I teach you what you need to know about each variable so that you can produce prizewinning campaigns for your business.

I have put a copy of this checklist on my home page at billgood.com. Every time you want to design a campaign, my recommendation is that you print out the checklist and go through it step-by-step. This checklist is so important that I am not going to let you have it unless you read this chapter. Buried somewhere in this chapter is the password to download this checklist.

But before I formally introduce you to this document, let's define three more key terms so we both know what I'm talking about.

More Definitions

Prospecting

We're going to be developing prospecting campaigns, so it would be a really good idea to have the definition of prospecting firmly in mind. In its dictionary definition, prospecting is the act of searching for something of value. In our context, that *something of value* is a person or company more likely to buy your product than someone else.

So, prospecting is the art and science of finding someone to sell to.

Prospecting can also be viewed as the art and science of discarding that which is of little or no value. What's left, then, are the keepers. Prospecting is primarily an act of discarding, of getting rid of.

Selling

OK, what is selling?

In selling, the salesperson takes a prospect—identified earlier through a prospecting campaign—who presumably already has a relatively high desire to own a product or service, and further increases that desire to the point where the prospect wants the benefits of the product or service more than the prospect wants to keep his or her money.

Selling, then, increases desire. Normally, this is done in a step-by-step fashion.

So, selling can be defined as the step-by-step procedure that increases desire to own the benefits of a product or service to the point the prospect wants those benefits more than the prospect wants to keep his or her money.

Selling and Prospecting Are *Not* the Same Thing

Quite obviously, *prospecting* and *selling* are two entirely different subjects: Prospecting gets rid of; selling keeps.

Prospecting takes an easy no. On the other hand, once a salesperson is convinced someone is a good prospect and should own the product or service, selling does not take an easy no.

Prospecting can be relatively quick. Selling can take a long time and cover a series of phone calls, meetings, proposals, and so on.

Campaign Dominant

This is a campaign-dominant book. Specifically, it's about *prospecting* campaigns, not retail advertising campaigns, definitely not political campaigns, certainly not selling campaigns. Those are covered in other books.

I hope that, after reading this book, the concept of campaign will come to dominate the way you think about prospecting. It should dictate the way you organize your files, your computer, your daily activities. Campaigns are the key to *sustained* successful prospecting.

As we progress through this book, we are going to proceed step-by-step through the development of a campaign. As we do, you would do well not just to read but to work through the steps so that at the end of the book you have one you can try out. If the campaign you develop produces predictably *profitable* results, it can make you rich. Each chapter will take up one of the variables from the Campaign Development Checklist. As you follow along, I will make absolutely certain you know how to use that variable in your own campaign.

But then, it's up to you, isn't it? If your campaign is a hit, you could be on your way to fame and fortune. If it produces predictably unprofitable results, it can drive you out of business unless you dump it quickly. But since you now know about the Four Basic Mistakes, you will keep good records and evaluate as you go. You will be able to continue changing unsuccessful campaigns until you get it right and then you'll lock it in.

Keep this in mind: To succeed in sales, *you must have one or more profitable campaigns.* I know people who earn seven figures who have only one. It worked so well they just kept doing it . . . and doing it . . . and doing it.

Introducing the Campaign Development Checklist

Since a campaign involves a series of steps, we'll develop it exactly that way—one step at a time.

The remaining text of this book will take each variable, discuss it, and give you lots of choices. If you have elected to follow the Campaign Development Checklist, you'll mark off that step on the checklist as you read along.

A Word About Checklists

At Bill Good Marketing, Inc., we use lots of checklists, and they serve two main uses:

1. By using a checklist, you are less likely to forget an important piece of your plan. And if you do forget, you just add the piece to the next version of the checklist.

2. If a key person decides to be sick, another member of the team can step in and complete the job.

So you might want to download the text of the checklist from billgood.com now and print it out. The password to download this checklist is: rosebud. (That's my German shepherd, who will bite you if you give the password to anyone who didn't buy the book.) Each chapter that deals with a step on the Campaign Development Checklist will have the corresponding step at the beginning of the chapter.

Campaign Development Checklist

BEFORE STARTING ANY CAMPAIGN

___ **A.** Get adequate supply of 5×7 Good Prospecting Cards (Chapter 7).

___ **B.** Ensure that lead tracking system is in place (Chapter 7).

___ **C.** Rewrite or adapt as necessary the Lead Processing Letters according to the Lead Processing Letter Guidelines (Chapter 15).

START DEVELOPING A CAMPAIGN

___ **1.** Identify the lists you need to buy or develop to use for this campaign and buy or develop them (Chapters 5 and 6).

_____

_____

_____

_____

___ **2.** Decide on the objective.

Your objective is the degree of "hotness" at which you intend to turn over a prospect to a salesperson.

POINTS TO CONSIDER

A. Strength of your offer   **C.** Resistance level of the market

B. Identity of your firm   **D.** Staying power of your callers

E. Value of salesperson's time in gross revenue per hour spent selling

MARK OBJECTIVE CHOSEN

A. Prequalified appointment   **C.** Cherry lead to follow-up

B. Requalified cherry   **D.** Interested in talking

___ **3.** Decide on the style.

❏ Phone/Mail/Phone   ❏ Mail/Phone

❏ Standard Direct Mail   ❏ Phone Only

❏ Drip   ❏ _____

___ **4.** Decide on your offer (Chapter 10).

List at least five end results someone might enjoy from owning your product or service. Then pick one to use as the offer in a campaign.

1. _____

2. _____

3. _____

4. _____

5. _____

___ **5.** Identify and then write or rewrite the scripts required for this campaign.

Name or description of script	Check off when done

___ **6.** Identify and then write or rewrite the letters (if any) required for this campaign. Start a "Creating a New Direct-Mail Letter" checklist for each letter listed (Chapter 16).

Name or description of letter	Check off when done

ASSIGNMENT

Using the secret password hidden in this chapter, download your copy of the Campaign Development Checklist, print it out, and then use it, as you read the remainder of the book, to develop your own campaign "by the book." (I was eleven when I came up with the "by the book" statement. My brother and I were constructing a giant building with our Erector sets. He wanted to get creative. I said, "Ed, let's do it by the book." A friend of my dad's ran a little publishing company, long since out of business, and he made this his advertising slogan.)

CHAPTER **5**

Filling the Bathtub
List Development
and Improvement

> *"Birds of a feather flock together."*
>
> —Bill Good, age nine

This statement actually forms the foundation of my entire system of developing lists. I first said it one cold Saturday afternoon when my dad and I were driving back from the Friendly Road Shopping Center, where we bought some birdseed. We were talking about birds, and I saw a bunch of pigeons on a telephone wire and commented, "Dad, it would appear that birds of a feather flock together." He thought that was clever, and mentioned it to his boss at Sears. He was amused and told the advertising director. Sears did an ad campaign for down pillows built around this slogan. It wasn't a very good campaign, but the slogan got around. No one bothered to find out where it came from.

> ___ **1.** Identify the lists you need to buy or develop to use for this campaign and buy or develop them (Chapters 5 and 6).

VERY IMPORTANT NOTE: This chapter and the next may not be for you. You may work for a large corporation that assigns you a number of accounts or even a single account. If this is the case, skip this chapter because your list, for better or worse, has already been developed.

As you begin working your way through your Campaign Development Checklist, you hit the first and probably most important step: develop or buy your list.

Right here at the outset, let me explain one very important concept: List development, properly done, is a series of steps. It's not a onetime thing. And, if done correctly, never ends.

The three steps of list development are:

1. *Develop* (or buy) a list of people you believe are likely prospects.

2. *Improve* your lists by adding the names of people who are like those now responding and, if possible, who know each other so that word of mouth can occur.

3. If the campaign is a winner, continually *refresh* the list, sometimes for years.

Develop. Improve. Refresh. These are the three *ongoing* steps.

So here's the plan: In this chapter, we'll cover how to fill the bathtub with good lists, developing and refining them. In the next chapter, we'll cover how to keep the bathtub full of good names without having to develop and refine them all over again. We'll deal with recycling and refreshing your lists.

So let's jump in.

Importance of List Development

Your lists are to you what a claim is to a gold prospector. It's where you find gold or not, succeed or not. Yet most salespeople don't spend even one percent of their time developing their lists. Too bad. To put a number to it, your list is at least 40 percent of your success in direct-response marketing.

Regrettably, too many salespeople are not willing to do the kind of work necessary to develop good lists. This brings to mind the classic story of two brothers who went up to their room and found it filled with horse manure. Needless to say, they were stunned. One burst into tears. But the other thought for a moment, smiled, and started digging like mad. The crybaby exclaimed, "What's wrong with you? Why are you digging?" The other brother said, "With all this crap, there's got to be a pony here somewhere."

The process of list development can, from one point of view, be compared to digging through a pile of manure looking for a pony. The work may be pungent and it's certainly no fun, but there is a pony in there. If you do the work, you'll find it.

Purpose of List Development

Every once in a while I have run into the old saw, undoubtedly held over from the Old School, that "it doesn't matter who you call, it's how many you call."

This is false. Not only does it matter who you call, but who you call can make a tremendous, indeed unbelievable, difference in your overall results.

On one of my many trips to Canada, I gave some prospecting seminars to some mutual fund salespeople. When I do seminars in-house, we always put everyone on the phone for the last two hours of the session. At the end of the phone session at this particular seminar, one of the reps asked me if I would get on the phone and make some calls.

"Sure," I said. "Give me a list."

Someone gave me a list from a street address directory. (For those who may not know, a street address directory is a phone book where the names and numbers are listed by street address. Some directories will grade the streets A, B, C, D, and so on, for income range of families living on given streets; others don't. To find a street address directory for your area, check your local library.)

I made about four calls and said, "How much do the people on this street make?"

"About twenty thousand a year," someone replied.

I said, "No good. Get me another street."

Someone else gave me the street he had been calling. I made four or five calls and said, "What do these houses look like?"

"Two- and three-bedroom bungalows," someone said.

"Would someone give me a street," I said, "where people have some money?"

Someone found a list with a building of condominiums worth several hundred thousand dollars each. On my second call, BINGO! The man I spoke with was very interested in a particular mutual fund. And he said the required minimum investment would not be a problem.

Granted, many such lists will already have been prospected to death. But others won't. That's why you have to switch lists quickly if yours is loaded with pits, or worse. Don't waste time wondering why they're pits. They could be pits because they don't qualify or because the people just aren't interested or because they have just received forty-two phone calls from the competition.

To find my cherry, I switched lists twice. I could undoubtedly have found one or two cherries on the less luxurious street—after all, people of all incomes do save money—but there just wouldn't be enough cherries to make the search worthwhile.

With this in mind, I use list development in much the same way a gold miner uses a device to concentrate his or her ore. Let's say you send off a sample of ore to the assay office and find that it could produce two ounces of gold per ton of ore. If you could get rid of half a ton of dirt and lose none of the gold in the process, you would be dealing with a sample of ore that had four ounces per ton.

In sales prospecting, creative list development serves a very important function. It concentrates your cherries, puts more of them onto a single list, so you don't have to make as many calls to find a good prospect. Or, to look at it another way, it will help you screen out the pits in advance. This enables you to use your nonoptimum calling time to develop lists and your optimum time to make your calls. After all, there is no virtue in calling pits. Why not eliminate them through list development if you can?

If you really hate picking up the phone, spend more time on developing your list!

The Basic Laws of Lists

After the first year of the California gold rush, the "easy" claims were already taken. It's the same with lists. In any highly competitive field, the easy lists have been clobbered by every new generation of salespeople that comes along. There is a point, after all, where repetition fades into harassment, and someone receiving several calls a day has long since passed that point. Attorneys, doctors, and other obvious categories from the Yellow Pages are cases in point.

This brings us to the two basic laws of lists:

1. The easier a list is to get, the more salespeople have it, and the less likely it is to be any good.

2. The harder a list is to get, the fewer salespeople have it, and the more profitable it's likely to be.

These laws explain why some salespeople ALWAYS find more cherries than others. They have put in the time and imagination to get better lists.

This I can tell you for sure: Your best lists will be developed through effort and creative thought. They won't be given to you by your sales manager, nor will you be able to buy them. This is not to say that buying lists is not important. It can be, depending on your market. But the very best ones are those you develop yourself.

What Is a Good List?

Let's define a Good list (named after me, of course) as follows:

A good list is any list of names, addresses, and phone numbers that has been selected according to any one or more characteristics that the individuals have in common and that produces better results than names taken from any major free source of information.

To evaluate "goodness," you need to compare it with something. So to justify the time and expense of developing a list, we need to know that it is better than something available for free.

Let me give you an example of "one or more characteristics held in common." If you define a list according to "occupation," the individuals have one characteristic in common. So, we could get a list of lawyers. When we specify "lawyers in New York City" we have added a second characteristic in common. Suppose we say "female lawyers in New York City under age thirty-five." We now have four characteristics in common.

And as a matter of fact, this is a list that one financial adviser used. She was a former attorney who understood attorneys, and she built up a fantastic clientele dealing only with people like herself, whom she understood, liked, and could relate to. As you develop your concept of a good list, you may also want to include the characteristic "someone I could like."

The more characteristics the prospects on your list have in common, the more likely you are to develop a presentation that will fit a relatively large percentage of them. Hence, more cherries per hour.

Go back to the definition of a good list again. Note the phrases "one or more characteristics that the individuals have in common" and "major free source of information."

Let's take the flip side of the female attorney list. Let's say that you think attorneys are of a lower life-form, along the order of algae. To you, spending time with an attorney is like an extra session of dental drilling. You would then, of course, take great care to exclude attorneys from your list. What's the point in coming to work in the morning if you are going to have to deal with people you don't like? I can't tell you how many sales-people I know who live half their lives in fear that some jerk they regret-tably sold something to will call. Why even sell to them in the first place? If there are certain types of people you don't like, try your best to exclude them from your list. Failing that, don't sell to them.

If it's not fun, don't do it!

How Good Is *Good*?

The definition of a good list we have been considering so far doesn't give you any idea how good is good. So let's expand our definition.

A Guaranteed Good List is any list that will generate a minimum of two or three cherries an hour.

In the earlier edition of this book, "three cherries per hour" was the definition of a good list. Period. In many areas, however, with the advent of voice mail, which slows down daytime contact, and with Caller ID, which screens out people in the evening, we need to be careful about defining away some good lists. So we will start with the idea that a good list is one that generates two or three cherries an hour. But your figures may be different, so let's pose an alternate definition: A good list is any list that generates a profitable response.

Let me give you an example from my own business. As this book was being revised, my company was engaged in a campaign to expand our client base into some high-tech companies. Our initial goal was 100 prospects in a month. Over a four-week prospecting cycle, we in fact generated 110 prospects. Since virtually all of that month was spent phoning, that worked out to 1.45 prospects per hour. Are we working with a good list? Well, since each of these prospects represents a massive corporation, and if just one sells (at this writing, we're at two), we could easily live with 1.5 cherries per hour as our definition of a good list.

So, my recommendation would be: Until you know differently, assume two or three cherries an hour. I have been able to get three cherries per hour in virtually every industry I have worked in—and this ranges from securities to insurance to residential real estate to commercial real estate to high tech and to long-distance communications firms. To achieve three or more cherries per hour, I keep working with the list, the message, and the time of day I call until I determine I can *or* cannot produce at least three cherries an hour. I'm more cautious now with lists that produce less. While I'm definitely shooting for the magic "three per hour," I'll settle for less . . . as long as it's profitable.

If you tell me you are getting three cherries an hour, I'm nearly certain you've got a campaign you can take to the bank. There is no question that some lists can be considered good at two cherries an hour, one an hour, or even one every several hours. The exceptions to the three-an-hour rule will depend in part upon the price of the goods or service you're selling and the resistance level of your market.

If you are selling an office building worth $40 million, you would have to have one mighty good list to get three people per hour interested in it. However, by researching real estate buyers for major insurance companies, private syndicates, and major public partnerships, you might well be able to come up with one.

If you are an insurance agent looking for pension fund money, one cherry every couple of hours might be the best you can do. This is an extremely competitive market, and some pension fund managers get literally dozens of calls a day from insurance agents and stockbrokers.

If you can't conceivably come up with three cherries per hour, then for you, a good list would be defined according to however many cherries you, or the best prospector in your firm, can produce per hour *with your best efforts.*

I should also add that I am assuming fifty to sixty dials of the phone an hour. If you're doing twelve calls an hour and not averaging three cherries an hour, don't blame me. Push up your numbers and then see what you can get (see Chapter 19).

List Selection Principles

In the balance of this chapter, I'll go over two of the three principles of list development we'll be using. Since there are so many applications for sales prospecting, it would be impossible to give detailed sources for each industry. So my objectives here and in the following chapter are twofold: I want to help you learn to "think lists," and I want to acquaint you with lots of different resources.

Once you know how to think about the subject, you can:

- Simply take your body down to the local public library, tell the librarian what you're looking for, and start from there.

- Pop in your favorite CD (lists, not music!) and begin working.

- Call your favorite list broker and find out what is available.

- Log onto the Internet and mine these incredible resources.

You will soon be on your way to developing likely names.

If you don't have access to a decent library, you'll just have to go to a city where there is one.

If you don't have an Internet connection, you'll just have to buck up and get one.

If you don't have a favorite list broker . . . well, you get the idea.

Develop Your Core List

It's time for your first assignment: develop or buy a list of *likely* prospects.

How many names do you need? Anywhere from a few hundred to a few thousand. At the end of this chapter, when you know more about list development, I will answer this question in greater detail.

We're going to use a single principle, the "Look-Alike Principle," to develop your lists. (Of course, it's based upon my famous statement, "Birds of a feather flock together.") Then we'll use the Look-Alike Principle again as well as the "Word-of-Mouth Principle" to improve your lists. Finally, in the next chapter, I will show you how to use the "Change Principle" to refresh your best look-alike lists.

LIKELY PROSPECTS: Your best prospect is someone who looks like someone who already buys your product or service. So we're looking for a list of people who resemble people who already buy your product or service. Obviously, I don't mean resemble *physically*. I mean resemble *demographically*. (Demographics is the study of population characteristics such as gender, income, and occupation, especially as these characteristics may affect buying decisions.) Where do we get such a list? Well, here are some suggestions:

Likely Prospects: Residential Market

1. Same neighborhood or street your current clients live on. If you are a brand-new salesperson, it's the same street that someone else's clients live on. Best sources: street address directory (page 67) or Select Phone (page 69).

2. Same club, organization, or activity. Best sources: *Encyclopedia of Associations* or *Directory of Directories* (page 68).

3. Same age, income, race, and gender. Best sources: List brokers (page 70).

Don't mess around getting started. Make a quick call to your friendly list broker.

Likely Prospects: Business Market

1. Same building. Best sources: street address directory (page 67) or Select Phone (page 69).

2. Same SIC (Standard Industrial Classification) code—a numerical coding system developed by the U.S. Department of Commerce to classify similar businesses. For example, the code for stockbrokerage firms is 6211. Best sources: Select Phone (page 69) or MarketPlace (page 70).

3. Same occupation (purchasing agent, human resources director). Best sources: List brokers (page 70), *Encyclopedia of Associations,* or *Directory of Directories* (page 68).

4. Same-size business. Best sources: List brokers (page 70).

Now, that wasn't hard, was it?

Once you have developed your core list, you will continue developing the rest of the campaign. When you have all the pieces put together, you will *test the campaign.* You will try your script and letters on the list. If you hit in at two or three cherries per hour, you probably have a campaign that you can take to the bank. If not, you need to change your script, the number of calls you're making, and so on and try to get the number up to two or three per hour. If you can't, you need to go back to square one and come up with a new core list. If you can get a list in range, it's time to improve it.

Improve Your Core List

Once you have some lists that produce acceptable results, the name of the game now is to improve them. You do this by adding names that, hopefully, are better. In order to add these names, you really have to know your clients and good prospects.

In short, to make these list improvements, you need to learn to think like a fisherman. Suppose you are going fishing in the morning, but your alarm doesn't go off, and you get a late start. As you walk down to the lake you see an old codger with a string of fish thrown over his shoulder. Naturally, you have some questions.

> YOU: Where did you catch 'em?
>
> CODGER: Down at the lake.

Now, if you are not much of a fisherperson, you would let it go at that and wander on down to the lake. But if you are a real fisherperson, you would continue the conversation.

> YOU: Where down at the lake?
>
> CODGER: By the big rock.
>
> YOU: You mean the one over by the willow trees?
>
> CODGER: Yep.
>
> YOU: What were you using for bait?
>
> CODGER: Plastic worm.
>
> YOU: Great. Thanks.

Take a look at your present clients as if they were that string of fish hanging down from the codger's back. What pond did they come from? Or to put it in sales prospecting terms, What list could they have come from?

You are looking for lists of people *on which your client's name appears.* Ideally, the people on the list will have some connection that will make word of mouth possible. Given a choice between a list of people who own a Mercedes-Benz and a Mercedes Owners Club directory, *always* take the list on which word of mouth can occur—in this case the club directory.

List Improvement Principles

To improve you core lists, you will use two principles:

1. You have already met one of these: the Look-Alike Principle. We used this to develop the initial batch of names. Now we're going to use it to improve the list by more precisely defining the characteristics to those that look just like our current clients. For example: You sell computer equipment and you got a big order from a medical practice. Now you put on your fisherman's hat and start asking questions: What kind of practice is this? Does the type of practice—say, laser eye surgery—have anything to do with them ordering a new computer system? If the answer is yes— because as a business, laser eye surgery is growing like weeds after a rainstorm—then obviously you don't want to focus just on doctor's offices but on medical practices performing laser eye surgery.

How would you find them? I would look up this type of practice in MarketPlace, find out what its SIC code is, and then pull all those SIC codes in your market area. You might only get a few names, but these still get added to your list.

2. The second of these principles is the Word-of-Mouth Principle. *If at all possible, find a list on which word of mouth can occur.* This is so important that if I could yell at you right now to get the point across, I would. It's what I did in selling seminars to various financial services and insurance firms. I cracked E.F. Hutton and Farmers Insurance by simply asking the one contact I had in each firm if I could have the list of branch managers. These were the best prospect lists I ever developed. They held the same job and knew each other. It was easy to spread the word because they all went to the same meetings and shared war stories.

Here are some possibilities that may combine tightly defined lookalike lists with lists of people who know each other. (I should point out that the best way to get these lists is by asking. So don't be shy.)

Improved Prospect Lists: Business

BEST PRACTICES LISTS: Major corporations have meetings with other companies they don't directly compete with to share "best practices." Can you get that list? You can at least ask, can't you?

TRADE ASSOCIATIONS: Chances are, your good corporate clients belong to several trade associations. Ask which ones your contact belongs to. If you feel comfortable doing so, ask for the list. Otherwise, call the association and ask how you can buy it. Check the home page of the association.

SAME OCCUPATION: Suppose your best client is the chief legal counsel of a publicly traded company. Naturally, you want a list of chief legal counsels. There might be an association, which you could find out about by asking your client. Or you might check the home pages of similar publicly traded companies. Worst-case scenario: You have to call all the companies and ask the receptionist for the name of the chief legal counsel.

Improved Prospect Lists: Residential

SAME CONDO DEVELOPMENT: You can get this from the street address directory, Select Phone, or from the tax assessor's office (page 66). This last may be very important, especially if you are doing a mail campaign. The U.S. Postal Service will not always deliver letters to an apartment or condo development unless you specify the apartment or condo number. I have run into people who have made a fine art of promoting to condo owners whose number is not listed in the street address directory. This means that many of the mail solicitations are being returned, and that means they are not getting their fair share of direct mail.

These top prospectors go to the property tax assessor's office and look up the condo numbers that are not listed in the street address directory. Those are the only ones they mail to. I have received reports of outstanding results.

SAME HOBBY: As you learn more about your clients, ask them how they spend their spare time. You may find they do everything from collecting stamps to playing ball to participating in square dance clubs. Ask for the lists. If you can't get them that way, call the club president and offer to join as an associate member. Many of these groups can be joined for $10 to $25, and you get the membership directory when you join. There are countless lists you can get, filled with people just like your best clients, and on which word of mouth can occur. As you develop these lists, you can be sure that your response rate to your mailing and phoning campaigns will improve.

List Development Resources

Since I don't know what company you work for and what kind of list you need to develop, I can't be certain I've given you any good ideas so far. So in the next few pages, I'm going to come at the problem from a different perspective. Instead of trying to help you identify lists of people that look just like your current clients, I'm going to give some resources I have used in various campaigns. As you look these over, you may be struck by the fact that your client appears on one or more of them.

Public Record Information

There is an absolute wealth of information available for free in public records and libraries. Don't complain about your bad lists if you haven't spent a few hours following the trails I'm outlining here.

LICENSES OR PERMITS: The best way to find out if public records, especially auto registration and driver's license records, are restricted in your state is to call a list broker. If the records are available, a list broker has them. Does one of your clients own a factory to dispose of toxic waste? I guarantee they have to have some kind of permit. The names of permit holders are available through a list broker or through the city, county, or state licensing agency.

PROPERTY TAX RECORDS: In the United States and Canada, and possibly other countries whose legal system descended from England's common law system, property tax records are open to public inspection and copying. The theory seems to be that in order to ensure that property is assessed fairly, we as citizens should be able to see what our neighbor is paying on his or her property. Among other things, you can tell when the property was purchased, its assessed valuation, how it's titled, how it's zoned.

Property tax records typically do not contain phone numbers. Property tax records are available in several forms, but they are always on microfiche at the local property tax assessor's office. In many areas, you can buy the fiche for a few dollars and a fiche reader for a few hundred dollars. You may also be able to buy the local property tax records on CD and use the search engine of the CD to locate, say, all the properties worth $1 million purchased before a certain date. You may even be able to access them over the Internet. Best bet: Go visit your local assessor's office and ask someone how the records are kept and to explain them to you.

Here are some uses for property tax records. If your prospect is likely to own or has owned property, you may find enormous use for these records.

- **Property and Casualty Insurance:** Very likely, the anniversary date of a fire insurance policy coincides with the date the property was purchased. There is no point in calling for an appointment to compare rates unless the policy is up for renewal.

- **Estate Planning:** From property tax records, you can tell how property is titled. You may wish to invite to a seminar people who live in a certain area whose property is not titled in the name of a trust.

- **Residential Real Estate Sales:** There is a phenomenon in real estate called "the empty nest syndrome." Couples, usually in their late forties and early fifties, sell the big home now that the kids are gone. How could property tax records be used to identify such couples? Well, you could search through the fiche or CD for people who have owned their home more than, say, fifteen years, and you would have a list of people statistically more likely to sell their home than you would if they had been taken at random from a street address directory.

- **Commercial Real Estate Sales:** If you are in real estate sales, you want to know two things: who owns a particular piece of property, and who the real estate investors are. By scanning the alphabetical list of property owners, you will often find the same name listed over and over. Each listing is a separate piece of property. By noting the names of people who own multiple pieces of property, you'll have found your list of real estate investors.

- **Rich People:** It has been said that 90 percent of the millionaires made their fortunes in real estate. Well, the property tax assessor's office will help you find them. Scan the alphabetical list of property owners for the names that keep recurring.

- **People with Unlisted Phone Numbers:** Obviously, you can't call this list. But you can send them mail. People with unlisted phone numbers don't get a lot of solicitations and could therefore be considered under-solicited. By comparing the street address list with the property tax list, you can develop a list of people who have unlisted phone numbers. You may get a better response to a mail campaign with these folks than you would with a mail campaign to people who get pounded by telephone solicitors.

Library Resources

STREET ADDRESS DIRECTORY: For virtually every city, there is a street address directory. The best way to find out the name of the directory for your area (if you don't already know) is to call the library. They will usually have a copy. They probably won't let you go in and photocopy names, but you can certainly find out if there is more than one directory in your area.

The few publishers of street address directories seem to have worked out an accommodation with each other, and for the most part there will be only one directory for an area.

My personal favorites are the directories published by Polk's. They develop their directory by sending people door-to-door, where they do a short survey. So from Polk's, you can usually tell a person's occupation.

DUN'S MILLION DOLLAR DIRECTORY: In this directory, you can obtain information about any company that does more than $1 million in sales. It will list the officers, something about the company, and how to contact them. The publishers have done a good job making sure you don't photocopy all the businesses you want to call instead of contacting them to buy names on disk, labels, or cards. If you have more time than money, you can build a very exact list of the kinds of businesses you want to call upon.

LIBRARIAN: Over the years, as I have researched different lists for different marketing campaigns, I have come to learn that if you take some time at the business desk of your local library, you may discover your very best resource. Remember, these folks answer questions all day long about library resources. If I were to give you an assignment to "learn all local resources for developing good lists," I would put at the very top these words: "Find out which librarian in your biggest library knows the most about directories, local publications, and Internet access. Befriend this person."

THE *DIRECTORY OF DIRECTORIES* AND THE *ENCYCLOPEDIA OF ASSOCIATIONS*: These two books taken together may help you develop the ultimate look-alike lists. They are comprehensive listings of the thousands of clubs, organizations, and associations that dot the social and political landscape. Here are some ideas for their use:

Residential Market: Let's suppose your best client is a dog enthusiast. He breeds champion greyhounds. I guarantee you that he knows every other greyhound breeder in the state. Therefore, the Greyhound Breeders Association directory is a list on which that all-important word of mouth can occur. There may be only a handful of breeders, or there may be a hundred. The place to start looking for the list is in the key word section of the *Directory of Directories,* or check the *Encyclopedia of Associations.* (A note on Kennel Club directories: Some of them will indicate which of their members employ an agent to show their dogs for them, for which they pay a lively $15,000-a-year minimum. So if you are looking for a look-alike list that also has a MONEY characteristic, rest assured that people who spend at least $15,000 a year on their dogs are not down to their last dime.)

By the way, many directories contain unlisted phone numbers. This is a windfall, because people with unlisted numbers don't receive a lot of cold calls. However, you will frequently be asked, How did you get my number? When you are, try one of these responses.

- "I got it from the Austin Kennel Club Directory" (or whichever directory you used).

- "I'm not sure. My assistant handles that. If you will hang on a few minutes I'll have him look it up." (*Pause*—No one in the history of the world has ever volunteered to stay on hold.)

- "I got it from a list of people who are supposed to have money. Did they make a mistake?"

This last response will usually get a chuckle and any resistance to your call will lessen with the laugh. Laughter is, after all, terrific medicine, for colds as well as cold calling.

If someone insists on knowing where you got their name, tell 'em.

Business-to-Business: Let's take a couple of examples: The ideal occupation list is one that is *not represented* in the Yellow Pages. Why? Because every salesperson selling anything with any kind of price tag at all is pounding away on the Yellow Pages. I asked a stockbroker one time who his best client was. He said, "It's a guy who designs packaging for different products."

"Would you like to have more like him?" I asked.

His reply was "Are you kidding? I've checked the Yellow Pages and there are none listed." He was certainly correct that package designers were not listed in the Yellow Pages. They tend to work for big corporations and advertising agencies, and so are not listed separately.

To get a list of package designers, we first checked a standard library book, the *Encyclopedia of Associations*. We found that there was an association of package designers based in New York with some three thousand members. The broker called them and asked, "How many members do you have in southern California?"

"Four hundred."

He then asked, "How do I get a copy of the membership directory?"

"Send me twenty-seven dollars" was the reply.

Now how many stockbrokers do you think regularly cold call the list of package designers? Not many. And that's the entire idea.

Suppose you sell a software product to human resource departments. Instead of cold calling companies trying to find out who the manager of that department is, find out which trade association they belong to and see if you can join as an associate member. It's easier than you think.

CD Resources

I consider the resources listed below extremely valuable. They should be in the list-building kit of every sales professional.

SELECT PHONE: I have examined several different CD White Pages and for my $100, this one is the best. It contains 100 million phone numbers and is maybe 85 to 90 percent accurate.

Its principal uses?

1. Locate the neighbors of your good clients.

2. Get names of people in the same building.

3. Locate the name of a company when all you have is a phone number. Maybe you're getting phone numbers from classified ads and want to know who the number belongs to. Look up the phone number; if it's listed, you'll know.

4. Get names within a certain distance of a specified address.

Needless to say, after this book is published, there may well be other sources. Please check the *Prospecting* site in the billgood.com home page. Select Phone is distributed by all major software distributors.

MARKETPLACE: MarketPlace is published by MarketPlace Information Corp. At this writing, it is the definitive CD for business listings, containing some 15 million names. However, they're not about to give you 15 million business profiles for just a few hundred dollars. With an initial payment of $595, you get $300 or so in credits and a little counter that goes into your serial port. When your counter runs out of credit, you get a message on your CD telling you to pick up the phone and call. Have your credit card handy.

Is it worth it? If you want very precise SIC code selections with the name and phone number of businesses, you bet. You certainly can't hire someone to call and gather that information for fifteen cents a name, which is what MarketPlace charges. For contact information for MarketPlace, visit billgood.com/prospecting.

List Brokerage Resources

A WORD ABOUT LIST BROKERS: There are thousands of companies who sell lists of various kinds. In most cases, list brokers are truly *brokers,* meaning that they *broker* a product they don't own. For example, a broker may sell a list of magazine subscribers. The magazine owns the list, not the broker, who just receives a commission for selling it. Depending on your needs, a list broker may be vital in your efforts to build good or even great prospecting lists.

If you want to see the primary source that list brokers work from, go to a good public library and ask to see a book called *Standard Rate and Data: Direct Mail Lists.* This is a catalog of thousands of commercially available lists. If there is a list of one-armed paper hangers in New Jersey, you will find it in this volume.

When you call a list broker, you need to know as much as possible about the kind of names you want. If you are prospecting people at their homes, you want to know age range, income range, location, status as regards home ownership, whether they have children, what kind of cars they drive, and so on. The more information you can give a list broker, the better job he or she can do in locating the ultimate look-alike list for you.

Internet Resources

So many resources; so little time.

Please understand: This book was completed in early 1997. By the time you read these pages, the particular sites I have listed below may have changed drastically. So be sure to visit the *Prospecting Your Way to Sales Success* site at billgood.com for updated information on Internet list-building resources. The password for the up-to-date section on list development is: goodlist.

SEARCH ENGINES: At this writing, there are dozens of search engines. What these Internet sites do is catalog information stored on the Internet and then enable you to find the sites that contain the information you are looking for. There are numerous places on the Internet that direct you to various search engines. Among my favorites:

Search.com	Lists ten different search engines
Microsoft.com	Provides links to many search engines
Netscape.com	Links to lots of search engines
Dejanews.com	Search millions of Usenet messages

In virtually all cases, these search engines will take you to home pages or newsgroups or both. If you learn that one of your clients races cockroaches, I guarantee you that somewhere you can find a home page or newsgroup featuring cockroach-racing enthusiasts. And they will know each other, thus adding our second principle of list development: Find a list of likely buyers on which word of mouth can occur.

HOME PAGES: There are many reasons you may wish to compile names of individuals at various corporations. Whatever the reason, the very first place to visit is the company's home page, which you can find through any of the search engines.

Many corporations will have a button somewhere on their home page that says simply <Contact Us>. In some cases, they will have names, direct extensions, and even photos of various staff members.

ONLINE YELLOW PAGES: At this writing there are two principal online Yellow Pages.

Big Book (www.bigbook.com)

Big Yellow (www.bigyellow.com)

Each location seems to have Yellow Pages for the entire United States. You can pick a category, several categories, a zip code, a city, whatever, and get a list of companies that meet those criteria. You can print out the list, and in some situations (for a fee), you can download a complete listing.

Suppose one of your new clients owns a welding gas supply store or something equally esoteric. I guarantee you that all the welding gas supply store owners in a given city know each other.

Best bet: Use online Yellow Pages to develop calling lists for a phone/mail/phone-style campaign because you will need to find out who the decision maker is when you call.

HOOVER PROFILES (WWW.HOOVERS.COM):   Hoover maintains profiles (at this writing) of about 2,500 corporations. These profiles include financial data, principal officers, and perhaps most important, competitors. You can get "capsules" for free but it will cost you $9.95 per month for up to 100 profiles per month.

Where a home page exists, there is a link from the capsule to the home page. If you are having trouble finding a corporate home page, you might check here.

ELECTRIC LIBRARY (WWW.ELIBRARY.COM):   For me personally, Electric Library has been the best find on the Internet. It is a library of hundreds of thousands of newspapers and magazine articles, thousands of books, pictures, and maps. It costs a big $9.95 a month for unlimited use. What do you do with it? Let's say you are going to be prospecting inside a large company. If any articles have been written about it, you may be able to find out who lives near it, who its competitors are, who sells to it, and who buys from it.

Marketing genius is in the details.

How Many Names Do You Need?

This is a tough question, and the answer varies tremendously by industry and by quality of list. You don't need an infinite number of names. When you get a good list, you'll keep it and contact it again by mail or phone in forty-five to ninety days, depending on your industry and product. So how many do you need? Here are some rules of thumb.

1. If you are prospecting a residential market, you will need about three thousand names *if you are new in the business.* Of these three thousand, you need approximately two thousand to call during the day and

one thousand for nighttime calling. Your daytime names may need to be developed with the help of a list broker because you want people who are home during the day. These are retirees, homemakers in older households, ages fifty to sixty-four, or people who work at home.

2. In other industries, you'll need to do some arithmetic to figure out how many names you need. First, figure out how many contacts it takes for you to achieve your weekly objective. Let's say you are a commercial leasing agent and that you want to see 10 new people each week. Let's further assume that to see these 10 people, you need to set up 15 appointments to allow for no-shows. To set up one appointment you need to contact 25 people on your look-alike list. So to set up 15 appointments, you need to contact 375 (15×25) people each week.

Now, multiply your weekly needs by 8. So in this case, you will need a "bathtub" of 3,000 names (8×375). This gives you enough names to last 8 weeks. Then, if you are getting your 10 people in the shop each week, and if that is profitable to you, start at the beginning of the list.

ASSIGNMENT

1. Sit down with your present account book or customer list. (If you don't already have clients, get your manager to spend some time with you and let you study other salespeople's clients.)

2. Open it to your best customer.

3. Write down what you know about him or her in business and, where appropriate, personally.

4. Ask yourself, where can I get a list of people *most like my client* and on which he or she appears?

5. Continue your look-alike analysis (include a survey if necessary) until you have five good list ideas.

6. Get the lists using the resources outlined in this book.

6

How to Keep the Bathtub Full

More on List Development

"The more things change, the more they remain the same."

—Bill Good, age twelve

This was actually the last famous statement I made before I realized I was being ripped off. I took my very first girlfriend—her name was Joan—to the movies one Saturday morning. They had a short film on the changing of the guard at Buckingham Palace. When we came out of the movie, she commented on how wonderful she thought the changing of the guard was. I was not particularly moved at all and was in fact bored with the whole thing. My comment: "Joan, frankly, between you, me, and the gatepost, the more things change, the more they remain the same." Someone took this one and made two famous statements out of it! As usual, all I got was a couple of Anon. mentions in *Bartlett's*.

Let's go back to our list development analogy. Using the principles in Chapter 5, first fill the tub with a likely list. If you need fifteen hundred names, you'll no doubt go through a lot more than that to find those lists that will get you two to three cherries an hour or whatever optimum number you've established for your particular product or service. These lists will then become the "limited market" that you are going to try to dominate. Even if you are able to *develop* lists in the two- or three-per-hour range, you will certainly want to take steps to *improve* your lists by adding better names.

If for no other reason, your lists will immediately start to shrink, because as you begin calling and mailing you'll remove the cherries. When you find a cherry, you'll simply either scratch the name off the list and start a 5×7 card, or you will already have affixed labels to cards and you will turn the card over to your computer operator (which might be you in a different time frame), and this person will change the list field from mass mail to prospect. So your mass-mail lists will start to shrink. (List management is covered very thoroughly in Chapter 7. So just bear with me until then and know that your list will begin to shrink just as soon as you begin working it.) Your green cherries will also come off your lists as will your info leads, jerks, and people who are no longer there.

A heavy prospecting campaign can remove as many as fifty to seventy-five names per week. Be careful not to cycle through your list too many times without replacing names; otherwise your list will get so small you'll be recycling it too often. Repetition can fade into harassment.

The solution is simple. Keep the list at fifteen hundred names by adding a name for each one you remove. I'll use the term "replacement list" to refer to the sources of names that will replace the names you have used up.

If you truly hate to cold call, you should pay very close attention to the three major sources of replacement names I will cover. They are:

Change lists

Referral lists

Connections lists

While I will be discussing these primarily as a source of replacement names—fresh water for your bathtub—some of you should consider only names from these sources. As a rule, they are so much better than the others available, it's a shame not to spend the time to start off with the best. A little time put in on developing lists from these sources means a lot fewer cold calls to achieve a given result.

A NOTE OF WARNING: It can be very time-consuming to develop replacement names in the manner I'll be discussing. You will have to decide for yourself whether you want to put in this kind of time. The trade-off is that the better the list, the fewer hours you have to spend to achieve a given result. Look at it this way: If you could develop a list of absolutely fantastic prospects, you wouldn't have to call very much. The principles of list development that I am going to discuss with you are so powerful that if you follow them only to replace names coming off your list, you will, over time, tremendously upgrade your list. If you were to develop an entire list using these principles, you would be a formidable competitor.

The Change Principle of List Replacement and Development

Let me first state the Change Principle of list development. Then I will give an example of it and discuss its application to various markets. The change principle can be stated as a variation of Newton's law of motion as follows:

☞ *Other things being equal, a person or company in process of change finds additional change easier to make.*

(Newton, of course, said, "Every body continues in its state of rest, or of uniform motion in a right line, unless it is compelled to change that state by forces impressed upon it.")

To show you how the Change Principle might apply, consider this example.

Suppose you are in one or another of the financial services professions. You call a person this evening who is forty-two years old. He has been working at the manufacturing company since receiving his M.B.A. from the University of Chicago seventeen years ago. He is now a senior vice-president earning $165,000 a year. He has been married to the same woman for eighteen years. Their oldest child is seventeen years old and a senior in high school, and the youngest is fifteen and a sophomore. They live in a four-bedroom home, and he has driven the same route to work for the past eight years. Their children have all gone to the same school system. Every Saturday night they play cards with the Stones, and for three weeks every summer they go to the same beach house. He has had the same financial adviser for the past twelve years.

As you imagine phoning up this person, ask yourself this question: Based on what you know about him and his lifestyle, how likely is he to change the way he invests his money? Not very likely, right? He's in a period where his life is stable, and he surely doesn't want to upset any apple carts.

Now, let's age him ten years. He's fifty-two. Five months ago he was made the executive vice-president. He earns $295,000 a year. All of the children are now out of college, and he and his wife have recently sold their four-bedroom house and bought a luxury condominium. She sold the station wagon and bought a Mercedes, and he sold the Oldsmobile and now drives a Porsche. Instead of going to the beach house, they now take three-week trips to exotic places. They have had the same adviser for twenty-two years. They just completed the redecoration of the new condo three weeks ago.

Let's ask the same question we asked about him ten years earlier. How likely do you think he is to change the way he invests his money when you phone him up tonight? Is he more likely to be open to a change than he was in the previous example?

The answer is an unequivocal YES. He will definitely be more open because other things are changing in his life as well. One more change won't upset the apple cart because *it is already upset!* It therefore doesn't make any difference if he changes something else. And chances are he may be tired of the old adviser anyway.

Here's another example: Suppose you have a list of five hundred homeowners and you want to know which ones are likely to sell their homes in the next year. To find out, you can call each and every one and ask. Or, if you're lazy, you can develop lists of homeowners *in the process of change*. I can state without question that in real estate, change lists are five to ten times better than geographic lists of homeowners.

To summarize: Our objective, then, is to add *replacement names* to your list that are better than the list to which they are being added.

A point of clarification: You might wonder, why not use only these lists? If you are willing to spend quite a few hours putting together enough names to keep you busy, go for it! Realistically, however, most salespeople need a quick start, and sales managers are leery of salespeople who run off and start organizing. That's why I recommend you start with look-alike lists and use the Change Principle as the source of your replacement names.

With this point of clarification in mind, let's talk about the application of the Change Principle in three broad markets: corporate, individual daytime, and individual nighttime. By corporate, I mean those markets where you are selling to businesses. By daytime, I mean those products and services you sell to individuals you can contact during the day. And by nighttime, I mean those markets you approach by calling people at home.

Change in the Corporate Market

The Change Principle is easy to visualize if you are accustomed to prospecting the corporate market. In many corporations, when someone new gets appointed to a position, he or she often sweeps out any remnants of the old regime. This holds great promise if you are on the outside trying to get in. If you are on the inside when the shake-up comes, you may find yourself swept away if you don't take quick action when the sweep starts.

As you search for corporate change, look for *any* change. When a corporation is in the middle of an expansion, a new product introduction, a reorganization, or a buy-out, the same principles apply: Change is easier when it is happening from some other cause.

There are four excellent sources of corporate change information:

1. Your best sources of corporate change are internal corporate newspapers and trade papers. Virtually every corporation with one hundred employees or more puts out some kind of in-house newsletter, or house organ, as it's sometimes called. These are unbelievably easy to get. The easiest way to get a corporate paper is simply to ask a client to put his copy in an envelope and send it when he's done with it. Better yet, send him or her a dozen self-addressed, stamped envelopes. You can also call the editor of the house organ and ask to be put on the list to receive the paper. Some corporations make theirs available as a public relations gesture to anyone who expresses interest.

If you are really serious about pursuing internal corporate papers, you should go to the library and study a book called *Working Press of the Nation,* volume 5. This is a source of major corporate papers and how to get them. Some may cost you a subscription fee, but I understand from speaking to senior executives in major sales organizations that salespeople are never prohibited from spending some of their own money to promote their own careers.

Another important source of change information is trade papers. A trade paper is a newspaper that goes only to members of a given occupation or industry. For instance, once, when I was doing some research in the Los Angeles City Library, which has one of the greatest collections of lists and librarians who know about lists, I came across a copy of the trade paper *Southern California Retailer.* As an exercise, I decided to count promotion announcements. I gave up when I passed ninety and still had more than half the paper yet to go.

On the front cover of this particular issue was a picture headlined "New Sony Marketing Team." Sony evidently had brought in heavy management to handle the southern California market. At a minimum, the members of this team would be good prospects for financial services, real estate agents, auto leasing, banking, furniture, clothing, credit cards, computer systems, office supplies, and so on, and so on.

To find out if there is a trade paper put out in the industry you are interested in, ask several people who are part of the industry. Find out if they belong to an association. Or go to the library and spend some time with the *Encyclopedia of Associations* and look up the industry in the key word index. Call the association. Also, check the Yellow Pages under "associations" and see what is available locally.

If you begin to check into some of the sources I've mentioned in this section, you will discover that *the amount of information available on people in the process of corporate change is staggering.* If for no other reason, calling new kids on the block is easier than old kids, because the new kids don't yet have their administrative defense screens in place.

2. Many corporations publish their press releases and news about the corporation on their own home pages. If you are targeting a corporate market, I would check in on these corporate home pages weekly.

3. One of the most marvelous sources of information about corporate change is a service of the *San Jose Mercury News* called News-

Hound. For $4.95 per month (at this writing), you can define five news profiles. Every hour, the NewsHound computers search through hundreds of stories and press releases and then e-mails articles to you that fit your profiles.

One of the sources used by NewsHound is PR Newswire. This is one of the channels on which corporate press releases are distributed. Frankly, most corporate press releases never see the light of day in print. But they can contain vital data about your market, and NewsHound is the best way I know to find them. Current subscription information on NewsHound is available at billgood.com.

4. Electric Library, as stated earlier, is my favorite resource on the Internet. Many cities have business publications—they are named *Salt Lake Business, San Jose Business,* etcetera. And Electric Library has lots of these local business publications on file. You could certainly search for various kinds of articles right in your marketplace. What will you find? All kinds of companies growing, changing, downsizing, promoting, laying off, and so on. For current information on Electric Library, of course, check in with billgood.com.

The Change Principle in Individual Markets

The Change Principle applies not only to corporations but to individuals as well. It's just a bit less obvious. It appears that individuals go through periods of stability and periods of change. And in these periods a lot of things change, many of them *apparently* unrelated. But there is something that unites the apparently different changes, and it is simply *the fact of change.*

In many industries, such as insurance, pieces of this principle have been grasped. For years, insurance agents have been advised to call a "new-birth list." The assumption is that a new birth in the family gives rise to heightened responsibility and additional needs for protection and coverage. Frankly, I don't think "additional needs" or "added responsibility" has much to do with it at all. I think the new-birth list is good because of the fact that it represents a *change in the family,* and where there is one change, there are likely to be others.

As we get into this topic, let me recommend a book that gives marvelous research on each of these changes: *Targeting Transitions: Marketing to Consumers During Life Changes* by Paula Mergenhagen. Information on the current availability of this work and other related works is, of course, available on our home page at billgood.com.

Life changes and where to look for their lists:

Life Change	Where to Look for Lists
New birth	New-birth announcement in local paper List broker County courthouse
Marriage	Marriage announcements in the paper. **Comment:** Then use Select Phone to look up both sets of parents. Keep in mind that one marriage announcement can be worth two or more sets of names. Here are people whose lifestyle is changing dramatically. Today, both sets of parents may be splitting the bill, and as soon as the wedding is over, their expenses are down and income is up.
Divorce	County courthouse. Divorce filings and completed divorces are matters of public record. List brokers will have lists of divorces in high-income zip codes. Of course, by the time it gets to the list broker, the divorce is a done deal and much of the change is over.
Long-term care and death	Get lists of elderly people from list brokers and offer services, generally with a direct-mail approach. Follow up on responses.
Job change	In *Targeting Transitions*, Mergenhagen cites a Bureau of Labor Statistics report that 7.8 percent of people who work in executive/administrative/managerial positions change jobs annually. For professionals the figure is 6.5 percent. The name of the game is to get in front of these people before the change occurs so that when it does happen, you can benefit from it. Befriend headhunters, employment agencies.
Retirement	Best source by far: In-house corporate papers. Set up NewsHound profiles to catch high-level corporate retirements.
Moving	Homes for sale listed through multiple listing services. Ask your friendly real estate agent for last week's copy. New telephone connections. Check with your local telephone company. In some areas you can download new telephone connections on the day the phone is turned on.

The Change Principle in Individual Daytime Market

In many industries, especially all areas of financial services, you can prospect individuals at work. You can't spend too much time at it because there is an inherent conflict of interest in handling a matter of personal affairs on the boss's time. But it can be done, especially since my method doesn't take much of your prospect's time.

RECENTLY PROMOTED EXECUTIVES: As an example, one financial adviser I know built his entire book of business on the change principle in daytime markets by focusing on recently promoted executives. He told me that when he was getting started, he and his wife used to go around every Thursday and pick up the local "shopper" newspapers in their area. They would cut out all the promotion announcements, and then he would give those promoted a call. His approach, which I have now incorporated into a recently promoted executive's script, went like this:

> Hello, Mr. Jones, this is (NAME) with (COMPANY). I am calling to congratulate you on your promotion and let you know that I have some excellent ideas to help you invest some of that new money.

His theory was that one way to grow as a broker was to get clients on the way up. He told me that several of his clients whose names he first got from local promotion announcements went on to become chief executive officers of Fortune 500 corporations.

Here are some sources of change names who can be contacted during the day. They would be prospects for almost any expensive item—securities, insurance, property, automobiles. Generally, when a promotion is announced in a major daily newspaper, a deluge of calls follows . . . and then silence. So wait a few days or even several weeks before calling. Better yet, scour corporate and trade papers. They're loaded, harder to get than daily newspaper promotion announcements, and therefore less likely to be hammered. Even better, set up a profile with NewsHound and periodically check in with Electric Library.

You can also purchase a list of recently promoted executives. Specify to your list broker that you want to subscribe to the change-of-address notices list made available from McGraw-Hill, the publisher of *Business Week* and other trade magazines. Don't contact McGraw-Hill directly. Contact your mailing list broker. A very large percentage of these change-of-address names have changed due to a promotion. Even when a person does not change location, if he is promoted from second vice-president to first vice-president, he will file change-of-address notices so that not even the people in the mail room will remember he was ever anything but first vice-president.

Buyers and Sellers of Commercial Property: In virtually every county in the United States, there is a *Journal of Record*. This is a publication that comes out anywhere from daily to quarterly and lists transactions of "public record," which means that anyone is entitled to know about them. It includes liens, divorces, marriages, wills filed for probate, and sale of real property. When a piece of commercial property, income residential property, or raw land is sold, you can be certain that a substantial piece of money changed hands. The seller got some. The real estate agent got some. There is surely a lawyer in there somewhere.

You definitely want to contact the seller of the property. Buyers, however, are also good prospects, because they have likewise gone through a major change. And don't forget the agent, broker, lawyer, and maybe the title insurer.

New Construction Projects: When a person or company is expanding, redecorating, or constructing a new building, a building permit is required. There is a company (McGraw-Hill again) that investigates these building permits, breaks them down into categories, and publishes them. The reports are called *The Dodge Reports* and are available in most public libraries. If you can't locate *The Dodge Reports* in your area, go investigate the city or county department that issues building permits. It will tell you who is expanding, remodeling, and redecorating. And that will tell you who has some money.

Legal Settlement: Some of the best securities accounts I know of have been obtained by calling people who have just received a legal settlement. These will frequently be announced in your local *Journal of Record* or daily newspaper. They will sometimes be announced in local business papers. So if you are selling any kind of expensive item, certainly consider people who have just received a good chunk of money. One of the few times to call a lawyer is when he or she has walked away with pockets stuffed with contingency settlement money.

Sale of Business: This information is available in the business pages of local newspapers, trade papers, and through changes in licensing at the local business license bureau.

The Change Principle in Individual Nighttime Market

If you are prospecting a residential market, there are lots of sources of change names.

People Selling Expensive Cars: This list is, of course, available in the classified section in the local newspaper. Given the search capabilities of today's electronic classified ads, you can specify price range and get a list of people in a flash selling a car worth more than, say, $20,000.

Some quick checking in Select Phone will give you the names of the people that have listed phone numbers. You will then at least know the names of some of the people you are contacting. And, if you have a bit of style and flair, you can usually tease the name of people who have published their unlisted number right out of them. Here's how:

YOU:	*(Ring, ring)*.
PROSPECT:	Hello.
YOU *(in a bright, cheerful voice)*:	Is this the person with the Mercedes for sale?
PROSPECT:	Yes.
YOU:	Very good. I have some good news and some bad news for you. Which would you like to hear first?
PROSPECT:	The good news.
YOU:	Let me give you the bad news first. I am not calling for the Mercedes. The good news is I am calling to let you know that I have a fantastic place for you to put some of that money when you sell it. May I mention an idea to you?
PROSPECT:	Sure, what is it?
YOU:	By the way, who am I speaking with?
PROSPECT:	Jack Jones.

Now you have the prospect's name and his unlisted phone number. By the way, classified ads are frequently filled with unlisted phone numbers, and this is one of the few sources for them. Like other hard-to-reach people, these individuals don't get their fair share of solicitation phone calls.

Owners Selling Their Own Home or Other Properties: These prospects are also available in the classified section of the newspaper. In the real estate industry, they are known as "Fizbos," which is the pronunciation for the acronym FSBO, which means "For Sale By Owner." Real estate people call Fizbos all the time, so it's not a bad idea to allow the ad to age for a week if you are going after them to sell them something other than a house.

Homeowners Selling Homes with Lots of Equity: This list can be extracted from an area's *Multiple Listing Book*. This is theoretically available only to members of the real estate profession who belong to a multiple listing board. But if you're friendly with a real estate agent, you can usually get someone to give you last week's copy. The *Multiple Listing*

Book is a record of all homes on the market that are listed with real estate agents. To get the list of homeowners with lots of equity, simply study the book and look for people who have owned their home for at least ten years. They will be the ones profiting from the real estate boom that began in the 1970s.

If you go after people who have owned their home for fifteen or twenty years or longer, you could be in for a major cash find. Anyone over the age of fifty-five who sells a home may take a onetime capital gains exclusion, which at this writing equals $125,000. This means that he or she does not have to pay any capital gains tax on up to $125,000 profit on the sale of a primary residence. Before age fifty-five, a person selling a home with a lot of equity has to invest in another home of at least equal value. Otherwise, he or she has to pay a tax. However, where there is lots of equity, there will usually be some cash available for other things. Here's how it might work even if the individual is not over fifty-five or is not going to take the onetime exclusion.

A homeowner may have purchased a $50,000 home in 1974 and sells it for $225,000 in 1986. He purchases a new home for $245,000 but instead of putting all of his $175,000 profit from the sale of his previous home into his new home, he may only put down the required 20 percent or about $50,000. As long as he has purchased a home of *equal or greater value,* he can do whatever he wants with his cash.

So if you can develop a prospect that will soon be getting his hands on a lot of money, why not!

HEIRS: Some people seem to think it is a terribly morbid idea to call the heirs of people recently deceased. My point of view is that this is a period of great and dramatic change. Estates will be restructured. Homes and property will be sold. Assets divided up. Someone will get this business. Why not you?

The obvious place to get these names is in the obituary notices in the local paper. If you want to take this one step further, you can go to the courthouse and ask to see the wills that have been filed for probate. These are all available to the public. When you read in the newspaper that a famous person has died and left $4 million to his cat, rest assured that the enterprising reporter who wrote the story used the same public record.

In dealing with the heirs list, it is in bad taste to call too soon and refer to your source of information. You would never call someone and say, "I was rummaging around in the basement of the courthouse recently and noticed that your aunt Matilda left you a bundle." Just deal with the person with tact and courtesy, as you would with any other person.

Tips on Developing Change Names

Copying down names at courthouses and cutting them out of newspapers does not require extraordinary amounts of skill and intelligence. In fact, it's a no-brainer. So I recommend that once you have developed your source of names and have tested it to make certain it produces worthwhile results, find a literate high school student and pay him or her to develop your names. If he or she gets ten names an hour, it's only costing you about thirty-three cents a name. And that's cheaper than you can buy some of the more expensive lists. It could cost you $10 to $15 a week to keep your list refreshed with first-rate change names.

The Referral Principle of List Replacement and Development

In the first edition of this book, I wrote:

> . . . salespeople in every industry will work hard, do a good job, develop a good rapport with a client, and not ever, not once, ask for referrals. One insurance company I ran across trains their agents to ask for "two but not more than three" referrals. Why stop at three? Why not ask for fifty or one hundred? Why stay on food stamps? Break loose! Ask for lots of referrals.

I now understand why it is so hard to get salespeople to ask for referrals. *They know, in their heart of hearts, it doesn't work.*

I was wrong, OK?

Why? Because what you get when you ask for referrals is:

a. A client put on the spot

b. A name or names that are not much better than cold call names

So if we're not going to be *soliciting* referrals, then what?

How about: *promoting referrals.*

Never ask: Who do you know . . . ?

Frequently remind: "If you run into anyone who might need help with their widgets, ask them to give me a call, would you?"

The first question solicits referrals. It generates names, not referrals. The second approach helps create a referral consciousness so that when your satisfied client runs into someone who can use your product or service he or she will refer them to you. A few referrals a month really strengthen your prospect lists and will be an important source of future business. Sometimes, with a very good client, you can strike gold.

I did a seminar a while back for one of the major insurance companies. At the end of the seminar, the general agent (GA) was very pleased. I first asked him for a copy of the GA directory for that company, which he gave me. Then I asked him to look it over—there were several hundred names on it—and check off the GA's he felt were big enough to afford one of our seminars. He took maybe ten or fifteen minutes to do this. Finally, I said, "Jack, would you mind if I contact these people and mention that you are a happy client?"

"No problem."

Bingo! I had over fifty referrals! Getting referrals doesn't necessarily mean just a few.

The Connection Principle of List Replacement and Development

People like doing business with people they know. As you progress with my system, you'll come to understand that it is *designed* to introduce you to lots of people and give you the opportunity to get to know them.

But what if you already know lots of people? Why not use them? Many, if not most, salespeople not only do not but will not use their connections. I even met a woman in Texas who explained to me that not only did she not use her father's very extensive connections, but she wouldn't even consider it. She said, "I'm going to do it on my own."

This idea is comparable to a race car driver at the Indy 500 who wins the pole position and who then says, "I'm going to do it on my own without the advantages of the pole position."

In other words, if you've got 'em, use 'em.

So let's talk about how to develop and utilize your family, social, and business connections. Follow my suggestions in the pages that follow, and, at the least, you'll develop superb replacement names in about six months. Best-case, you'll develop and utilize the best list you're likely to see.

Some Industries Built on Connections

It used to be that if you didn't have connections, you wouldn't get hired in some industries. That's how important connections were and are.

This was true in the securities industry, and it was also true in life insurance. As a matter of fact, the life insurance industry today has benefited enormously from the connections of failed agents. Most every insurance company I know has a program called something like Project 100 or Project 200. Before agents are licensed, they are expected to write down the names of one hundred (or two hundred) people they know so that as soon as the license is approved, they can call their connections, get appointments, and sell them something. The problem is that when the agents run out of connections, they are all too often out of business, because they don't know how to cold call. The insurance companies, in the meantime, wind up with the accounts.

So as you see, I recommend you *start* with cold calling. Let your connections be your second year's business.

Why Don't Salespeople Use Connections?

In every industry I've worked in except insurance, I have found that salespeople are reluctant to use connections. In asking countless salespeople why, the answer I hear over and over is "I just feel awkward" and "I feel like I'm taking advantage of them." I have a theory on where this awkwardness comes from and, therefore, some ideas on how to overcome it.

The awkwardness comes from the fact that your connections don't perceive you in your new identity. Let's say you grew up in a wealthy family. You are known as the son or daughter of Joe Doakes. You're not recognized as Joe Doakes, account executive, or Joe Doakes, Jr., insurance specialist, or Josephina Doakes, real estate agent. So when you're attempting to communicate to someone from the "wrong identity," it smacks of "taking advantage." And it does create problems. Never mind that many of your connections do a great deal of business with your father at the country club. Never mind that people like doing business with people they know. Because they are not aware of your new identity, they feel awkward and that makes you feel awkward as well. The solution, quite obviously, is to change the way your connections perceive you.

Using Family Connections

Quite obviously, the way to use family connections is to get the family member with the connections to help you. I met an account executive one time whose grandfather was an extremely well-known and influential man in the community. He was active in sports, community affairs, business, and politics. So while the young broker was aggressively cold calling to build an identity of his own, he was following a very low-key approach with his grandfather. The grandfather was making a point of including him in golf foursomes, of inviting him to the country club, of making certain he participated in political meetings, and everywhere he went he took the opportunity of introducing the grandson as "This is Joe Doakes the third, a stockbroker with Merrill Lynch."

In time, the grandfather's connections would come to perceive Joe Doakes the third as Joe Doakes, a stockbroker with Merrill Lynch. And in time, they would begin to discuss investment ideas, and when that occurred, Joe Doakes the third could safely assume that it was OK to be a bit more aggressive in prospecting what are now his grandfather's *and his own* connections.

In my opinion, it is a pity to use connections too soon. You must first alter the perception that people have of you and create a new one. And frankly, this takes time and effort. So don't try to live on your connections at first. Look at them as next year's business.

Utilizing Your Own Connections

Many people, when coming into a new sales position, know lots of people. These connections may come from college fraternities or sororities, business clubs, former selling jobs, former employers and coworkers, neighbors, and so on. And as with family connections, you are likely to be reluctant to pursue them actively as prospects.

The cause of the reluctance is the same. Instead of perceiving you as Joe Doakes, real estate agent, they still know you as Joe Doakes, fraternity brother at Beta Theta Pi, or Josephina Doakes, copier salesperson at Acme Company. The fraternity brother or copier salesperson has no reason to call his or her friends and talk about real estate, insurance, or whatever.

So the name of the game, once again, is to create a new perception. There is no reason why the old perception as fraternity brother cannot remain in place. But the new perception should become "fraternity brother who is now a real estate broker for Coldwell Banker." Then, when that new perception has been created, you can run with that old truth that "people like doing business with people they know." When your old fraternity brother decides to sell his house, he'll want to call someone he knows who is in the business.

Creating New Perceptions

So how do you create this new perception with your personal connections?

1. Make up your list. Think of *everyone* who might have need of your services. Review your old address and phone books. Fraternity or sorority directories. Old customer lists. Directories from former employers, neighbors, dentists, doctors, lawyers, cleaners, plumbers, TV repairpeople, home repair professionals, and so on.

2. If at all possible, get these names entered in a computer. If you don't have a computer, you will have to hand-address the envelopes or type them. Mailing labels are not desirable. These are, after all, your friends, family, and associates. At least treat them with enough respect to address their letter individually.

3. Send your prospects a letter. All you want to do is send them information of general interest. Magazine articles are preferable (and generally better written) than company promotion. The first letter might read like this:

> Dear Fred:
>   As you may recall from the announcement I sent you several months ago, I am now associated with Smither & Snorfleet, insurance agents.
>   From time to time I will be sending you some material you might find of interest.
>   I hope you and your family are doing well.
>   Sincerely,
>   Cortney Blather, III

Please note: At no point does this letter ask for *any response of any kind.*

This is an example of the "no-key" campaign I will define for you in a later chapter. Remember, "low key" is low pressure. "No key" is NO PRESSURE. None. Not a hint of "If you have any questions, call me." Just get your name in front of your connections, and your good name and previous association will work magic over a period of a few months.

Send a letter like this to get the process started. Next month, send some other information and another *no-key* letter. And the next month something else.

If you're in the securities industry, send along an article on mutual funds or a change in the tax law or what your favorite stock analyst is recommending. You can even print up some notes on small pieces of paper that say, "Here's something I thought you could use." Signed, Joe Doakes. And then all you have to do is initial it. A secretary, service assistant, or you can then hand-address or type the envelopes; or, if you have access to a computer or word processor, you can have your list input into the memory of the machine, and run the letters and envelopes in a moment's notice.

The new perception might take months to achieve. And you'll know when it's done because you'll start to get calls. Once you start receiving calls, that's your signal that the new perception is in place. Now you can safely call your connections!

If you persist, you will build a list of people who know who you are and who will contact you when they are interested and ready. Also, by that time you will feel confident that when you contact them, your call will be welcomed. In other words, if you've got the pole position, use it. There is no glamour or magic to being forever condemned to cold calling. And as a matter of fact, if you really analyze the whole cherries and pits theory, you'll see that the style I'm recommending is really designed to create warm lists. Ultimately, wouldn't it be nice to have connections with a list of fifteen hundred prospects? Well, that's what I'm proposing.

Rules for Mailing to Your Connections List

Here are some rules for managing your connections list:

- Never use mailing labels. Grant your connection the appearance and consideration of *first class.* Either put your connections list in a computer that can individually address envelopes with a letter-quality printer, or hand-address the envelopes.

- Use individual stamps, not metered mail. Again, this is part of creating the look of first class. Something that looks like an individual letter gets opened first.

- Frequency is more important than brilliance. By this I mean if you don't have anything especially brilliant to say to your connections, send them an article about something of interest about your product or service.

- To be taken off the list, a person must ask to be removed. Otherwise, leave them on the list.

Contacting Your Connections by Phone

When I began working in the securities industry, it was very common for branch managers to recommend a service approach for cold calling. The only problem was it did not and does not work well for cold prospecting. A service approach, however, *is the way to go in calling your connections.* It goes like this:

YOU: Hello, Fred, this is Joe Doakes. As you've probably heard, I'm affiliated now with Ditchwater Securities. You have been receiving my mailings for a while, correct?

(RESPONSE): Great! What I would like to do is renew our acquaintance, get together for lunch, and see if there isn't something we can do for you. What time would be best for you?

Remember, in its heyday, this was *the* approach since only people with connections were hired to begin with. If you don't have connections, you'll have to do it another way. But if you have connections, this is the way to go. No key. Go see them and don't pressure.

As you plan a connections approach, keep in mind that this is business that will materialize in six months. You can't live on it now.

If you have the connections and can use them in your business, dig 'em out and get those envelopes addressed.

Summary

Once you have *developed* and then *improved* your list to the point that you are generating a profitable response, you can maintain the list through:

Change names

Referrals

Connections

ASSIGNMENT

Get enough sources of change names, referrals, and connections flowing in to balance the names falling off your list.

CHAPTER 7

List Management

> *"A place for everything and everything in its place."*
>
> —Francis Williamson Good, age forty-two

Very probably I got my flare for famous statements from my mother, who undoubtedly came up with this one. At least that's what I thought when she kept saying it to me for years on end. This timeless truth is the key to list management.

In the chapter, I am going to show you:

How to keep track of all your lists.

How to use a personal computer *as part of* your record-keeping system.

I will tell you this with absolute certainty: If you do not have a good list management system in place, you will drown in a sea of paper, and lose valuable prospects and clients.

So let's jump right in.

Definitions

Keeping track of hundreds or even thousands of names is quite a trick. So let's first separate our lists into three very broad lists: Mass Mail, Prospects, and Clients.

MASS MAIL: These are just names on a list. You don't know any more than name, address, phone number, and perhaps some basic demographic data. They've never responded. *Or* you've downgraded somebody you know more about but who wasn't worth keeping as an even minimally active prospect.

PROSPECTS: A prospect, for our purposes, is anyone who has responded with whom you would like to do business. Our prospects are broken down into different grades of goodness:

Hot prospect (these have started the selling cycle).

A=cherry

B=green cherry

C=info lead

D=pitch and miss

F=won't return calls (These are on the way out the door unless you elect to save them by assigning them pitch and miss status and rescuing them from sales oblivion.)

Unless you have decided you do not want to do business with someone because of general disagreeableness or jerkdom, the rule is that a prospect remains on your list until he or she buys, dies, or becomes a jerk.

Quite obviously, the best way to store such names is on computer. But I have some thoughts on the computer I would like you to read before we begin a discussion of the use of the computer to store your names and addresses.

A Word About Computers

I am very much opposed to salespeople *personally* doing much more with computers than using them to look up information. This doesn't mean they aren't very important to the entire process. But when salespeople—who can be worth many hundreds or even thousands of dollars an hour—spend time printing letters, updating records, or even worse, entering records, well, you might as well pour hard cash down the porcelain bowl. Salespeople acting as computer operators may alone account for the fact that recent studies do not show much productivity gain from computer use in business.

There are two reasons, gleaned from long and bitter experience, why I think computers are being misused by salespeople. First, entirely different frames of mind are required for computer operations, as opposed to selling. A salesperson operates on the mind-set best described as "Ready, Fire, Aim." In the course of my company's helping build over 2,400 sales teams in the financial services industry, we have learned this lesson well: A salesperson operating with a salesperson frame of mind will commit horrible mistakes, change things, and otherwise muck up a database. But a salesperson selling with a computer operator frame of mind, which is based on sameness, consistency, logic, and sequence, will starve to death.

The two mind-sets are contradictory, inimical, and just downright hostile to each other.

Second, computer use generates unproductive time. Consider this: To keep a computer system up to date—which means letters sent, reports run, back-ups attended to, records updated—requires ten to fifteen hours a week *per salesperson*. At my company, my sales force is worth $1,200 an hour in gross revenue to my firm for time spent making presentations to interested, qualified prospects. Do I want them spending ten to fifteen hours a week doing computer work? I don't think so.

So here's what I recommend:

First, if you personally have to do computer operations right now, set up entirely different time blocks for selling and computer operations. In your sales time block, the only thing you do with the computer is look up information. In your block as computer operator, do the updates, letters, back-ups, and so on. Your computer operator time block should obviously be scheduled in nonoptimum prospecting and selling times. If your manager sees you touching the blasted thing in optimum selling or prospecting times, he or she should chop the thing up into little pieces and be done with it. You can make a lot more money on the phone and seeing clients and prospects than you ever will pecking away at the computer.

Second, as soon as possible, get your company to let you hire a part-time high school or college nerd or geek to run your database.

So, as we develop our list management system according to the pages that follow, I am going to direct my remarks at two job descriptions: you as salesperson and as a computer operator. I fully understand that you may, for now, be holding both jobs.

The Good List Management System

The system I'm going to recommend may keep information in as many as three places:

1. A computerized database. Basically, we are going to be using the computer for mailings, both individual letters and mass mailings.

2. On 5×7 cards. You'll keep your notes here and use a date-ordered file system to trigger callbacks.

3. On cold calling lists stapled to a copy of my List Evaluation Sheet. If all you are doing is calling these folks, there's no point in going to the time and effort to enter the names in a database.

Here are the rules of the list management system:

- Mass-mail names, especially if purchased from a list broker, should optimally be imported into your electronic database. Nonelectronic mass-mail names, most likely derived from various printed lists, should be pasted to List Evaluation Sheets and kept in a big notebook.

- When someone becomes a prospect, basic data such as name, address, interest, and so on, should go into the computer (if it's not already there) so you can do targeted mailings.

- Notes, actions to be taken, and such should go on 5×7 cards that are then kept in a file box I shall shortly describe.

- Each month, every prospect gets a drip letter. Every three months every prospect gets a phone call (that's dripping).

With these basic principles in place, let's take a closer look at the details.

Managing Mass-Mail Lists

We are going to begin the establishment of this system with mass-mail lists.

There are seven rules to mass mailings. This may not be the most exciting reading, but once you have studied, understood, and then implemented it, you may very well be excited, because you will see an end to stuff slipping through the cracks, or worse, whooshing through the floorboards. So here goes. The seven rules:

1. Mass-mail lists are kept in one of three places.
- On a computer.

    If you're going to do any serious prospecting, you will need several thousand names. But as you set up your computer, DO NOT set up different files for different lists. Put all names into one file. Otherwise, your computer operator will spend hours hunting through various files for mass-mail names returned "addressee unknown." (It's not a bad idea to test whichever program you have to determine how many names it can easily process in a single database. If it's just a few hundred, get another program.)

    By putting all your names in a single database, you can easily move names from one category, such as mass mail, to another category, such as prospect, without retyping data. You can also more easily locate names that have to be deleted.

    Your database should be set up so that at least one of the fields enables you to trace the source of the mass-mail list. This "source field" should contain enough text space to describe where you got the list from. This enables you to evaluate at some later date the responses from that list.

Your database should also have a "list" field. There should be four choices in the list field: client, prospect, connection, and mass mail. As a name upgrades from mass mail to prospect, instead of having to retype the name into another database, just change its list field.

- Printed on labels, with the labels affixed to 5×7 cards.

If you don't have a computer, whenever you order names from a list broker, you should order them on labels. You are absolutely not going to use labels for your mailings, as letters with labels on them simply get thrown out. Rather, you're going to affix the label to a card.

As you will see in Chapter 19, you can make many more calls when your lists are already affixed to a *properly designed* card. Any card is better than trying to call off a printed list, because when you get a prospect, you don't have to then rewrite the name. If you have a well-designed card, such as the one in this book, you can use the card design to further speed up your calling. Sales is, of course, a numbers game.

As you will see when you study the card, when certain conditions change, all you have to do is check off an option already printed on the card and then hand the card to your computer operator, who will know what to do. You, in the meantime, are back at work prospecting!

The design of the card and your refusal to do computer operations in optimum prospecting time can increase your results per hour by 50 percent or more.

Even if you do have a computer, the correct thing to do is use it to print out labels and then affix those labels to cards.

- Paste lists of names to List Evaluation Sheets and keep all such lists in a notebook so you can evaluate them. (On page 84 is a copy of a List Evaluation Sheet. You can download an MS Word file of this sheet from billgood.com.)

The List Evaluation Sheet is designed to track results from each time you call a list. If you copy a list out of a street address directory or other source, instead of just having it lying around loose, paste it to a List Evaluation Sheet and keep it with your other lists in a List Evaluation notebook. Whenever you call the list, keep the appropriate statistics (which will be discussed in Chapter 19).

For each mass-mail list that you keep on computer, you should also print out a hard copy and use it to start a List Evaluation Sheet. This way you have, in a single place, a complete record of all your mass-mail lists. Only by keeping the records can you evaluate who to call.

Sounds simple, doesn't it?

List Evaluation

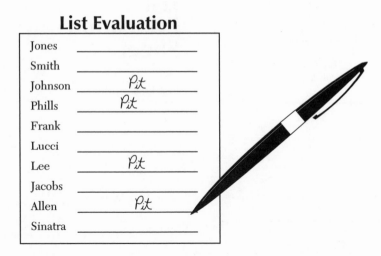

Jones	
Smith	
Johnson	Pit
Phills	Pit
Frank	
Lucci	
Lee	Pit
Jacobs	
Allen	Pit
Sinatra	

2. As you make contact with mass-mail names by phone, never identify those not interested as pits. If you pulled out a list and it looked like this, would you call it? Of course not! It's nothing but a bunch of pits. But remember: As long as a list produces profitable results, you will continue to recycle it. Recycle means a series of low-key calls. It does not say anything about taking names off the list.

If you have "pitted" many of the names on the list, you will not be interested in calling it back. Don't write down the negatives; just remove the jerks from the list. Saves time, too.

3. Refine and refresh lists producing more than one and a half cherries per hour and then push up the minimum results you will accept to three per hour. Naturally, if you don't have any lists that will produce a large number of cherries per hour, you're not going to throw down your phone and quit. But by maintaining the documentation in your mass-mail notebook, you will identify some lists that always work better than others, and even if they're not yet up to our definition of a "good list," you will be focusing on the ones that produce more than others.

We can arbitrarily say that you should initially keep those that produce 1.5 cherries per hour. As you get other lists that produce even more, drop the non- or underperforming lists. As you do this, the total responsiveness of your mass-mail list increases. The effect on the value of your prospecting time is enormous.

4. After attempting several variations of scripts on a list, replace lists producing less than 1.5 cherries an hour.

5. Don't mix lists. When you're doing a campaign, don't combine the names from several lists. It completely messes up your ability to evaluate your results. Enough said.

BOX SCORE

Date ___/___/___ Caller ___/___/___
Start : End : Elapsed :

Script _____
Dials _____
Contacts _____
Appts _____
Cherries _____
Greenies _____
Info Leads _____
Cherries/Hr _____
Comment: _____

List Evaluation Sheet

List Description:

_____
_____
_____

Date List Acquired: ___/___/___

Source: _____

_____
_____

(Paste list here, or use space for other notes.)

BOX SCORE

Date ___/___/___ Caller ___/___/___
Start : End : Elapsed :

Script _____
Dials _____
Contacts _____
Appts _____
Cherries _____
Greenies _____
Info Leads _____
Cherries/Hr _____
Comment: _____

BOX SCORE

Date ___/___/___ Caller ___/___/___
Start : End : Elapsed :

Script _____
Dials _____
Contacts _____
Appts _____
Cherries _____
Greenies _____
Info Leads _____
Cherries/Hr _____
Comment: _____

6. For each new mass-mail list on label, or computer, take a hundred labels or so, affix them to cards, and test the list. Since getting good cards printed can be expensive, you don't want to take a bad list and burn up five hundred cards. So take a small amount, add the labels to the cards, and test. If the list is decent, print out the rest of the list on labels and attach these to cards. Keep the cards for a given list together with a rubber band. Record each calling session on a List Evaluation Sheet. Keep all List Evaluation Sheets in a notebook. When your mass-mail lists are on cards, you can make many more calls, so it's worth the extra expense to buy the cards.

7. When a mass-mail lead becomes a prospect, make sure you remove it from the mass-mail list, preferably by changing its list field from mass mail to prospect. When the prospect buys something, change the list field again from prospect to client. Prospects will be getting mailings urging them to become clients or to respond in some way. You need to make certain that client mailings do not go to prospects.

Managing Prospect Lists

- Keep all prospect names on cards. Update the computer *only when there is an interest change or when a letter otherwise needs to be sent. Then refile the card according to the principles that govern its new interest status.*

OK, what do we mean by "interest change"? When a mass-mail name first becomes a cherry, green cherry, or info lead, that person is now more interested than before. When a current lead, say a cherry, wants a follow-up later, it becomes a green cherry. That person is now less interested.

All you have to do is check the appropriate box on your card and hand it to the computer operator. He or she will consult the Computer Operator's Cheatsheet, send the correct letter, and refile the card.

The Lead Processing Letters

I have created for you eleven Lead Processing Letters. Thoroughly covered in Chapter 15, these letters are used to send out information and to maintain contact with the prospect until he or she is ready to begin a selling cycle. I will be making reference to these letters in this chapter.

With this as an introduction, let's meet the Prospect Record Card.

The Prospect Record Card—Side 1

Red	Yellow	Green	Blue	White	Orange	Black

_____ M/F _____ _____
First Person's Name   Office Phone   Home Phone

_____ M/F H/W/O_____ _____
Second Person's Name   Relationship   Fax Phone

_____   _____
Home Address   Company Name

_____   _____
Mailing Address   Company Address

_____   _____
City/State/Zip   Address

_____   _____
Important Information and/or   City/State/Zip
E-mail Address

First Contact (mark one): **A** Chry **E** Other/Ag/Bkr

C Send Info on: _____

B Opportunity: $ _____ on ____/____/____

Situation: _____

From List: _____ By a Caller: _____

Date	Action to be done

Fold the colored dots over the top of the record card.
Use our sample meanings or your own.

The Prospect Record Card—Side 2

| Black | Orange | White | Blue | Green | Yellow | Red |

Notes: _____

_____

_____

_____

Salesperson: Mark Record Status Changes, Then Submit This Card to the CO

Updated __/__/__	Updated __/__/__	Updated __/__/__
❏ Purchased!—Show as New Client	❏ Purchased!—Show as New Client	❏ Purchased!—Show as New Client
❏ Appointment, 3 or more days away	❏ Appointment, 3 or more days away	❏ Appointment, 3 or more days away
❏ Upgrade to **A** Cherry	❏ Upgrade to **A** Cherry	❏ Upgrade to **A** Cherry
❏ Up/Downgrade to **B** Greenie:	❏ Up/Downgrade to **B** Greenie:	❏ Up/Downgrade to **B** Greenie:
$_____	$_____	$_____
on __/__/__	on __/__/__	on __/__/__
from _____	from _____	from _____
❏ Downgrade to **C** info lead	❏ Downgrade to **C** info lead	❏ Downgrade to **C** info lead
❏ **D** Pitched & Missed	❏ **D** Pitched & Missed	❏ **D** Pitched & Missed
❏ **F** Won't return calls	❏ **F** Won't return calls	❏ **F** Won't return calls
❏ Downgrade to Mass Mail	❏ Downgrade to Mass Mail	❏ Downgrade to Mass Mail
❏ Jerk—mark for NO calls/letters ever	❏ Jerk—mark for NO calls/letters ever	❏ Jerk—mark for NO calls/letters ever
Include info with letter:	Include info with letter:	Include info with letter:
_____	_____	_____
_____	_____	_____
Add/Remove Interest(s):	Add/Remove Interest(s):	Add/Remove Interest(s):
Red Yellow Green Blue White Orange Black	Red Yellow Green Blue White Orange Black	Red Yellow Green Blue White Orange Black

To have your CO add an Interest (sticker and in computer), circle it in the lower part of this side of the card.

To have CO remove an Interest from the computer, cross it out on this side and pull the sticker off yourself. For Interests color codes, see preceding page.

Interest Changes and the Card File System

Most of this card is self-evident. Some of it, though, is not, so let's take a couple of examples.

> **Event:** You get a new cherry.
>
> **Actions:** Salesperson fills in basic data on Side 1 (if not already covered by a label), circles A Chry in the "First Contact" section on side 1, and indicates what information is to be sent. The card is then put in the basket to be handled by the computer operator, who, of course, might be you.

First Contact (mark one): **A** Chry **E** Other/Ag/Bkr
C Send Info on: _Widget Report_
B Opportunity: $ _____ on _03_ / _31_ / _98_
Situation: _____
From List: _Widget Eaters Association_ By a Caller: _____

Until completely familiar with the lead management system, the computer operator should consult the cheatsheet and determine what is to be sent to the letter named NuChrySP (explained on page 108).

As instructed by the Computer Operator's cheatsheet, the card is refiled in your 1–31 file (See "Date ordered," page 104) seven days from the day the information is sent out.

Let's take another example.

> **Event:** You find a green cherry. This person is interested in your widgets but only after the end of their fiscal year.
>
> **Action:** Salesperson circles B Opportunity, supplies the data, and adds other information as shown. The card is then given to the computer operator.

First Contact (mark one): **A** Chry **E** Other/Ag/Bkr
C Send Info on: _Widget Report_
B Opportunity: $ _____ on _03_ / _31_ / _98_
Situation: _Interested at end of fiscal year_
From List: _Widget Cooking Club_ By a Caller: _____

After consulting the cheatsheet, the computer operator prints NuGrnSP.doc and also prints Info1.doc and Info2.doc (see page 108). These last two letters are set aside to be mailed ten days from the day of call and twenty days from the day of call. The card is filed with next month's green cherries so that continuous dripping can occur.

Now, let's take a look at an interest change of an existing prospect.

Event: Green cherry, contacted three weeks before the opportunity date, sets up an appointment.

Action: Salesperson, in one of the "action blocks" on side 2 of the card, checks off "Appt" and notes the date. In the "Notes" section of the card, the salesperson writes down the date and time of the appointment. The card is then given to the computer operator.

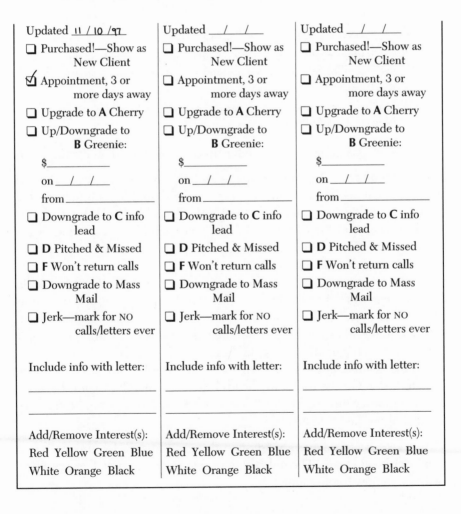

Updated 11 / 10 /97	Updated __/__/__	Updated __/__/__
❏ Purchased!—Show as New Client	❏ Purchased!—Show as New Client	❏ Purchased!—Show as New Client
☑ Appointment, 3 or more days away	❏ Appointment, 3 or more days away	❏ Appointment, 3 or more days away
❏ Upgrade to **A** Cherry	❏ Upgrade to **A** Cherry	❏ Upgrade to **A** Cherry
❏ Up/Downgrade to **B** Greenie:	❏ Up/Downgrade to **B** Greenie:	❏ Up/Downgrade to **B** Greenie:
$_____	$_____	$_____
on __/__/__	on __/__/__	on __/__/__
from_____	from_____	from_____
❏ Downgrade to **C** info lead	❏ Downgrade to **C** info lead	❏ Downgrade to **C** info lead
❏ **D** Pitched & Missed	❏ **D** Pitched & Missed	❏ **D** Pitched & Missed
❏ **F** Won't return calls	❏ **F** Won't return calls	❏ **F** Won't return calls
❏ Downgrade to Mass Mail	❏ Downgrade to Mass Mail	❏ Downgrade to Mass Mail
❏ Jerk—mark for NO calls/letters ever	❏ Jerk—mark for NO calls/letters ever	❏ Jerk—mark for NO calls/letters ever
Include info with letter:	Include info with letter:	Include info with letter:
_____	_____	_____
_____	_____	_____
Add/Remove Interest(s): Red Yellow Green Blue White Orange Black	Add/Remove Interest(s): Red Yellow Green Blue White Orange Black	Add/Remove Interest(s): Red Yellow Green Blue White Orange Black

Following the instructions on the cheatsheet, the computer operator prints the letter and sets it aside in a tickler file to mail four days before the appointment. The card is then filed in the salesperson's 1–31 file one day before the appointment. The salesperson will then call the prospect and confirm the appointment the day before it is scheduled.

The File System

The file system I recommend is a *date-ordered, prioritized callback file cross-referenced by area of product interest and set up on the computer so that drip mailings can occur.* To implement it you need:

A few hundred to several thousand 5×7 good prospect cards

5×7 file card box

1–31 dividers

5×7 dividers marked January to December

A 5×7 divider or folder marked "No Calls" (You will have to make your own label for this. The 1–31 and monthly dividers are available commercially.)

Up to seven colors, Avery, ¾" pressure sensitive dots (red, yellow, green, blue, white, orange, black)

Let's take each piece of the definition and see how it all fits together.

DATE ORDERED: This means we are going to file the card according to when it again needs a personal contact. We will not file it alphabetically. Rather, we will drop it into the appropriate slot in the 1–31 dividers, if it needs a contact in the next month. If not, we will file it according to the month it should be called. In this case, it just drops into the appropriate slot in a series of January–December dividers.

At this point, I know what your concern is. "What if Zelda Zorch calls in and I can't find her card?" Yes, this will happen . . . once in a blue moon. However, if she's important enough to have been scheduled for a future contact, then you've also got her filed on your computer! So you can look up some or all of her data there.

If that's not enough, here's what you say: "Zelda, I file all my records in date order. Off the top of my head, I do not remember when I scheduled you for a callback. While I'm looking, would you remind me of the subject of our last conversation?"

PRIORITIZED: We have already laid the groundwork for this with our Prospect Food Chain. The only thing remaining is to officially assign priorities and how to file them.

Here's a Good file system cheatsheet for you. You can download an MS Word copy from billgood.com.

Good Filing Principle Cheatsheet

Prospect Priority	How Filed
AA=Hot Prospect	Filed in 1–31 file according to the day additional action is required. If this is an in-person or phone appointment, there will also be a confirmation letter, filed four days before the appointment—unless there's no time between now and then.
A=Cherry	Filed same as Hot Prospect, except callback (never an immediate appointment). Note that ONLY Hot Prospects and Cherries are filed in the 1–31 file.If you clutter this section of your file with other stuff, you will no longer have a *prioritized* callback file. So everyone else goes in your Jan–Dec file.
B=Green Cherry	If funds are due toward end of a month, file in that month's slot. Otherwise, file in *previous* month's slot. In that month, the greenie will receive a call.
C=Info	When a lead first becomes an Info lead, it is filed in next month's slot with a note in the Actions section of the card to call and requalify (see Lead Processing Scripts). The objective of that call is to upgrade to a red or green cherry, and failing that, to ensure the prospect specifically wants to continue on your mailing list. After requalification, if the prospect remains an Info lead, the card is set ahead three months, at which time it will receive its three-month call.
D=Pitch and Miss	When a lead is pitched, it is set ahead three months, at which time it will receive its three-month call.
F=No Calls	When someone won't return a call, they are sent the No Call letter and then dropped into the No Calls file divider. If they do not then respond, you have the option of *pitting* them or, for whatever reason you deem them especially desirable, assigning them Pitch and Miss status and treating them accordingly.

CROSS-REFERENCED BY AREA OF PRODUCT INTEREST: Unless you sell only one thing, you will be very interested in how to cross-reference your file by area of product interest. It will make you a lot of money.

What people are likely to buy depends on what they are *interested in.* To cross-reference by area of product interest, you just need to define the likely areas of product interest, assign each a color, and buy some ¾-inch colored dots corresponding to the colors you have assigned to the interests. As you learn more about your prospect's interests, you just affix the appropriate colored dot to the correct spot on the card. Voilà! You've cross-referenced by area of product interest.

Here is a possible interest table from financial services. Obviously, a client or prospect could have one or more of the following interests:

COLOR	INTEREST	EXPLANATION
Green	Growth	Interested in their portfolio growing
Blue	Income	Want or need current income from their investments
Red	Safety	A primary concern is safety of principal
Orange	Tax-Free	Not only do they want income, but in their tax bracket, they are interested in tax-free income
Yellow	Speculation	This person wants lots of growth and is willing to assume risk to achieve it
White	Estate Planning	Wants to ensure heirs inherit the estate, not Uncle Sam
Black	Life Insurance	Interested in protecting assets or family income in case of an unpleasant surprise

You can download an Interest Table from billgood.com if you like. In this case, you can probably do it quicker in Word if you are even minimally proficient.

Here's how it works: As you learn about your prospect's interests, you check off one or more of the half-moons where the dots are supposed to go. Give the card to the computer operator, who will affix the appropriate dot and, if your computer is set up correctly, add an interest to the computer record. These colored dots enable you to conduct various campaigns built around interest.

To stay with our financial services example, suppose you sell stocks. Some of your clients are interested in, say, speculation. You get a few hundred extra shares of a hot IPO (initial public offering) and decide to prospect. Who should you call? Answer: Anyone with a yellow dot. Just pull all your cards with a yellow dot and call them. Some will be hot enough to buy *right now!*

So there you have it: a date-ordered, prioritized callback file system cross-referenced by area of product interest . . . and set up on computer so that drip mailings can occur.

Here's THE LAW: If you offer someone something they are genuinely interested in, they will find the money. As you call your yellows, you will find some become hot, some upgrade to cherry, some become green, and undoubtedly some are downgraded. Yes, I know, some of the cards are not set for a callback for months. It doesn't matter. When you have something they may be interested in, call them!

The Full System Know-how

Following are cheatsheets for the salesperson and for the computer operator. It is important that you study these well. To operate the filing system correctly, you need to understand:

The card itself (pages 100–101)

The Good Filing Principle Cheatsheet (page 105)

The Computer Operator Cheatsheet (pages 107–8)

The Salesperson's File System Cheatsheet (pages 110–11)

The Interest Table (page 106)

Computer Operator's Cheatsheet

File System Cheatsheet

* *Processing New Leads*

ALL New Prospects (not yet in database)

a. Enter or update basic data.

b. If computer: Change List field to *Prospect.*

c. Add interests, if any.

d. Add important information.

e. Continue with appropriate choice below.

NEW A CHERRY (INTERESTED AND QUALIFIED NOW)

a. Send: *NuChrySP* (initial contact by salesperson), *NuChryC* (initial contact by caller), or *NuChryM* (initial response by direct mail), enclosing promised material indicated on the card.

b. Place in 1–31 file for follow-up call seven days from mailing information.*

NEW C INFO LEAD (INTERESTED, BUT CAN'T PIN DOWN OPPORTUNITY OR FUNDS DUE DATE)

a. Send *NuInfoSP* or *NuInfoC* letter, enclosing promised material indicated on the card.

b. Print *Info1* letter, file ten days from mailing. (If that is not a working day, choose first working day *before* that date.)

c. Print *Info2* letter, file twenty days from mailing (adjusting earlier if required).

d. File with next month's Cs.

NEW B GREEN CHERRY (INTERESTED, FUNDS DUE OR OPPORTUNITY AT KNOWN LATER DATE)

a. Send *NuGrnSP* or *NuGrnC* letter, enclosing promised material indicated on the card.

b. Print *Info1* letter, file to go out ten days from first mailing. (But if that is not a working day, then choose first working day *before* that date.)

c. Print *Info2* letter, file it to go out twenty days from first mailing (adjusting to an earlier date if required).

d. File with next month's Bs.

• *PROCESSING CURRENT LEADS (BACK OF CARD)*

ALL EXISTING LEAD CARDS (ALREADY IN DATABASE)

a. Be on the lookout for new or changed information. Salesperson *should* have crossed through anything old and added new info.

b. When you make each change called for—as instructed below—put a tiny check so you and the salesperson will know how it has been done.

c. If nothing else is required from you, then *if* a future "Actions to be done" is filled in on the front of card, transfer it to the 1–31 file.*

PURCHASED—SHOW AS NEW CLIENT

a. On computer: Change List field to *Client*.

---

*Or, if office policy, return card to salesperson to do same.

b. Send *TksNuCl* (thanks, new client) letter.

c. Transfer to 1–31 file, seven days from date of *TksNuCl,* to be called and checked up with "just staying in touch."

SET APPOINTMENT

IMPORTANT NOTE: *Most appointments will be set with current leads, not new leads. However, if your salesperson gets a hot prospect on a cold call, use this procedure.*

a. If appointment set *less than three days* away: Salesperson *should* have kept the lead card and filed it for a confirmation call one day before; if not, either return to salesperson or file it yourself, depending on office policy.

b. Appointment set *three or more days* off: Modify *ApptConf* (appointment confirmation) letter so that it notes the date, time, and place of the appointment. Print the letter. File letter for mailing four days before appointment. File card in 1–31 file for day before appointment for salesperson to make confirmation call.

UPGRADE TO A CHERRY (ALREADY IN DATABASE, NOW INTERESTED AND QUALIFIED)

a. Send *UpChry* letter, enclosing requested information.

b. Transfer to 1–31 file, seven days ahead of mailing, for follow-up phone call.

CHANGE TO B GREEN CHERRY (ALREADY IN DATABASE, NEW FUNDS DUE OR OPPORTUNITY DATE)

a. Send *UpGrn* or *DownGrn* letter depending on whether the lead has been upgraded from an info lead or pitch and miss or downgraded from a hot prospect or cherry.

b. File with next month's Bs.

DOWNGRADE TO C INFO LEAD

a. Send *DownInfo* letter.

b. File with next month's Cs.

DOWNGRADE TO MASS MAIL

If list is on cards, just file with mass-mail cards. Otherwise, throw out the name rather than try to locate it.

JERK

Mark in computer never to receive calls or letters.

Add/Remove Interest(s)

a. If color name(s) circled, add matching color sticker(s).

b. If color name(s) crossed out, pull off matching color sticker(s).

c. If computer: Make changes called for in interest field(s).

d. Continue with any other appropriate process.

For sample color code, see Interest Table, page 92.

D Pitch and Miss (salesperson made presentation but no sale)

a. Send *Pitch* letter.

b. File with next month's Ds.*

F Won't Return Calls

a. Send *No Call* letter.

b. File as an F in no-calls slot.

Still Won't Return Calls

Downgrade to mass mail (see previous page).

Salesperson's File System Cheatsheet

Appointment

IF less than three days away, file for confirmation call one day before appointment.

IF more than three days away, mark card. (Confirmation letter will be sent four days before and card refiled for confirmation call.)

A Cherries

In process of active follow-up

Track. Send requested info. Call back in seven days to begin relationship. As long as prospect is progressing step-by-step toward a decision, leave in 1–31 file. As names fall out—buy or don't—upgrade to Client or downgrade to lower priority.

Filing Principles. File in 1–31 appointments file, moving to new slot whenever you make an additional appointment or promise additional follow-up.

---

*Or, if office policy, return card to salesperson to do same.

Phone Contact Objective.   Get initial appointment. Then, via phone, move prospect through various steps of selling process.

Contact Frequency.   As often as necessary. Most likely, lots—several times a week.

Script.   First call, *Cherry Callback*

Target #.   Twenty-five to fifty As at any one time.

Goal.   Four to six appointments per week from As.

B Green Cherries

Interested with known amount of "funds due" at known later date

Track.

> *If new B:* Send three letters over twenty-day period, then "drip" (see "Contact Frequency" below).

> *If kept as or changed to B:* Send any info requested, keep dripping.

Filing Principles.   If funds are due toward the end of a month, file in that month's slot. Otherwise, file in previous month's slot.

> General note: Separate different priorities in given month by inserting colored cards within slot—*or* placing in separate filing box(es).

Phone Contact Objective.

> *Until funds due:* Keep name before prospect; forestall surprises.

> *When funds due:* Get appointment (or if info requested, send cherry letter), upgrade to A Cherry. Failing that, requalify as B Greenie Cherry for different future date. If not, downgrade to C Info Lead or D Pitch and Miss.

Contact Frequency (until funds due).

> *Mail:* One letter each month *even if also called.*

> *Phone:* Stay-in-touch call every ninety days.

> We call this mail/phone pattern "dripping."

Script.   *Greenie Recontact.*

Target #.   Forty Bs coming due each month.

Goal.   Ten new-business appointments a month from dripped-on Bs.

C Info Leads

Interested, but you couldn't determine even approximate funds due date.

Track.

> *If new C:* Send three letters over twenty-day period, then *requalify by phone* (see "Phone Contact Objective" below).

> *If kept or changed to C:* Send any requested info, keep dripping, periodically *requalify by phone.*

Filing Principle.

> *If new C:* File for next month (see above).

> *If kept as or changed to C:* File to *requalify by phone* three months (ninety days) away.

Phone Contact Objective.   If you can, upgrade to A Cherry or B Green Cherry. If not, but contact specifically requests to remain on mailing list, keep as C. Otherwise, downgrade to MM.

Contact Frequency.

> *Mail:* One letter each month *even if also called.*

> *Phone:* Requalification call every ninety days.

Script.   *Info Drip/Requal.*

Target #.   One hundred Cs at any one time.

Goal.   Ten As and ten Bs per month from Cs.

D Pitch and Miss

Received salesperson's presentation but didn't buy.

Track.

> *If new D:* Send one letter, then drip.

> *If kept as D:* Keep dripping.

Filing Principle.   File for *upgrade phone call* three months away. (Note: *Applies no matter how often kept as D.*)

Phone Contact Objective.   If hot, set appointment. If not, offer info, hoping for upgrade to A Cherry. If neither, try requalifying for funds due—B Green Cherry. If can't, keep as D.

CONTACT FREQUENCY.

Mail: One letter each month *even if also called.*

Phone: Stay-in-touch call every ninety days.

SCRIPT.   *Pitch and Miss Upgrade.*

TARGET #.   One hundred Ds at any one time.

GOAL.   Twenty As and twenty Bs per month from Ds.

E Other—Agent/Broker Leads (Agents, stockbrokers, etc., only)

"But I already *have* another guy."

TRACK.   Call monthly.

FILING PRINCIPLE.   After calling each in this month's slot, move to next month's. (Note: *Applies no matter how often kept as E.*)

PHONE CONTACT OBJECTIVE.   Sell something! Otherwise, offer info, hoping for upgrade to A Cherry. If won't budge, try requalifying for funds due—B Green Cherry. If can't, keep as E.

CONTACT FREQUENCY.   *Phone:* Monthly or more often.

SCRIPT.   *Other Broker*

TARGET #.   Fifty to one hundred at any one time.

GOAL.   Five As and five Bs per month from Es.

F Flunking, In Danger Of

Won't return your calls.

TRACK.   When you grade an F, send *No Calls* letter, then wait until they call back or next month, whichever comes first.

FILING PRINCIPLE.

If new F: Keep separate, tag for thirty-day review. If then does not call you: (a) downgrade to MM; (b) downgrade to Jerk; (c) try calling one more time.

If kept once as F: Choose between (a) and (b) above—only!

PHONE CONTACT OBJECTIVE.   Same as before consignment to junk heap.

CONTACT FREQUENCY. Once or never again, as case may be.

SCRIPT. None.

TARGET #. Not many, if any!

GOAL. Wasting as little time on Fs as possible.

MM Mass Mail

Combination of (1) potential future prospects and (2) former prospects with no remaining priority.

TRACK. *Mail and/or Phone:* Four times per year.

FILING PRINCIPLE. File separately from prospects with priorities assigned.

PHONE CONTACT FREQUENCY. Four times per year, if phoned.

SCRIPT. None provided.

TARGET #. Two thousand daytime and one thousand nighttime.

GOAL. Constant flow of prioritized prospects.

Dripping

The way I've set it up, the card system keeps the information about a prospect until the prospect becomes a client or gets thrown out as a jerk.

The computer stores basic name/address data, plus list (client, prospect, connection, mass mail), source (where the list came from), and interest. Naturally, it can store other information that you require. Just don't get too bogged down in updating the database instead of selling.

In this model, we are only using the computer for two reasons as far as prospecting is concerned.

1. To send lead processing letters, and

2. to send monthly drip letters.

Your phone contact is controlled by the card.

ASSIGNMENT

1. Download the relevant documents from billgood.com.

2. Buy 1–31 dividers, Jan–Dec dividers, and create a no-calls divider.

3. Buy the seven colors of Avery ¾-inch colored dots.

4. Run off a hundred labels and affix them to cards.

5. Study all the cheatsheets.

6. Do it!

8

The Campaign Objective

Two More Reasons Salespeople Don't Like to Prospect

As we begin thinking about how to pick a campaign objective, you need to give some thought to two additional reasons salespeople hate prospecting. The biggest reason by far is the kind of rejection generated by Old School–type prospecting. To the extent one adopts the "cherries and pits" mentality, the negative effects of that will very nearly, if not entirely, go away.

This brings us to two additional reasons many salespeople don't like prospecting. Following hard on the heels of Old School rejection is this: When a professional salesperson is prospecting, he or she is taking a big pay cut.

Consider this: Based on time management studies that I have done in the financial services, I know that if a financial adviser has survived the first two or three years and made it up to the average income level of the industry ($117,000 as of 1996), that person is worth *$1,000 an hour in gross revenue to the firm when she or he is* selling *to interested, qualified clients and prospects.* In financial services, the adviser gets 33 to 40 percent of the total revenue, and much more if self-employed.

Quick math will show that there is a big discrepancy between $117,000 a year and this theoretical $40,000 per week, assuming the salesperson was *selling* full time.

Well, our time management studies showed that this salesperson is spending only a little more than an hour a day in actual contact with clients and prospects. The rest of the time, he or she is doing service, cold calling, dialing and waiting, sorting out operational problems, and sharing war stories at the water cooler.

Since I learned this, my entire focus in designing marketing and prospecting systems has *not been* to make financial advisers better in selling. Rather, it has been to help them spend more time selling in front of better-qualified clients and prospects.

Part of our strategy is this: A caller can be hired for less than $10 an hour. So let's get these high-producing salespeople to delegate some portion of the prospecting process by hiring it out. You don't like prospecting? Chances are you are worth hundreds or thousands of dollars an hour and you know in your heart of hearts that every time you pick up the phone to prospect, you are taking a huge pay cut. This is certainly one of the real reasons for so-called call-reluctance.

So, if you're high-producing salesperson or you manage one or more high-producing salespeople, consider solving your prospecting problem by hiring someone specifically to do it. Naturally, their first course would be to read this book.

By the way, even if you know you are worth $1,000 an hour, you need to master prospecting once and for all. I have noticed that people tend to hire someone worse than they are. If you're lousy, your pocketbook will gush as you pay someone even worse. Which brings us to the second reason some salespeople hate prospecting: They're really not good at it.

There are actually at least two separate skill sets normally required for success in sales. You have to be good at getting the horse to water (prospecting) and good at making the horse drink (selling). I have seen great salespeople die because they can't prospect. And I have seen great prospectors perish because they didn't know how to sell.

I have been instrumental in creating literally hundreds of sales partnerships along a model we call *hunter/skinner.* One person *hunts* and finds the new account. The other person *skins,* or develops the new account. The thoughts presented here will have bearing in a few pages, as we consider how to set the campaign objective.

Campaign Objective Defined

The term "campaign objective" refers to the hotness a lead must attain before it is turned over to a salesperson. Now, I am fully aware that many salespeople will be doing their own prospecting. As you will recall, in Chapter 7 I recommended that you separate computer operations and sales into time blocks. Well, here, I also need you to separate sales and prospecting. Perhaps you cannot, right now, get anyone else to prospect for you because there is no one to do it, and *it must be done.* However, just as you separated computer operations and prospecting by assigning each a separate time block, it is at least if not more important that prospecting be done in its own time block and sales in another.

So, in the balance of this chapter, I am going to be speaking to you, the prospector. As such, you need to give very serious consideration to how much you want your salesperson (you) to deal with cold or luke-warm leads. Do you just want to run interference for your salesperson and find someone who is just willing to talk? Or do you want to send your salesperson out only on prequalified appointments? Once you decide on the campaign objective, you will have answered this question.

With these thoughts in mind, let's take a look at some possible objectives and some things that you'll need to think about in choosing one.

Possible Campaign Objectives

In sales, you have obviously heard the term "hot prospect." The problem with hot prospects is very simply that there are not enough of them, or they are just too hard to find and create. If they exist, obviously prospects that are not as hot must also exist.

A hot prospect, remember, is someone ready to begin the selling process. When someone says, "I want to see you," they're hot. If they will set a telephone appointment, they are pretty hot. But if they request information first, they are not as hot. And if they only express a mild interest in talking, they are even less hot, perhaps even cool. So I guess you could say we have some kind of a "lead hotness thermometer."

The four different gradations on this thermometer refer to campaign objectives. So let's look at them more closely.

The Prospect Thermometer

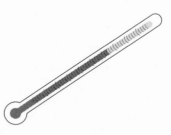

- Prequalified appointment

- Requalified cherry

- Cherry callback

- Interested in talking

PREQUALIFIED APPOINTMENT: This is as good as it gets in terms of a lead. This is what all sales people live for. To produce prequalified appointments for a salesperson, you need someone on the telephone getting them; and you may need direct mail or other advertising as well. Someone other than the salesperson would be following up on these leads, prequalifying, and then setting up appointments with the hot ones.

REQUALIFIED CHERRY: Remember, a cherry is anyone who is interested and qualified NOW. We send information and then follow up.

If a requalified cherry is your campaign objective, your prospector finds the cherry using one or another of our campaign styles, sends the information, and then calls back a second or even a third time to find out if the person is ready to talk to a salesperson.

A really good prospector will set up telephone appointments with the salesperson, because one of the great drains on salespeople's time is telephone tag. Phone tag has now degraded into voice-mail tag. Many salespeople can spend hours a day trying to get back to other busy people. It would make a salesperson's day to give him or her six or eight telephone appointments with requalified cherries.

CHERRY CALLBACK: A cherry lead in this context would be someone who has responded, is preferably qualified for decision-making capability and funds now, and has been sent requested information. Again, the response can have come from a standard direct-mail campaign, a phone/mail/phone, or a mail/phone campaign. The salesperson then follows up to see if the person is hot enough to begin the selling process or needs to be downgraded to green cherry or info lead status.

At my company, our marketing department generates cherry leads for the salespeople to follow up. Sometimes, depending upon the availability and skill level of callers, we have the lead qualifier (as we call them) make an initial follow-up call and set up telephone appointments with those who are really interested. In some cases, a caller will follow up on leads and get people to attend a conference call. It's only after the conference call that the salespeople make a follow-up call.

What we do is send out lots and lots of letters to both prospect and pitch and miss lists. The focus of our mailing is to get people to call in. When they do, they speak to one of my lead qualifiers, who gives them a bit more information and then verifies that the price is not a problem at this time.

If they meet the money as well as some other qualifications, information is sent, and then the lead is routed to my salespeople's in-basket in seven days.

INTERESTED IN TALKING: The lowest lead on this thermometer is someone who would just be interested in talking to a salesperson. This lead would most likely be generated through a mail/phone campaign in which letters are sent out and a caller follows the letters in three to five days. When the caller gets the prospect to the phone, he or she simply says, "This is Joe Blow's office calling with Reliable Widget. Mr. Blow sent you some information about our new vibrating widget. Would you like to speak with him about it?"

If so, the prospector turns the lead over to a salesperson or sets a time within the next few minutes that the person would receive a phone call from the salesperson.

So these are our objectives. Now, how do we pick one?

How to Pick an Objective

There is no hard-and-fast rule in picking a campaign objective. It's not mechanical. But there are some things you might consider.

1. Consider your resources.

If you have nobody to set up appointments for your salespeople, obviously they have to do it themselves. So the highest your campaign could go would be cherry lead to follow up. If you have a very small mailing list, you can't afford to miss a single opportunity. So you might want to invest a lot of resources just to get your best salesperson talking to one of these prospects. So think about your resources.

2. Strength of your offer.

Let's assume your offer is a 50 percent price decrease on a well-known product for a limited period of time. You could have your salespeople jump on the phone and do a blitz and set prequalified appointments. But if your offer is the same thing they've heard for years, you have to sell it harder, which means you may have to settle for someone interested in talking.

3. How well known is your firm?

If you are the lead dog in the pack, it may be very easy to make appointments. If nobody has ever heard of you, you may have to go down the thermometer and focus only on finding someone willing to talk.

4. Resistance level of the market.

If lots of similar companies are pounding the same market for the same product, you may want to take your very best salesperson and focus your campaign just on getting people to the phone for him or her so that this talented persuader can get the door opened more than a crack.

5. Skill level of your callers.

If you have people on the phone whose job it is, say, to set up appointments for your salespeople, the better they are, the higher up the thermometer you go. But if they are just starting out, their first assignment might well be simply to connect people to the salesperson without any or with very little explanation.

6. Value of your salesperson's time.

A huge impact on a salesperson's and company's bottom line can be produced by shifting the objective up the thermometer or down. If you have a star salesperson, my inclination would be to surround that person with the best support staff you can develop. The more time that star is in front of your clients and prospects, the more revenue will be brought in.

Assignment

Your assignment, then, is to turn to your Campaign Development Checklist and decide upon the objective for your campaign. You will find that checklist, as always, on pages 52 and 53 in Chapter 4.

CHAPTER **9**

The Campaign Style

"There's more than one way to skin a cat."

—Bill Good, age eleven

Our fifth-grade class went on a field trip to the DeVille Kitty Kat Coat Factory, which was located right next to the DeVille Dalmatian Puppy Coat Factory near Greensboro, North Carolina, where I grew up. As I watched the skinners at work, I noted to a classmate, "Charles, there's more than one way to skin a cat." It seems he remembered that and quoted me in a paper he wrote on cats and coats for our teacher. She showed the paper to her husband, who worked for the American Society for Prevention of Cruelty to Animals. The husband was outraged to learn that puppies and kitties were being raised to be made into coats. He ran a national ad campaign about the puppy and kitty-cat coat industries, resulting in its demise. He used my statement as the headline for the campaign! In later years, I found it amusing that my idle comment had not only come to mean "There's more than one way to do something," but also that it resulted in the shutdown of an entire industry. Thousands of people were laid off. As I said later, "The tongue is mightier than the sword." Someone else altered that, obviously!

More About Campaign Styles

Let's go back and review for just a moment. A "variable" is anything over which you have control that can change the outcome of a campaign. "Campaign style" is a variable. Changing the "style"—the medium or combination of media used to produce the campaign objective—will normally have a huge impact on the outcome because so much is affected when you change it.

While it may not take very long to execute this step on the Campaign Development Checklist, it is worth taking a few minutes to think about the style and pick one according to the guidelines laid down here. The style lays down the sequence of actions for a campaign; it also defines its parts. So let's give some thought to this step.

How to Pick a Style

In picking a style, you want a campaign that will achieve the objective with the least time and effort yet with due consideration given to how you like to run your sales business.

Just as there is no rote way to choose the campaign objective, there is no rote way to pick a style.

If you hate direct mail and think it doesn't work, don't do it. If you don't want anyone working for you and want to do it all yourself, you would probably want to do a phone/mail/phone style. If you work a residential market but hate working nights, you'd better do direct mail. Otherwise, you or a caller that needs to be supervised will need to be phoning in the evening—by far the optimum time to call residences.

So, with your campaign objective in mind, you should look over the list of styles and pick the one most consistent with your objective. To put it another way, pick a style and try it. If it doesn't work, try a different one.

To quote myself again: "There is more than one way to skin a cat."

Campaign Styles Expanded

In this chapter, I am going to take each campaign style, describe it, and give some thoughts on its effectiveness. In addition, I will list the *promotional elements.* These are the scripts, letters, and other pieces that are needed to run the campaign.

To jump ahead for just a moment, all these campaigns generate the same kind of prospects: cherries, green cherries, and info leads. These leads are processed with the same set of lead processing scripts and letters. These are covered in Chapters 14 and 15 and will not be treated here. In dealing with each campaign style, the promotional elements I will deal with now are the letters and scripts necessary to create the response.

Phone/Mail/Phone

This is the first campaign style I developed. I got the idea for it probably in 1979, when I separated the prospecting call from the selling call and created a multicall system. Tens of thousands, even hundreds of thousands of salespeople who have attended my seminars and read earlier editions of this book have implemented this style campaign. Here goes.

1. Call to find out if people are interested and qualified now. If yes, they are cherries. If no, find out if they will be qualified later. If yes, they're

green. If you cannot pin down a date, are they at least interested? In that case, they are an info lead.

2. Send requested information.

3. If a cherry, call back in seven days. If green or info lead, follow the procedures of the Lead Processing System in Chapter 7.

REQUIRED ELEMENTS:

1. First-call script

2. Information to send out

3. Second-call script

COMMENT: If you're not sure which style to use, choose this style. In a very few calls, you can get a good idea of how resistant or responsive the marketplace is. The start-up costs for this style of campaign are close to nothing. Plus, it's very easy to revise this campaign without having to change a whole bunch of printed material or other expensive items. Very possibly, you should consider this campaign style as the *campaign before the campaign.* It's your survey. Your testing ground.

Mail/Phone

In this style, you send a letter and follow it three to five days later with a phone call. Depending on whether you have a caller or not, and how good the caller is, you would choose one or the other of the follow-up scripts.

1. Version one of the phone call can simply be from a rookie caller or brand-new salesperson asking if the recipient of the letter would like to speak to a salesperson. What this accomplishes is very simple: You delegate the dialing and waiting, and very important, you delegate the rejection. You, the salesperson, have a *designated rejectee.* When a person is found who wants to speak to the salesperson, the caller or *connector* either transfers the call or sets up a time, preferably within the next few minutes, but possibly later, for the salesperson to call.

2. Version two of the call has the salesperson or an experienced caller making the follow-up call. In this script, the salesperson or caller is qualifying and, where possible, setting immediate appointments.

REQUIRED ELEMENTS:

Preapproach letter following the guidelines in Chapter 16

Business reply envelope (Some people will reply by mail to the letter. Why not make it easy for them to do so?)

Follow-up script, version 1 (caller follows up)

Follow-up script, version 2 (salesperson or experienced caller follows up)

COMMENT: If you have a brand-new caller or even want to try out a style using someone from a temp agency, this is the way to go. Where you are calling well-defended business executives or professionals, the fact that you have sent a letter gives you something to talk to the screener about. You can ask if the boss received it, and if not, ask if the screener will show it to the boss. This is also generally the best style to use when putting on a seminar.

To promote a seminar, send a letter describing the contents of the seminar and sell it hard. Follow the letter with a phone call asking if the recipient would like to attend. Always enclose a reply card. Your best replies will normally come in by mail, because people who go to this trouble are clearly interested. However, in many marketplaces, mail response is just too costly, and you'll have to really beat the bushes to turn out the crowd.

Mail/phone normally works quite well except in the most highly resistive markets.

Dripping

Dripping is, first, a series of low-key letters and/or phone calls designed to build or maintain an identity so that when the client or prospect is ready to buy, your name will be in first position. Second, through the low-key phone calls, lower-grade prospects or clients can be upgraded to hot, cherry, or green.

Dripping is normally done on clients (people who have bought something) or on people who have already responded. However, I am familiar with several cases in which highly targeted groups of people were dripped on and then, after some period of time, were contacted or simply sent in a reply.

REQUIRED ELEMENTS:

Interesting information, generally in letter form or in the form of an enclosure accompanied by a brief note

Business reply envelopes

Low-key phone script

COMMENT: Well over half of your new business will come from a well-dripped-on prospect file. So if you do not maintain contact, the number of new clients will be less than half of what it could otherwise be. Remember, people like doing business with people they know. A tasteful series of letters and low-key phone calls give people the feeling they know you, or at least that they know you better than they know the competition.

Standard Direct Mail

In a standard direct-mail campaign, you send out letters with some form of information, request, coupon, or reply card. If it's a good letter, list, offer, whatever, a profitable number of people will respond. When the response comes in, you typically send out what was promised. Then, seven days later, you follow the information request with a phone call.

I treat direct-mail responses like the cherries they are. If someone is interested enough to put something in the mail to you, he or she is probably interested enough to buy. The materials sent out can be anything from a letter to a very fancy brochure to a videotape.

At Bill Good Marketing, we do seventy thousand or so standard direct-mail letters a month. We use letters instead of a lot of fancy color printing because of my own personal inability to be happy with something for very long. I like to mess around and test different things. If you invest some thousands of dollars into color separations, that's the end of your messing.

REQUIRED ELEMENTS:

Letter

Business reply envelope

Information to be sent out as requested

Direct-mail follow-up script, or

Incoming-call qualification script

COMMENT: Over the years, I have heard many sales managers say, "The mail doesn't work." That's just a confession that they don't know how to make it work. Properly designed and tested, direct mail can generate very high quality leads. It's especially valuable where the response rate to a phone/mail/phone-style call is very low. Normally, to make a standard direct-mail campaign work, you need a highly profitable item to sell, because it can cost as much as $100 or more to get a lead.

I once designed a campaign for someone in the financial services industry not too far from where I live. We sent out a thousand letters and received one response. Profitable? You bet. That one response was a very specialized client that generated in excess of $25,000 in commission revenue *per year.* Had we tried to call all of those people just to find that one, we would undoubtedly have grown discouraged and thrown in the towel.

Phone Only

In a phone-only campaign, you just pick up the phone and call a group of people and either try to sell something or set up an appointment. You do not offer information.

REQUIRED ELEMENTS:

A script.

COMMENT: Normally, to pull off a phone-only campaign, you have to do a lot of preparatory work on your list and know in advance that your offer is of interest to the people you're calling. When combined with genuine scarcity, this can be an especially powerful campaign. It can also be used to harvest a list of dripped-on prospects, especially where you have kept very careful records of areas of interest.

ASSIGNMENT

On your Campaign Development Checklist, pick a style.

10

The Offer

". . . an offer you can't refuse."

—*The Godfather*

Wish I'd said it first, but, oh well . . .

The offer of a campaign is so important that it deserves its own chapter, even though it never stands alone in any of your written or scripted material. You have to think it out, know how to use it, and then use it correctly. Ultimately, it governs the entire focus of your campaign letters and scripts. So, let's define it, give examples, give you the laws, and then you'll know how to develop it and what to do with it.

The *offer* is what you think people want to achieve by owning your product or service. In prospecting, you basically make an offer. If your offer is in fact what people want, a profitable number will respond to a well-crafted, properly delivered telephone script or a well-written direct-mail letter. This end result that you're going to use as an offer is *always a benefit.* It is *never* a feature.

So let's make sure that we understand the difference between feature and benefit.

Benefit

Very simply, a benefit is what people perceive or believe a product or service will do for them. Let's take some examples. A person might buy a laptop computer to *increase productivity,* or they might buy it to *save time.* You might have purchased this book because you felt it would help you *make more muh-ney.* Or perhaps you are under the gun from your boss to find more prospects. So the desired end result was to *keep your job.* Or perhaps you felt that more prospects would enable you to *get promoted.*

Let's take another example: You go buy a microwave. Why? You just don't have time to cook a conventional meal so you buy it to *save time.* Or perhaps you believe that some of the new microwave recipes will enable you to *cook better.*

All of these are examples of product benefits.

Now, what enables a product to deliver its benefits? Its features.

Feature

A product feature is some aspect or part of a product or service that enables the product or service to deliver certain benefits to the consumer. Let's follow through with our examples above.

You buy a laptop computer with a 1.2 gigabite hard drive. So what? Why do you need that? Well, the size of the hard drive might enable you to increase your productivity by making it possible for you to carry all of your critical files with you on the road.

Here's another feature: Your friendly computer salesperson says, "It has twenty-four megabites of RAM." Again, your question should be, so what? Well, by having a large RAM, your computer performs certain functions much faster, thereby enabling you to save time.

Consider this book: A feature is detailed information on list development. Again, so what? Answer: By being able to develop and manage good lists, you will be able to find more prospects and therefore make more money. This book also contains detailed instructions on campaign development. Why on earth? By knowing how to develop a campaign, you can deliver more prospects to your boss, definitely keep your job, and possibly even get promoted.

Got the idea?

At this point, you may find it helpful to list several features of your product and their corresponding benefits.

Finding Interest

OK. You know what an offer is, and you know the difference between a feature and a benefit. Now let's use these to find interest. *Interest is our first requirement for a qualified prospect and it is the interest that we must find.* With no interest, qualification is pointless. So here are the principles that, when applied, will enable you to find interest.

1. People buy benefits, not features. This should be so obvious as to require no comment, but based on my own experience being sold various products and services, I can tell you that very few salespeople understand what their prospects really buy. As I write this, I am in the process of buying a car for my daughter, and one particular salesperson rattled off that the car has antilock brakes, power injection, and a whole bunch of other things that I'd never even heard of. But I did know this: They were all features, and that's not what I was buying. What I wanted to buy was something safe, with excellent mileage, and stylish, so my daughter would enjoy it and take care of it. The first two benefits are for me. The last for her.

2. But they ask questions about features, not benefits. This is odd, isn't it? We buy benefits but ask questions about features. How many bonds in the fund? or How long has the manager been with the fund? Now why on earth, if a person buys benefits, not features, does he ask questions about features, not benefits?

I think there are really two answers to this question. People ask questions about features because they need to know how the product or service delivers the benefit they want to buy. And perhaps more important, they don't want to appear a total pushover to the salesperson. They want to demonstrate that they are reasonably sophisticated and can't be sold a bill of goods. So they ask the most technical question they can possibly think of in order to prove that they are analytical, not emotional, buyers.

Now here's where all of this is leading: *If a person does not ask questions, you can be sure he or she will not buy.*

Since most salespeople fill up their presentation with features, it leaves any but the most sophisticated buyer with nothing to ask. With no questions to ask, *they will not buy.*

3. Therefore, in your initial script, letters, and sales presentation, stress benefits and withhold features so that the client or prospect can ask questions about the features if they are interested in the benefits.

Feature/Benefit Examples

Let's take some examples of features and benefits.

The product I'm interested in buying right now is a car for my daughter. The benefits that I want are that it be safe, economical to operate, and that my daughter likes it. Now what are the features that support these benefits?

Certainly air bags and a solid construction would support *safety*, and thirty-plus miles per gallon and low maintenance contribute to *economy of operation.* That takes care of *my* needs. But another benefit for me is that she likes it. That means styling and a built-in CD player. Since she nearly requires a forklift to carry around her CD collection, I know that a car without a built-in CD player would not do the job at all.

So, do the features as enumerated support the expressed benefits? Absolutely, and that's why I'm buying.

Now let's just suppose I receive the following phone call.

> Hello, Mr. Good, this is Bob Hammer at Blasto Audi Dealership. Our new Audi A4 is safe, economical, and very stylish. If you happen to be looking for a car for your son or daughter, I would like to take a second and run a few questions by you. Yes? No?

Would I be interested in talking to this fellow? You bet.

Would I necessarily buy from him? It would depend upon whether or not he could deliver the benefits that I want. But by *making me an offer I can't refuse,* he at least has a chance to show me his wares.

So how do we pick the offer? Two ways, both of which have their merits.

First, you can survey, and then test the results of your survey in a script or letter. Very literally, you can call up people and ask them why they would buy such and such a product. Once you have an idea, you can plug it into one of my letters or scripts. Piece of cake. (I hesitate to tell you where this expression came from.)

Second, based on experience, you can pick an offer and try it. I probably use this method more than the survey methods, although I do use both. I have found that the most valid survey is to call up people and offer them something and see if they are in fact interested in it. I start with a phone/mail/phone campaign or even a phone/mail. If I can punch out two or three cherries per hour, I know I may have a winner.

ASSIGNMENT

List at least five end results someone might enjoy from owning your product or service. Then pick one to use as the offer in a campaign. To provide a point of comparison, I have given you five end results a buyer of my marketing system might expect.

I have circled the end result we have offered for ten years. Works like a champ, as I say.

Yours	Mine
	Double sales on half as much work
	Become more organized
	Stop things from slipping through the cracks
	Grow business faster
	Do a better job fighting off competition

CHAPTER 11

To Script or Not to Script
What You Say

"What you say makes a difference."

—Bill Good, age fourteen

I'm sure, by now, that you are just *bowled over* (mine) to know how many statements you grew up with that are mine. But what you don't know—at least not yet—is that I have a whole bunch of statements I haven't yet released. As I mentioned, when I was twelve, I shut up. Don't get me wrong, I didn't stop coming up with great statements. I just kept them to myself. Instead of telling my mother or Sunday school teacher, I wrote them down. I trust that as I release these now, *credit will be given where it's due* (mine). So I hope you enjoy the never-before-released statement I have chosen as the theme for this chapter. It does have a lot to do with our next subject. By the way, I first used this statement when I asked the prettiest girl in school, Anne, for a date. I said, "You probably don't want to go to the hay ride with me, do you?" She said, "You got that right." I almost said aloud, "Hmmmm. What you say makes a difference," but I squelched it and jotted it down instead. My next attempt I said, "I have an invitation here to go to a party at Joyce's. Would you like to take a look at it?" She said, "When is it?" And you know *the rest of the story* (also mine).

If you are going to have a campaign, at the very minimum, you will need some scripts, in addition to the lead processing letters that I will discuss in Chapter 15. If you are going to be using a mail/phone, standard direct-mail, or drip campaign, you will also need some prospecting letters. So we have arrived at a critical juncture. You can keep doing what you've been doing so far, which is to fly by the seat of your pants, or you can buck up and take your prospecting to the next level of professionalism.

Work with me, would you? I promise I will help you with the letters and scripts you have found difficult to develop in the past. Developing your scripts and letters are critical parts of campaign development. So don't wimp out on me, OK?

Your Message Counts

Suppose you work for Beam of Light Financial Services and you call up a prospect and say:

> Jack, this is Fred Smithers at Beam of Light Financial Services. We've got a terrific opportunity here. So I want you to empty out your bank account, bring it down to the office, and we'll load you up. How's that sound?

Frankly, with that message, I think Jack would be crazy to set foot out of his house, unless it was to come down to your office and punch your lights out. Quite obviously, the words you say are important. According to me, "What you say makes a difference." The wrong words will stamp out whatever interest you might find. The right words will fan a spark of interest into a flame. So let's dig into the subject of the message. Your prospecting message is a very important variable. If you have an excellent list but deliver a tired, boring message to it, you won't get outstanding results.

Before actually getting into the mechanics of designing the message, let's talk about whether you should have a written script or not. Then we'll take a look at some important strategic questions that will shape your words.

To Script or Not

Very early in my sales training career, I encountered two phenomena that have always puzzled me. On the one hand, there is no question that a good *written script* gets better results on any list than no script; on the other hand, most salespeople would rather cut off a body part than use a script. So, what exactly is a script? By "script" I mean a word-for-word treatment of key parts of the prospecting presentation. I do not mean that every single word is scripted—that would be impossible—but the *key sections* should be.

Since most salespeople would rather pay parking tickets than use a script, and since I believe a written script to be vital, let's take a look at both sides of the issue.

Reasons Not to Use a Script

At many of my seminars, I ask the salespeople attending to write down three reasons why it might *not* be a good idea to use a prepared script. I want you to do that right now. Then I want you to compare your reasons to the reasons below. The ones I'll give, by the way, are the very same ones that crop up in every sales group I have ever worked with. It is absolutely amazing how consistent salespeople are, from one area of the country to another, from one company to another.

Sales managers take note. The items listed below *are the reasons* your sales crew will give as to why they don't want to use a script. So if you're big on scripts, you better know these well.

- *It sounds canned.*

  By this, salespeople mean that the script sounds as if it's being read, not said. Who needs that?

- *It's "not me."*

  By this, most salespeople mean that the script isn't written in words they would use, and someone else's words make them uncomfortable. And they sound it. So naturally, since it's "not me," they don't want it.

- *It's not spontaneous.*

  Surely, an inspired, spontaneous presentation has more life and vitality than an unspontaneous, "canned pitch."

- *It makes me talk too fast.*

  When people try a prepared script, they find themselves blabbering on at two hundred words a minute. And once again, the poorly written script takes the blame.

- *It's impersonal.*

  Obviously, a presentation that is impersonal won't create a rewarding relationship between salesperson and prospect. Since the script is not written with any one person in mind, it is quite obviously impersonal.

- *It's inflexible.*

  This is fairly obvious. A salesperson with decent verbal skills should be able to adapt his or her presentation to each individual rather than lose business due to an inflexible script.

- *I can't listen.*

  People feel that when they're reading, they have difficulty listening. And everyone agrees you should listen to the people in your life, prospects included.

- *I get thrown off.*

  One of the worst dreads a salesperson has is getting thrown off a script and then groping around at a loss for words. And that definitely can happen.

- *It's boring.*

  Frankly, people just get tired of doing the same old thing over and over.

These are the negatives. I'll bet if you did what I asked and wrote down your reasons for not using a script, at least two out of your three are on my list! (Most likely all of them are.)

Reasons to Use a Script

Now let's look at the positive. Take just a moment and write down three reasons why it might be a good idea to use a prepared script. Here are the positive reasons salespeople come up with once they've given it a little thought:

- *You sound certain.*

  If you have something to say, you'll sound as though you know what you're talking about. This will handle the "ah"s and "um"s and dead spaces that you fear.

- *You can test.*

  If you're using a different script on every person you talk to, there is no way you can tell what worked and what didn't work. You've got to hold all variables constant in order to test.

- *You cover all your important points.*

  I can't tell you how many salespeople have told me that they have gone through their presentation only to learn that they have forgotten to get the client's bank account number or some other piece of qualifying data without which they don't have an order.

- *You can listen better.*

  When you've got your message worked out, you can concentrate on what your prospect is saying.

- *You can make more calls.*

  If ever there was truth said, this is it. If your message is written down, you're more likely to stick to it. But if you start winging it, you'll thrash around until you have created a bloated message. And your bloat will take much longer to say. Thus a short, neat phone call becomes a blubbering, lumbering, twenty-minute, pit-polishing phone call.

Let's go back and review the reasons not to use a script, and see if I can't get you to look at scripts in a different light.

- *It sounds canned.*

Certainly many salespeople, when using a script, do sound canned. As a matter of fact, when we get into Chapter 18 I'll show you exactly which speech elements cause a canned sound. Once you understand this, and once you have a good script, you can avoid sounding canned.

After all, there is a difference between script preparation and script delivery. Some of us may be good at developing a sales message. Others may be excellent at script delivery, and delivery of a script is really just a question of performance, isn't it? An actor does not create the script. He makes it come alive, and as more than one writer on the subject of sales noted, great salespeople are also great performers.

- *It's "not me."*

This objection is obviously true. To the salespeople who complain "It's not me," I tell them to "Be someone else." There is no reason anyone should be restricted to one style of sales. Surely you would sell to New York lawyers one way and to North Carolina grain dealers another. If I'm giving my seminar in the Deep South, I'll speak more slowly. I'll let my old North Carolina accent come out. But if I'm in New York City, I will adjust my speech, humor, and many of my examples (script, if you please) to a faster-paced audience.

- *It's not spontaneous.*

True, a script is not spontaneous. But the art in delivering a script is to know it so well that you can deliver it the thousandth time with the same spontaneity as the first. (Realistically, the first time you gave the speech, you probably stumbled through it and didn't sound spontaneous at all. It probably won't even begin to sound good until the hundredth time.)

- *It makes me talk too fast.*

This is a problem when using a prepared script. Many people, when they have the written word in front of them, act as if they haven't read aloud since the third grade. (Many haven't.) Instead of reading as they speak, they just fire away at machine-gun rate. The only way I know to overcome this is to take the script and read it aloud about fifty times. Then record it. And then compare a recording of the script with a recording of yourself speaking naturally. Force the script to conform to the way you speak as a human being, not necessarily as a salesperson reading a script.

- *It's impersonal.*

If you just read the script and make no spontaneous comments, it will be impersonal, but that's not necessarily bad. There are only so many ways to qualify prospects for interest and money. There is no problem if you want to get off the script *briefly* to personalize it.

- *It's inflexible.*

A good script *is* inflexible. Any *good* script is designed to find a certain type of prospect. As you try to develop a script that will appeal to everyone, you will wind up appealing to no one.

Here is part of an inflexible script. I call it a gorilla script, and it's designed for people in financial services who want to find BIG prospects. A gorilla is someone who is qualified to write a check for $100,000 right away. As you can understand, gorillas are few and far between, and they don't respond the way an ordinary investor does. They are accustomed to being treated differently. The following is the opening line from a gorilla script I wrote that has proved to be very effective in prospecting for big money.

> Mr. Jones, this is Bill Good with Acme Securities. You know who we are, don't you? I'm looking for a very unusual investor this evening. This investor could raise $100,000 for an exceptional opportunity. Does the idea of a $100,000 investment just blow you right out of the saddle? [This script was written in Texas.]

Another gorilla script that I wrote for a Richmond, Virginia, campaign contained the phrase, "Does the idea of $100,000 blow you out of the water?"

As you can see, this particular script is *very inflexible;* it's looking for a particular type of investor. The idea behind the inflexibility of a good script is that you, as a prospector, have set in your mind the kind of prospect you want, and you are going after that type of person. If someone does not meet your requirements, you find someone who does. Remember, we're not trying to sell everybody. Just those who are interested, qualified, and with whom *you want to do business.* A good script is inflexible and will find you the kind of prospect you're looking for.

- *I can't listen.*

You really can't, until you've rehearsed the script. If you'll spend somewhere between ten minutes and an hour reading your script aloud, over and over, you'll find that you can actually listen better because you won't be wasting mental energy thinking about what you're going to say.

- *I get thrown off.*

There is no question whatsoever that you can be thrown off. I'll never forget a young man in Des Moines, Iowa, who was reading a particular paragraph of a script, got asked a question, forgot his place, and then began to read the same paragraph again. All the color suddenly drained from his face, and I heard him stutter, "I'm . . . not . . . doing a very good job. Suppose I call you back later, OK? Thankyouverymuch. *(Click. Dial tone.)*" Remember, the system you're learning in this book contains an ejection seat. If you get in trouble, press the eject button!

- *It's boring.*

We did a study at Harvard and discovered, to everyone's surprise, that salespeople like making money. We then asked 4,085 salespeople: If they had a script that was making money for them, would they be bored? Three replied yes, they would be bored. On further investigation, it was found that two of these were independently wealthy anyway, and one was a part-time welfare worker who believed that money was the root of evil. But the other 4,082 salespeople interviewed replied they most certainly would not be bored.

So what's boring about using a script?

Getting no results is boring, very boring. *So when you find yourself getting bored, chances are you're doing something wrong and are not getting results!*

Two More Reasons to Use Scripts

The reasons salespeople give *to use a script* are all true. I would like to offer two more of my own.

- *Top salespeople use scripts.*

It may not seem as if they have their scripts written down, but they are. They're in their heads. If you ever have the opportunity to listen to a top salesperson give a presentation a couple of times, you will notice not just similarities but identical passages. He or she has worked these words out over the years and wouldn't change them for anything.

I was fortunate on two occasions to sit through a seminar given by one of the top financial advisers in the United States. This man is a specialist in managed commodity accounts, and when I heard his one-hour seminar the first time, I learned a lot, not only about managed commodities but about seminar structure and design. It was brilliant. Then I heard it again. The thing that struck me the second time was that the speech was virtually identical to the first.

Over lunch at a conference in Reno, Nevada, I asked him, "John, don't you get tired of giving that same old seminar over and over again?" He looked at me as if I had just asked one of the world's most stupidest questions. He answered with a shrug: "If it ain't broke, don't fix it." (He quoted me without knowing it. Most annoying!)

He had his script. The idea of changing it was incomprehensible. It was putting a lot of money in his pocket year after year. I've listened to other great salespeople. And I find that they do the same thing over and over again. It's the new kid on the block who feels compelled to be unique and creative each and every presentation. The old kid on the block long since tried that and found that some sets of words work better than others. And since he wanted to go to the bank instead of the poorhouse, he stuck with the one that worked. And even if it causes brain damage to give the same presentation over and over again, he'll laugh all the way to the bank.

- *Words create effects.*

This may seem self-evident. You were, I hope, taught by your parents that honey catches more flies than vinegar. To put it another way, it's not just what you say, it's *exactly* what you say that counts. Consider these very slight changes in classic advertising slogans.

McDonald's: We do it all to you.

E.F. Hutton: When E.F. Hutton talks, some people listen.

AT&T: Reach out and grab someone.

Changing even a single word can alter the meaning and therefore the effect. If you have a good script, one that delivers predictable and profitable results, changing it is a sign of advanced brain damage. Don't do it.

You Will Use a Script

As a final argument for using a written, word-for-word script, try this: If you're going to be making high-volume phone calls, there is no way, after the fiftieth call, that you will have failed to develop a script. It is impossible to make fifty rapid *and unique* phone calls. It won't happen. By the fiftieth call, you will have a script whether you intended to or not. And it will be one that you have settled into and, more likely than not, will contain such gems as "Mr. Jones, I was wondering if maybe . . ."

So you will use a script. The only question is: Will you write it down in advance or just fall into it?

Now that the argument is settled and you are using a script, we need to discuss some basic strategy of the script. The questions I am about to go over will shape your script. So please give very careful thought to these questions, my comments, and your own answers.

Should Your Offer Involve Service, Concept, or Product?

We've already defined your offer as: the end result you think people want to achieve by owning your product or service. Let's assume you have a choice between an offer related to a product, a service, or a concept. Let's first define some terms:

Service: Something you can do for someone.

Concept: A group of related products. Blue-chip stocks, apartment buildings, photocopiers are all concepts.

Product: Something you can write an order for. You can buy or sell a thousand shares of IBM; you can buy or sell the apartment building at 405 Dokes Street; you can rent or lease a Xerox photocopier. These are all products.

In almost any industry, there is some choice about what to talk about on the first call. Take fire extinguishers. You could talk about a service— this would be a free home safety examination that would, most likely, end in finding that the prospect needs more fire extinguishers. Or, you could talk about a specific fire extinguisher that you would like to sell or at least get an appointment to show. So where do you start? Service? Concept? Product?

My answer is: PRODUCT. A specific product. If you are selling fire extinguishers, talk about the fire extinguisher that sells best in the type of market you're calling, and do that *even if you have an entire catalog full of fire extinguishers.*

Why? Simple. As a rule, you'll get better results that way.

With every company with whom I've worked, in every market, in every part of the country, I have been able to get better results talking about the RIGHT PRODUCT. And that's true even for such service-oriented industries as life insurance. I have found that the more specific you make that first contact, the more likely you are to discover interest and qualification. And the more likely you are to get people to make up their minds one way or the other.

Let's take the securities industry, where I have done my most extensive research on this question. When I began doing my research in the securities industry in the fall of 1978, the conventional wisdom stated that a stockbroker should offer a service. A typical first call went like this:

Mr. Jones, this is Brad Bradshaw. I'm over here at Wiggins and Wanstrop. If you don't mind, I'd like to take a few minutes of your time, run a few questions by you, and see if there isn't something we can do for you.

As I watched and listened to rookies make this kind of call hour after hour, it became apparent that it was one tough row to hoe. Worse, after forty-five minutes or so, the brokers themselves had become extremely discouraged, and that discouragement had begun to color their voices and bring about the negative result they sought to avoid. Yet despite what seemed to me to be highly unsatisfactory results and low morale, "everyone" seemed to agree that "service" was the way to go. "Need satisfaction" selling was, after all, the order of the day.

As I studied this approach, I began to realize that the era in which the service approach came of age was quite different from the late 1970s. The approach was born in an era when young men were only hired if they had family or social connections. This service approach, then, is appropriate when *connections already exist.* But what about the young man whose father drove a garbage truck? His connections are certainly not going to make him rich. Will the service approach work for him?

So I began a series of tests that went on for quite some time. I split a group of rookies in half. The first group would use the usual service approach. The second group would call on a product. Or the first half would call on a concept and the second half on a service. You get the idea.

Sometimes, my results on calling with a product absolutely bombed, and service was better. My breakthrough came one night when I was testing a particular product approach. Nothing was happening. I was calling the Palos Verdes Peninsula in southern California (lots of money), and I got tired of the script I was using. So I pulled another one out of my file and tried it. Results *instantly* improved. No one in Palos Verdes wanted to hear about annuity, which is what I was experimenting with on my first script. Within twenty minutes, however, I found four prospects for a tax-free bond fund. Looking back, I had found a *specific product that a list was interested enough in to make my calls extremely profitable.* What else did I need? Nothing. End of test.

☞ Conclusion: *You have to get the right offer about the right product crafted into the right words in the right script and then call the right list to make it work!*

If you absolutely cannot find a product that is profitable to talk about on the first call, then fall back and try a conceptual approach. And finally, as a last resort before using your list to line the bottom of your birdcage, try service.

If what you really want to do is talk service, FIRST TALK PRODUCT. Why? Because it works. Just try it.

If You Only Sell a Service

If your product is a service, you're in deep trouble on this approach, right? No. Just sell it like a product. Suppose you sell a consulting service. Just package it so that it has a fixed price and accomplishes a verifiable result. For $1,200 (or whatever), you will tell your customer "what's wrong and what it will take to fix it." Or if you sell "financial planning," sell the plan, not the process. If you sell janitorial services, sell clean buildings. If you sell carpet cleaning, sell "clean carpets." If you sell architecture, sell "planned buildings."

Take seminars, which I sell. A seminar is really a packaged consulting service offering a solution that applies to similar businesses. So while I deliver a service, I package and sell it like a product.

So if you sell service, figure out what the end result of it is, assign a fixed price to at least the first sale, and sell it like a product. I used to wonder why there was so little good material in sales literature on selling services as opposed to product. The reason, of course, is that those who have mastered "service sales" sell a service like it's a product. There is no separate subject of "selling intangibles."

ASSIGNMENT

No assignment! You get off easy. I just had to get you pointed in the right direction and committed to developing a script.

CHAPTER 12

Script Rewriting

How to Have Professionally Written Scripts If You're Not a Professional Writer

Although I have never done it, I am sure that writing radio commercials requires some of the same discipline that writing telephone scripts imposes.

Both radio commercials and telephone scripts must be short. Each deals with voice only. A wrong word can blow either out of the water. Also, as with telephone-script writing, I imagine it would be difficult to become a good radio-commercial writer. And as a matter of fact, if I had to learn to do it, I would get hold of a collection of the best radio commercials ever written, and I would rewrite each several hundred times, adapting them to suit a different product or service. By so doing, I would learn the structure and form of a good commercial. I know I would never learn it by just reading one. Nor will you learn how to write good telephone scripts if you just read this chapter. I will teach you the best way to learn how to write them, which is to rewrite them. In this chapter, I will walk you through rewriting a phone/mail/phone-style first-call script. You can then apply your know-how and then rewrite any of the numerous scripts in this book and on our home page.

As you get into rewriting this and other scripts, you will note I have used some very direct questions. Don't worry about offending people with directness, since the only people you'll offend are most likely people who cannot make up their minds. By asking direct questions, we separate the fisherpersons from the bait cutters.

As you will see, the questions you'll be asking are normally "closed ended." A closed-end question is one that can be answered with a yes or a no. They are point-blank, and in addition to weeding out the bait cutters, they'll get rid of the bush beaters as well. Remember, one definition of a pit is someone who cannot make up his or her mind. We want to find those early, since the major killer of salespeople is not the ones who say no, but the people who say maybe.

Different Kinds of Scripts

Very broadly, there are two kinds of scripts we'll be dealing with in order to complete this step on our Campaign Development Checklist. The step we're working on requires us to identify and then develop the scripts required for the campaign.

You will need two kinds of scripts: a Lead Generation Script, and a Lead Processing Script.

Lead Generation Scripts are the one or two scripts that you need for each campaign to find the prospect and get him or her properly classified. Is this prospect a cherry, green cherry, info lead? pit? jerk? Lead Processing Scripts are those you need to recontact your prospect base by phone.

You will meet the Lead Processing Scripts in Chapter 14. In this chapter, I will teach you how to rewrite a script. In the process, I'm going to teach you a lot about qualification. So even if you are a hot-shot scriptwriter already, you might learn a thing or two about qualifying the prospect. In the next chapter, I'll be giving you sample scripts for each style of campaign. And you know what? Without much effort at all, you'll be able to follow my simple rewriting guidelines and make my scripts into your scripts.

A Note on How to Get the Most Out of This Chapter

I would definitely recommend that you hustle your browser over to billgood.com. Pop into the materials for Chapter 12 and download *scripts.doc*. You will need a special password for this section. The password is: bretgood. (Bret is my adopted son. What a great fortune to have him a part of our lives!)

So download these now. When you open the document, you will see that the first script is called My Script Worksheet. We'll be going through this document, throwing away much, keeping some, and rewriting the rest. The end result is that you will have a complete script if you prospect the residential market. We will have a little more work to do if you prospect the business market, but not a lot.

My recommendation: As you go through the rest of this chapter, have *scripts.doc* open on your computer to My Script Worksheet. We're not going just to talk about scripts; working together, we will produce one for you.

Before You Start: What You Need to Know

As you see from the worksheet you have downloaded, you have to answer two questions. I need this information in your face. These questions are:

1. What is your offer? Remember, the offer is the end result someone may expect from owning your product or service. You make the offer to attract interest. We're going to take your offer and hammer it into the opening line of the script. The offer is *always* a benefit, because people buy benefits, not features.

Quick review:

FEATURE: *What something is.*
BENEFIT: *What that feature does for the prospect. Here are some examples:*

ITEM: *Coffee cup*
FEATURE: *Made of bone china*
BENEFIT: *Not only lovely to look at and hold but something you would want your grandchildren to have.*

ITEM: *Ball-point pen*
FEATURE: *Has blue ink*
BENEFIT: *Easy to read.*

If you wimped out on me earlier, go back to Chapter 10, study it well, and write an offer. Just type it right into our worksheet.

2. Write down the bare qualifications necessary to purchase your product or service. There are really more than the two I'm listing here, but these will serve us for now.

Need. Do they need or want your product or service? If you are selling an air filter for allergy sufferers and no one at this household suffers, don't waste your time.

Money. Do they have the money or credit?

There's no point in spending time with someone who does not have a need for your product or service.

When we do in-house training seminars for big companies, we always ask: "Do your salespeople need more prospects?" If the answer is no, we're truckin' on down the road.

You might think, "Every salesperson needs more prospects." But that's not true. Some companies have defined territories and they know exactly who their clients and prospects are in each territory. Some salespeople may be assigned only to one massive account, say AT&T. They don't need any more prospects.

On your worksheet, complete the two assignments listed above. Don't worry. When you're all done, you will delete all the stuff from this assignment except your actual script.

Creating Great Scripts

In the title of this chapter, I said we're going to rewrite instead of write. Why? Well, the most important rule I have learned in teaching people this skill is: *It's easier to rewrite than it is to write.*

So, we're going to start with developing a phone/mail/phone script, because this is the most important of the campaign styles. I will be giving you examples from three different scripts I have written. Your final script may consist of rewritten parts of each. Do this exercise even if you don't intend to use a phone/mail/phone campaign. It will give you the practice you need to be able to be a good script rewriter.

Just to make sure you know what I mean by rewriting, here's an example:

> **Original for Financial Services:** M/M_____, I have some important information for investors on what's called a tax-free municipal bond fund. Have you ever heard of one of these before?

> **Rewritten for Computer Sales:** M/M_____, I have some important information for computer hardware buyers on our new Armadillo computer. Have you seen the ads we've been running on TV?

As you rewrite, I want you to pay attention to these rules:

1. No sentence should contain more than fourteen words. Long sentences are fine for school compositions, especially when you don't have much to say and need to pad. But they are not good for sales, which is spoken, not written. In spoken English, your listener can't go back to the beginning of one of these long, tortured sentences to see what you started out to say. Very often, in rewriting a script, you will find that you have produced one of these fifty-five-word monster sentences. Rewrite the sentence into several shorter ones.

2. No technical words. It is never safe to assume that a prospect is as well educated as the salesperson. Some prospects think a debenture (which is a kind of bond) is what you put in a glass of water on your bedside table each night. So edit out complex and technical words.

3. Don't talk more than fifteen seconds without asking a question. If a prospect does not get involved in the conversation, you've lost.

Questions are the salesperson's tool for creating involvement. Also, they help you establish control. In the conversation below, you tell me who is in control.

DAUGHTER: Daddy, why does it rain?
FATHER: Well, uh . . . tiny little drops of water get together and become big drops. They fall down.
DAUGHTER: Why do they fall down instead of up?
FATHER: Uh . . . gravity. It's gravity that calls them down to the earth, sort of like you call your dog.
DAUGHTER: But why?
FATHER: Well, uh . . .
DAUGHTER: How far is it to the moon?
FATHER: Uh . . . it's . . . uh . . .

Another reason for asking lots of questions is: How else will you know if your prospect is still awake?

Finally, asking questions enables you to control what the prospect thinks about. If you simply stop talking, the prospect's attention can just wander off. But the question directs his or her attention to the area you want the prospect to think about.

With these rules in mind, let's rewrite a script.

Finding Out Who Buys at Home

OK, we're not quite ready to start. You have to know who to ask for when you are calling a residence. If you don't call residences, just skip ahead to the next section.

If I'm ever going to be shot for being a male chauvinist, it will be for what I am about to recommend to you. Forgive me if it sounds chauvinistic; it is not intended to be. But the fact remains that in most American households, there is a certain division of labor and responsibilities. This division, while certainly not as defined as it was even a few years ago, is more or less traditional, and quite frankly, it's a waste of time to ignore it. If you follow the advice below, you'll get through to more decision makers than you would if you do it any other way.

1. Where the phone is listed in the man's name, ask for the man *IF:* Your product or service has to do with the structure of the house, the outside of the house, or any of the major systems, such as heating, air-conditioning, or insulation.

Since there are a lot of widows and divorcees out there who have left the phone listed in the man's name, be alert. If the woman says, "He's not in" or, "Who's calling?" immediately qualify with: "Is this Mrs. Jones? Mrs. Jones, this is Fred Smithers with Acme Company. Do you take care of the chain saw purchase decisions for your family?"

"He's not in" and especially "Who's calling?" when spoken by an adult woman is a dead giveaway that you may have a female living alone who does not wish to broadcast that fact.

2. Where the phone listing at a home address is by initial only, assume a female head of household but qualify if the product or service is a "guy thing" as in item 1 above. Frankly, women are well advised not to list their first names, since this encourages crank calls. Some men, such as Alphonse Theodorakis Jones will be listed as A. T. Jones. In prospecting, our only interest is in determining if A.T. is the buyer or not.

Here's how your script goes for calling A. T. Jones.

YOU:	*(Ring, ring.)*
WOMAN'S VOICE:	Hello.
YOU:	Is this Mrs. Jones?
WOMAN'S VOICE:	Yes, it is.
YOU:	Mrs. Jones, this is Fred Smithers with Acme Insurance. Does the name Acme Insurance ring a bell?
MS. JONES:	Yes, I have seen your sign.
YOU:	Good. Tell me, Mrs. Jones, do you take care of the financial decisions for your family?

3. If your product involves the inside of the home, its decoration, cleanliness (carpets, drapes), education (books, subscriptions), or other service providers, ask for Mrs. Jones. In test marketing a phone/mail/phone campaign for dentists, we found that our buyer was *Mrs.* Jones.

4. Here's the wild card. Many female heads of households are divorcees or widows. For reasons of safety, as I've said, they have left the phone listed in the man's name. So if you call and ask for "Mr. Jones," you may occasionally hear a recent widow respond, "He just died." But after they have had time to collect themselves a much more common answer from a divorcee or widow is "He's not in." Or even more strongly, "Who's calling?" *Always,* when you hear "Who's calling?" qualify if a female answered the phone.

5. With some products, notably financial services, ask for whomever answers the phone. If you hear a male voice, ask to speak with "Mr.

Jones." Here's why: According to a 1996 survey commissioned by the Securities Industry Association, 55 percent of investors are men, 45 percent are women. There would be a slight percentage advantage in asking for a man but not so great as to justify a sleight to your female buyers.

Phone/Mail/Phone First Call

OK. Time to jump in. Get your *scripts.doc* document open to My Script Worksheet.

A phone/mail/phone first-call script is designed to find cherries. It is not designed to set up an appointment or to sell. We'll reserve that for the second call.

To find a cherry, in your first call, offer your prospects some written information. Your *offer* then explains why they should want the information. Then ask if the prospect is interested. If the prospect is interested, you ask up to five qualification questions. One qualification question is ALWAYS about MONEY.

Here's the procedure we will follow: I'm going to take the script apart to make sure you understand why I did it the way I did. Then I will give you several examples from the three scripts I have written for this section. (These examples are reproduced in your worksheet.) As we work our way through each section, you will throw out what you don't want, keep what you do, and rewrite what's left. Simple?

1. The Introduction

The introduction gets the prospect to the phone, and if done correctly, will do one of two things.

1. It will cause the prospect to quickly say, "I'm not interested," or

2. It will buy you fifteen seconds of the prospect's time.

EXAMPLE OF INTRODUCTION

May I speak with M/M_____, please? (RESPONSE) Very good. M/M _____, this is_____, with (FIRM). (a) Does the name (FIRM) ring a bell? OR (b) You know who we are, don't you? OR (c) Can you hear me OK on this phone?

> **Don't Know You:** We're the (PHRASE IDENTIFYING FIRM). Does that ring a bell?

> **Verify Decision Maker:** M/M_____, do you take care of the_____ decisions for your family?

Obviously, you have some choices here. So let me raise the questions that are probably on your mind.

Who is M/M?   "M/M" stands for Mr. or Mrs. or Ms. When addressing women at home, according to Judith Martin, who writes under the pen name "Miss Manners," use Mrs. unless you know otherwise. When addressing women at work, use Ms. and the name under which the woman built her professional reputation. This may be a maiden name, previously married name, hyphenated name, or some other name. Miss Manners refers to this as "The Conservative Lady's Solution."

Why are you using the person's name twice?   The more times you can use a person's name the better. It pulls them right into the conversation.

What's with this "you know who we are" stuff and its variations? The first two questions give people an opportunity to say, "Yes, I know who you are and I'm not interested." If they haven't heard about you, it gives you the choice to explain who you are. The third choice, "Can you hear me OK on this phone?" would be for use in a highly resistive market. If you aren't even getting a chance to make your offer, try this one. It ALWAYS gets a yes or no and then gives you the opportunity to go to the next step.

What about this "phrase identifying firm"?   You need a couple of words that will tell people who you are. When I started my business, my line was "We're the company that specializes in helping salespeople find more business by phone." (Thirteen words exactly.)

Assignment

Go through Section 1: Introduction on your worksheet. Take out anything that does not apply. Fill in the blanks. Make any changes necessary for your market.

2. The Offer

Once you have the prospect's attention, make an offer. In a phone/mail/phone-style script, the offer must be some written information that explains the primary end result someone will receive as a result of owning your product or service. If it takes you longer than one or two sentences to make the offer, you need to break up the long-windedness with a question. If you suspect that your prospect may not be familiar with your offer or product, you may also need to use a question to determine familiarity.

Here are some examples of "offers" from different scripts.

Tax-Free Bond Fund—Securities Industry

M/M_____, I have some important information for you on what's called a tax-free municipal bond fund. Have you ever heard of one of these before? (Response) OK. Then (as I'm sure you know), it's a portfolio of top-quality tax-free bonds that have been selected for both *income and safety.*

Comment: The yes-or-no phrase indicates that we really don't care whether the person has or has not heard about tax-free municipal bond funds. We're going to tell 'em anyway. I have found that a lot of people thought they knew what such things were and didn't. The phrase "as you know" is inserted if the prospect claims he or she has heard about it.

Commercial Real Estate

The Offer

I have some information available on an eight-unit apartment building we have for sale. Are you familiar with the eight-plex on the corner of 14th and State streets? (Response) Because of its location near the university, this building has nearly 100 percent occupancy, which could give you a *steady income stream, which could be an important part of your goal to retire well off.*

Computer-Based Marketing System

I have some information available on the Bill Good Marketing System. This is a computer-based marketing, prospecting, and office management system. Did you read about this in Bill's book *Prospecting Your Way to Sales Success?* (Response) Then (as I'm sure you know), this is a system designed to enable salespeople to *double their business or work half as much.*

Assignment

On your worksheet in Section 2: The Offer are the three offers listed here. Pick the one that is closest to the way you would make your offer. Delete the other two. Rewrite the remaining offer to fit your product or service.

3. The Interest Question

Immediately after making your offer, it is time to fish or cut bait. Is your prospect interested? To find out, ask a question. But you need to make certain your question matches your offer and is not, at this stage, a thinly disguised closing question.

Here's how to do it wrong:

M/M_____, I have some very important information for investors on what's called a tax-free municipal bond fund. Have you ever heard of one of these before? (YES OR NO) Basically, as you know, it's a portfolio of top-quality, tax-free municipal bonds. These have been selected for both income and safety. Are you interested?

Comment: The question "Are you interested?" is too strong at this point in the conversation. Many people will feel that a yes to that question commits them to buy, and so they'll say, "No, I'm not." A better question would be "Could I send you some information on it?" This lets the prospect express interest without making too much of a commitment so early in the relationship. So keep in mind that the interest question is designed to see if the prospect is interested in your offer and not, at this point, in getting together with you or in buying your product. If you offered information, your question should ask if they are interested in that! Here are two examples:

Would you like to take a look at a report on this (product/concept/ service)?

Could I send you some information on it?

While I have used the first question for a long time, my current favorite is the second. It seems to be a bit easier for people to answer.

ASSIGNMENT

On your worksheet, in Section 3: The Interest Question, pick the interest question closest to the way you would say it. Get rid of the others. Rewrite as necessary.

4. Not Interested at All

This is a line that is standard in every script. When you hear a firm "I'm not interested," your response is always "Thankyouverymuch."

ASSIGNMENT

None. Just leave it alone.

5. Fallback

If you don't study very carefully what I am about to say, you will think I just undercut what I said in Number 4 above and that I have opened the door to pit polishing. Let's define the fallback as "that portion of the script you use when the prospect is not interested in your offer but his or her behavior indicates there may be interest in something." *If the prospect says firmly, "I'm not interested," believe! Go on to the next call.*

Here's a piece of a phone call.

> YOU: Could I send you some information on our new candy, which is made from vitamins, algae, and soy meal?
>
> PROSPECT: I don't eat candy.
>
> YOU: OK. What are some of the things you eat that you know you shouldn't?
>
> PROSPECT: I have a doughnut every morning.
>
> YOU: Great! If we come out with a line of fat-burning doughnuts, you wouldn't mind if I called you back and let you know, would you?
>
> PROSPECT No. That would be fine.

Comment: This "fallback" section of our script requires some explanation.

First, I didn't offer to send the prospect information right away. Why not? Because I didn't want to appear to be one of those salespeople who have something for everybody. I called him on a bond fund idea, and quite frankly, I really don't want to appear too interested in another area. I am, but I don't want to appear to be.

Second, use a fallback when your primary offer fails. But do so ONLY when the prospect indicates in manner or behavior that some interest or openness exists.

Third, let's consider, for a moment, what kind of prospect we have identified with our fallback and where to file him. Let's call him an *A minus* and phone him in a week or ten days. At that time, we'll qualify for money if we haven't done so already and, if he's qualified, then go straight for the appointment.

Fourth, you will usually fall back when your prospect is not interested in your offer. *If you have qualified for money and the prospect is broke, don't fall back.* Find out when the prospect will have some money.

Here are some fallbacks.

Tax-Free Bond Fund—Financial Services

Let me ask you this: What kind of investments have you been making lately? (Response) If I came up with an idea in (Investment Type Mentioned), you wouldn't mind if I called you back and mentioned it, would you?

Commercial Real Estate

Let me ask you this: Are there other commercial real estate transactions you would consider at this time? (Response) Very good. If something comes up that meets these requirements, you wouldn't object if I gave you a call and mentioned it, would you?

Computer-Based Marketing System

Let me ask you this: What would you most like to improve in your business right now? (Response) If we had a cassette tape series that dealt with that, is this something you would consider? I'll look through our inventory and if something comes to mind, I'll give you a jingle, fair enough?

Comment: Since we don't sell a lite version of our marketing system, I have to look for another product area entirely. Your choices in developing this section depend entirely on what else you sell.

Assignment

In Section 4: The Fallback choose the fallback closest to the way you want to do it and rewrite as appropriate. Throw away the versions that do not apply to you.

6. Qualification

Once you have established interest, it's time to see if your prospect has the *capability* to carry through. This capability is absolutely dependent on five conditions that must be met. Any one condition not met means no sale. No question about it.

Commitment: Are you speaking with someone who is at least minimally committed?

Need: Do they need your product or service? If you are selling an air filter for allergy sufferers and no one at this household suffers, don't waste your time.

Money: Does the prospect have or can he or she get the money?

Decision: Are you speaking with someone who can make a decision or who is at least on the team?

Time: Can the prospect make a decision in the near term or will he or she have to put off a decision for some reason?

To *completely* establish these conditions requires a lot of time. No way can it all be done in a one-minute phone call. By touching on each of these points very briefly in a first telephone contact, you can get some prospects qualified as cherry, green, info lead, or even pit and do it in short order. Will you make mistakes? You bet. But the biggest mistake of all is trying to sell everyone you talk to.

Here are three examples of qualification scripts.

TAX-FREE BOND FUND—FINANCIAL SERVICES

Commitment: If I send this information out today, you should receive it by (DAY). Will you have time to look it over by (DAY)? (RESPONSE)

Need: To benefit from tax-free income, you need to be at least in the 99 percent* tax bracket. Would you say this applies to you? (RESPONSE)

Money: If you like the idea, would an investment of ($_____) be a problem for you at this particular time? (RESPONSE)

Decision: When making this kind of decision, are you the decision maker or do you consult a significant other? *(If there is an "other":)* Who else would be involved in the decision?

Time: What's the time frame you feel comfortable with for making a financial decision of this magnitude?

COMMERCIAL REAL ESTATE

Commitment: If I send this information out today, you should receive it by (DAY). Will you have time to look it over by (DAY)? *(If the response is no:)* When would you be able to review the material?

Need: How do you see an eight-plex fitting into your long-run investment strategy?

Money: This eight-plex would require a down payment in the area of $40,000. Plus, your credit would need to be good enough to guarantee payments around $3,200 a month in case the building isn't rented. Any problem with the $40,000 down payment? (RESPONSE) What about your credit?

> **If money is a problem:** When would you expect to have the funds available? (RESPONSE) OK. Suppose I give you a call in (MONTH) and we'll set a time then to take a closer look. Fair enough?

Decision: Would you make this decision on your own or would you consult with a significant other, CPA, or attorney? *(If there is an "other":)* Who else would be involved in the decision?

Time: And if you like the idea, how long does it typically take you to make up your mind one way or the other?

> **If response is "not now":** When would you be better able to seriously consider a real estate investment?

---

* This figure has changed many times over the past fifteen years and by the time this book is out of print in the year 2097, it will have changed many more. I chose 99 percent just because I needed a number. If you are in financial services, you will know how to calculate what this figure is, based on current tax law.

Computer-Based Marketing System

Commitment: I know how busy you are and how much paper comes across your desk. If I send this out today, you should get it in three to five working days. Realistically, you need about an hour to look it over and jot down some notes and questions. When will you have time to do this?

Need: On a scale of one to ten, how effective do you feel you are with your current database program?

Money: Our system sells for $9,400. If you like what you read, could you write a check or put it on a credit card?

If money is a problem: When would you expect to have the funds available? (Response) OK. Suppose I give you a call in (Month) and we'll set a time then to take a closer look. Fair enough?

Decision: How many people would ultimately be involved in making a decision to proceed?

Time: When you are making a decision of this kind, what is the procedure you typically go through and how long does it take?

Assignment

In Section 5: Qualifies of your worksheet, rewrite "qualifies" portion of your script. Delete everything that does not apply.

1. Qualifies

If your prospect does qualify, wrap up the conversation and get off the phone. Here are two versions of a standard wrap-up, one for residential prospects, the other for business prospects. The phrase in parentheses is optional. Use it if too large a percentage of cherries tell you on a second call that they do not in fact have the funds available right now.

Residential Wrap-up: *(Are these funds available now?)* Just one other question and I'll let you go. In case I can't get in touch with you during the (Day/Evening), how can I reach you during the (Evening/Day)? I have your address down as _____. Is that correct? Great! Haveagoodday and thankyouverymuch.

Business Wrap-up: *(Are these funds available now?)* Just one other question and I'll let you go. In case I can't get in touch with you during normal business hours, are you ever reachable earlier in the morning or later in the afternoon at your direct extension? (Response)

If no: What is the best time of day to contact you?

If yes: And that number is?

I have your address down as_____. Is that correct? Great! Haveagoodday and thankyouverymuch.

Comment: Questions about making contact at other times may be the most important questions in the script. The answers really tell you if you have a *committed* prospect.

Assignment
In your worksheet, delete the version of "qualifies" that you will not be using and modify, as necessary, the remaining version.

With the completion of this assignment, if you sell to residential customers, you have a complete script. If you sell to business customers, you need to add some material on the front end to help you with receptionists, screeners, and voice mail. So here goes.

Determining Authority to Buy

In selling products or services directly to a consumer, you really won't have much of a problem identifying your decision maker. There are a few difficulties, and we'll come to those. It's much harder, however, to determine "authority to buy" when dealing with a corporation. So let's spend a few minutes on that first.

Finding Out Who Buys at a Corporation

Surely, one of the biggest time wasters is talking with someone who cannot spend money. Regrettably, many corporations are populated by people who can say no but not yes. Ideally, you want to spend your time with the decision maker, but a lot of decision makers got to be that way by learning how to delegate parts of their job. They'll use subordinates, for example, to screen salespeople and their proposals, while reserving for themselves the right to say yes. Unfortunately, if you try to sneak past the people who can say no but not yes, they'll sabotage you. So go through channels, but try to find out as quickly as possible what the channel is and if the person who can say no can also lead you to the person who can say yes.

So let's learn how to identify and contact the decision maker.

The Players: The Receptionist, the Screener, and Voice Mail

To identify decision makers today and get to them, you have to deal with at least three players. In some cases, there is a fourth player: the savior. We'll talk about this person in a moment.

When you call a business, the first person who answers the phone is the receptionist. In a corporation of any size, the receptionist *will not screen calls.* His or her job is simply to route calls to their correct destination. In many cases, voice mail answers the phone. However, in most companies, if you quickly press "0," you will get the receptionist.

The *screener* is normally the second person you talk to. With one exception, you want to talk to the screener because your only other option is voice mail. That's like being sent to purgatory or even the ninth rung of hell.

The third player, then, is *voice mail,* which can be a wonderful tool once you have established a relationship, or a daunting hole to fall into if you haven't established meaningful contact. From the point of view of the prospector, it's mostly a black hole, wall, barrier, pit, slough of despond— call it what you will. I have a lot to say on the subject of voice mail, most of it later. For now, you just need these two rules:

1. When you hit voice mail in making a first call (no screener, just a person's voice mail), disconnect. Try to get the screener or just recycle the list.

2. Until you have made contact with a decision maker, the ONLY reason to use voice mail is to persuade a decision maker to look at material you are sending to his or her screener.

SCRIPT DEVELOPMENT FOR IDENTIFYING AND
GETTING THROUGH TO THE DECISION MAKER

First, I will give you a piece of the script that will take you through a single step of the corporate maze. Then we will go through the script, not necessarily line by line, but as appropriate.

Receptionist: Identify the Decision Maker

To Receptionist: Good morning/afternoon. (PAUSE) My name is
_____.

Decision Maker Unknown: I need to speak with the person in charge of (AREA NEEDED). Could you tell me his or her name please? (RESPONSE) In case I get disconnected, what is his/her assistant's extension? (RESPONSE) I would actually rather talk to (DECISION MAKER)'s assistant. Could you tell me his or her name, please?

(RESPONSE) And could you connect me, please? (RESPONSE) Thank you.

Decision Maker Known: I understand (NAME) would be in charge of (AREA NEEDED); is that correct? *(Clarify as needed)* I need to speak with his/her assistant. Could you tell me his or her name, please? (RESPONSE) In case I get disconnected, what is his/her direct extension number? (RESPONSE) Could you connect me with (ASSISTANT'S NAME), please?

ANALYSIS: OK. Now let's go back over this first section. I will reproduce portions of the script on the left and comments on the right. It is essential that you understand why I'm doing certain things so that you won't change them. If it ain't broke . . . (age 12)

To Receptionist: Good (MORNING/AFTERNOON).

(PAUSE) My name is_____.

Give a loud, friendly greeting and SHUT UP. This causes the receptionist to pause for just a moment. Remember, he or she may be fielding hundreds of calls an hour. Our objective is to get the decision maker's name from the first person you talk to. When the receptionist replies, introduce yourself. If you want the receptionist to give you a name, give yours first. You do not have to state your company name, just yours.

Decision Maker Unknown: I need to speak with the person in charge of (AREA NEEDED). Could you tell me his or her name, please? (RESPONSE) In case I get disconnected, what is his/her assistant's extension? (RESPONSE) I actually want (DECISION MAKER)'s assistant; could you tell me his or her name, please? (RESPONSE) And could you connect me, please? (RESPONSE) Thank you.

Decision Maker Known: I understand (NAME) would be in charge of (AREA NEEDED); is that correct? *(Clarify as needed)* I need to speak with his/her assistant. Could you tell me his or her name, please? (RESPONSE) In case I get disconnected, what is his/her direct extension number? (RESPONSE) Could you connect me with (ASSISTANT'S NAME), please?

RULES

1. *Get as much information from the receptionist as possible.*

2. *Until you have established a relationship, don't even try to speak with the decision maker. You will only get his or her voice mail.*
   We're going to use the screener or assistant to help us contact the decision maker. However, realize that today many decision makers do not have assistants. So this won't always work.

3. *Always get the assistant's direct extension. It saves a step when you call back.*

The Screener

WARNING: The procedure given here should be used ONLY on a corporate decision maker who buys on behalf of the corporation. If you are prospecting people as individuals at their places of business, you will wind up sending out a ton of information and wasting a lot of time. For the individual buyer who is contacted at a business location, I recommend a mail/phone campaign.

In Chapter 19 I will give you the full theory on various ways to deal with screeners. In this section, I am going to incorporate the best methods into our script.

That method here is: *Answer the screener's questions first.* The rule is: The person who asks the questions controls the conversation. So that's exactly what we are going to do in our attempt to get right through to the decision maker. Sometimes it works, sometimes it doesn't.

TO SCREENER:

Decision Maker Known: Good morning/afternoon, (SCREENER'S NAME). My name is_____. I work at (FIRM) in (CITY). I need to speak with M/M_____about (OFFER). Could you connect me, please?

Decision Maker Unknown: Good morning/afternoon. This is (NAME) with (COMPANY). Whom am I speaking with? (OR SCREENER'S NAME), I have available some information on (PRODUCT/CONCEPT/SERVICE) that will show (COMPANY) how to (OFFER), and I need to verify who should receive it. Could you tell me who would be in charge of_____? (RESPONSE) Do you report to him/her? In case I get disconnected, what's his/her direct extension? (RESPONSE) Could you connect me, please?

Decision Maker Not Available: Let me ask you this. Do you think this is something he or she would be interested in?

> **Yes or Maybe:** OK. I'm going to send this information to him/her and then check back with you. If he/she is not interested, I'll just go on my way; but if he/she is interested, perhaps you could relay back to me how to proceed further. Would that work? (RESPONSE) Great. Could I have/confirm your mailing address? (RESPONSE) Your fax number? (RESPONSE) Thankyouverymuch. And do you suppose you could connect me to his/her voice mail now?

> **Don't Know:** OK. Let's try this. I'm going to send the information to your attention, but I would like to leave a voice-mail message telling him/her to expect it. Then I will check back with you and perhaps you could relay whether he/she is interested. Would that work? (RESPONSE) Great. Could I (have/confirm) your mailing address? (RESPONSE) Your fax number? (RESPONSE)

Thankyouverymuch. And do you suppose you could connect me to his/her voice mail now?

Voice Mail

Good morning/afternoon. This is_____with (FIRM). We are (PHRASE OR MORE IDENTIFYING FIRM). I have some information available on (OFFER) and will be sending it to you via fax/mail to the attention of (SCREENER). I will be following up on (DAY). If you have any questions, my name again is_____. You can reach me at_____. If this something you are not interested in, please inform (SCREENER). Thank you very much for your time. I hope to speak with you soon. That phone number again is_____?

ANALYSIS

Decision Maker Known: Good morning/afternoon, (SCREENER'S NAME). My name is_____. I work at (FIRM) in (CITY). I need to speak with M/M_____about (OFFER). Could you connect me, please?

If you did a good job with the receptionist, you already know the decision maker's name and the screener's name. Act like he/she is expecting your call.

A screener normally tries to find out who is calling, the company that person is with, and what the call is about. To save time and get control of the conversation, answer those questions first. Sometimes you will be put right through. More often than not, the decision maker is in a meeting or otherwise unavailable. So you will need another leg of the script.

Decision Maker Unknown: Good morning/afternoon. This is (NAME) with (COMPANY). Whom am I speaking with? (OR SCREENER'S NAME), I have available some information on (PRODUCT/CONCEPT/SERVICE) that will show (COMPANY) how to (OFFER), and I need to verify who should receive it. Could you tell me who would be in charge of_____? (RESPONSE) Do you report to him/her? In case I get disconnected, what's his/her direct extension? (RESPONSE) Could you connect me, please?

Frequently, you will not be able to dig out the decision maker's name from the receptionist. All too often you just get transferred to a voice or, worse, a voice mail.

RULES

1. *If you get transferred to a screener's voice mail, disconnect and try later.*

2. *Gather as much information as possible from the screener, especially the decision maker's direct extension number. Our second voice-mail strategy is: Call when the screener isn't there, especially early in the morning.*

Decision Maker Not Available: Let me ask you this. Do you think this is something he/she would be interested in? Would that work? (RESPONSE) Great. Could I have/confirm your mailing address? (RESPONSE) Your fax number? (RESPONSE) Thankyouverymuch. And do you suppose you could connect me to his/her voice mail now?

Don't Know: OK. Let's try this. I'm going to send the information to your attention but I would like to leave a voice mail message telling him/her to expect it. Then I will check back with you and perhaps you could relay whether s/he is interested. Would that work? (RESPONSE) Great. Could I have/confirm your mailing address? (RESPONSE) Your fax number? (RESPONSE) Thankyouverymuch. And do you suppose you could connect me to his/her voice mail now?

This is the usual result of a first attempt. Our objective is to befriend the screener. We want to send the information to the screener, if possible, and then have the screener get us to the boss if the boss is interested.

VOICE MAIL ANALYSIS

Good morning/afternoon. This is_____with (FIRM). We are (PHRASE OR MORE IDENTIFYING FIRM). I have some information available on (OFFER) and will be sending it to you via fax/mail to the attention of (SCREENER). I will be following up on (DAY). If you have any questions, my name again is_____. You can reach me at _____. If this is something you are not interested in, please inform (SCREENER). Thankyouverymuch for your time. I hope to speak with you soon. That phone number again is:_____.

Here we are using Persuasive Voice Mail. Our objective is to persuade the decision maker to look at the material we are sending. It also follows the basic rules:

1. *Speak slowly.*

2. *Give your telephone number at least twice.*

3. *Stress the offer. This is what creates the interest.*

4. *Sound upbeat and positive.*

ASSIGNMENT

On your worksheet, the item just after My Script Worksheet is Identify the Decision Maker Worksheet. Go to that document and create your own Identify the Decision Maker script by rewriting the one I have created. Other than putting in identifying information about your firm, you really should not change a whole bunch.

Sample Scripts

On the pages that follow are complete scripts for the three examples we've been developing so far. These are also in the *scripts.doc*, which you have downloaded. I am including the copies in the book for the benefit of those who may not yet have Internet access. If you don't, time to buck up and plunge into the new millennium.

Tax-Free Bond Fund Script

May I speak with M/M_____, please? (RESPONSE) Very good. M/M _____, this is _____, with (FIRM). (a) Does the name (FIRM) ring a bell? OR (b) You know who we are, don't you? OR (c) Can you hear me OK on this phone?

> **Don't Know You:** We're the (PHRASE IDENTIFYING FIRM). Does that ring a bell?

> **Verify Decision Maker:** M/M_____, do you take care of the_____ decisions for your family?

The Offer: M/M_____, I have some important information for you on what's called a tax-free municipal bond fund. Have you ever heard of one of these before? (YES OR NO) OK. Then (as I am sure you know), it is a portfolio of top-quality tax-free bonds that have been selected for both income and safety.

Interest: Could I send you some information on it?

Not Interested at All: Thankyouverymuch.

Fallback: Let me ask you this. What kind of investments have you been making lately? (RESPONSE) If I came up with an idea in (INVESTMENT TYPE MENTIONED), you wouldn't mind if I called you back and mentioned it, would you?

QUALIFICATION

Commitment: If I send this information out today, you should receive it by (DAY). Will you have time to look it over by (DAY)? (RESPONSE)

Need: To benefit from tax-free income, you need to be at least in the 28 percent tax bracket. Would you say this applies to you? (RESPONSE)

Money: If you like the idea, would an investment of ($_____) be a problem to you at this particular time? (RESPONSE)

Decision: When making this kind of decision, are you the decision maker or do you consult a significant other? (*If "other":*) Who else would be involved in the decision?

Time: What's the time frame you feel comfortable with for making a financial decision of this magnitude?

Qualifies (Residential): *(Are these funds available now?)* Just one other question and I'll let you go. In case I can't get in touch with you during the (Day/Evening), how can I reach you during the (Evening/Day)? I have your address down as_____. Is that correct? Great! Haveagoodday and thankyouverymuch.

Commercial Real Estate

May I speak with M/M_____, please? (Response) Very good. M/M _____, this is_____, with (Firm). (a) Does the name (Firm) ring a bell? or (b) You know who we are, don't you? or (c) Can you hear me OK on this phone?

> **Don't Know You:** We're the (Phrase Identifying Firm). Does that ring a bell?

> **Verify Decision Maker:** M/M_____, do you take care of the _____decisions for your family?

The Offer: I have some information available on an eight-unit apartment building we have for sale. Are you familiar with the eight-plex on the corner of 14th and State streets? (Yes or No) Because of its location near the university, this building has nearly 100 percent occupancy, which could give you a steady income stream, which could be an important part of your goal to retire well off.

Interest: Could I send you some information on it?

> **Not Interested at All:** Thankyouverymuch.

> **Fallback:** Let me ask you this. Are there other commercial real estate transactions you would consider at this time? (Response) Very good. If something comes up that meets these requirements, you wouldn't object if I gave you a call and mentioned it, would you?

Qualification

Commitment: If I send this information out today, you should receive it by (Day). Will you have time to look it over by (Day)? (Response) *(If no:)* When would you be able to review the material?

Need: How do you see an eight-plex fitting into your long-run investment strategy?

Money: This eight-plex would require a down payment in the area of $40,000. Plus, your credit would need to be good enough to guarantee payments around $3,200 a month in case the building isn't rented. Any problem with the $40,000 down payment? (RESPONSE) What about your credit?

If money is a problem: When would you expect to have the funds available? (RESPONSE) OK. Suppose I give you a call in (MONTH) and we'll set a time then to take a closer look. Fair enough?

Decision: Would you make this decision on your own or would you consult with a significant other, CPA, or attorney? *(If "other":)* Who else would be involved in the decision?

Time: And if you like the idea, how long would it typically take you to make up your mind one way or the other?

Qualifies (Residential): *(Are these funds available now?)* Just one other question and I'll let you go. In case I can't get in touch with you during the (DAY/EVENING), how can I reach you during the (EVENING/DAY)? I have your address down as_____. Is that correct? Great! Haveagoodday and thankyouverymuch.

If not now: When would you be better able to seriously consider a real estate investment?

Computer-Based Marketing System

May I speak with M/M_____, please? (RESPONSE) Very good. M/M _____, this is_____, with (FIRM). (a) Does the name (FIRM) ring a bell? OR (b) You know who we are, don't you? OR (c) Can you hear me OK on this phone?

Don't Know You: We're the (PHRASE IDENTIFYING FIRM). Does that ring a bell?

Verify Decision Maker: M/M_____do you take care of the _____ decisions for your family.

The Offer: I have some information available on the Bill Good Marketing system. This is a computer-based marketing, prospecting, and office management system. Did you read about this in Bill's book, *Prospecting Your Way to Sales Success?* (YES OR NO) Then (as I am sure you know), this is a system designed to enable salespeople to double their business or work half as much.

Interest: Could I send you some information on it?

Not Interested at All: Thankyouverymuch.

(Alternative) Let me ask you this. What would you most like to improve in your business right now? (RESPONSE) If we had a cassette tape series that dealt with that, is this something you would consider? I will look through our inventory and if something comes to mind, I'll get it out to you, fair enough?

Qualification

Commitment: I know how busy you are and how much paper comes across your desk. So you tell me. If I send this out today, you should get it in three to five working days. Realistically, you need about an hour to look it over and jot down some notes and questions. When will you have time to do this?

Need: On a scale of one to ten, how effective do you feel you are with your current database program?

Money: Our system sells for $9,400. If you like what you read, could you write a check or put it on a credit card?

> **If money is a problem:** When would you expect to have the funds available? (RESPONSE) OK. Suppose I give you a call in (MONTH) and we'll set a time then to take a closer look. Fair enough?

Decision: How many people would ultimately be involved in making a decision to proceed?

Time: When you are making a decision of this kind, what is the procedure you typically go through and how long does it take?

Qualifies: *(Are these funds available now?)* Just one other question and I'll let you go. In case I can't get in touch with you during normal business hours, are you ever reachable earlier in the morning or later in the afternoon at your direct extension? (RESPONSE)

> **(If no:)** What is the best time of day to contact you?

> **(If yes:)** And that number is?

I have your address down as_____. Is that correct? Great! Haveagoodday and thankyouverymuch.

CHAPTER 13

More Lead Generation Scripts

Lead Generation Scripts

For our purposes, we are going to divide telephone scripts into two categories.

1. Lead Generation Scripts: These are the scripts we use on the first one or two contacts to get the prospect properly categorized as: hot, cherry, green, info, pit, jerk.

2. Lead Processing Scripts: These are the scripts we use to call back existing prospects. These include: phone drip, green cherry callback, info lead requalification. You might want to download these now. (Password: erg, my Dad's initials.)

In this chapter, we will be covering the remainder of the primary Lead Generation Scripts, plus walk you through more exercises in script-rewriting.

Know Before You Go

Very probably you have read or heard about the large amounts of money American corporations pay to send their salespeople on even one face-to-face appointment. It's for this reason that it is especially important to qualify before you go.

Certainly one way to do this is to get a cherry, by virtually any campaign style, send information, call back and requalify, and then, if, *and only if,* the person is now a hot prospect, set up the appointment.

Another way to find a hot prospect is with a mail/phone campaign. Sometimes you can get the appointment on the first call because someone has already read your material. With only a little prompting from you, he or she is ready to begin the buying process, which, in most cases, means setting up an appointment.

Mystery Appointments

Before getting into the techniques on rewriting appointment scripts, I want to take a couple of shots at a type of appointment setting I find particularly objectionable. It is practiced in many industries and I call it the mystery appointment. If it sounds bizarre, trust me; this is the way many major firms teach their salespeople to prospect.

In setting a mystery appointment, you don't let the prospect know anything more than your name, your company, and that you have some important but unspecified need to see him or her right away. Basically, you just bully your way in the door. Those who work for the offending companies will recognize this style instantly.

> M/M_____, this is Joe Doakes with Acme Company. I have a few new ideas which I'd like to share with you. I'm going to be in your neighborhood between four and six o'clock on Friday. When can I see you?

Another version is practiced extensively by multilevel marketing companies whose distributors are explicitly told not to tell a prospective distributor *anything about the meeting.* Here's how one of these might go. (And this is for calling your friends!)

> FRED: Jack, it's your old fishing buddy, Fred.
>
> JACK: Hey, when we going?
>
> FRED: I got some place else I want to take you and Alice.
>
> JACK: What you got in mind?
>
> FRED: It's something I think will be very important for you and Alice. Suppose I pick you both up at seven o'clock Thursday evening.
>
> JACK: What are we going to do?
>
> FRED: That's exactly what I'm going to show you. Thursday at seven?
>
> JACK: Yeah, I guess.
>
> FRED: Great! Thursday at seven. See you then.

One multilevel distributor I know went to pick up "Jack," found all the lights on, the TV on, dinner on the table, and no one home. I wonder why.

Here's a promise: If you trick your friends and prospects into seeing you, you'll come to hate your job. Remember that, and don't set mystery appointments. Instead, take on faith, for now, that in the time you spend driving out to see one of these mystery leads—or anyone else you have forced yourself on—you can sit down at the phone, find five or ten excellent prospects,and set up some quality appointments. So no bully tactics. And no mystery, please.

Cherry Callback Scripts

Let's start with a cherry callback script. It's a relatively easy script to develop since you already have a foot in the door because of last week's qualification call. However, we first have to handle a problem with second calls.

Here's the problem. Last week you sent some information. This week you call back. This is how the all-too-typical second call goes.

FRED: Jack, it's Fred Smithers over here at Acme. How are you?

JACK: Fine.

FRED: I sent you that information last week. Did you get it?

JACK: Doesn't ring a bell.

FRED: Remember the big package? Brown envelope?

JACK: Oh, yes. I've got it. Haven't had time to look at it yet. It's about number six down from the top.

FRED: When do you think you'll get to look at it?

JACK: Try me next week some time.

Let's do a triple whammy handle on the "I didn't get it/I didn't read it" problem. You'll probably never stamp it out entirely. But we can sure cut down on it. Here's what we'll do.

1. Mutilate the material you send out. By "mutilate" I mean write all over it, circle items, draw arrows, and so forth. If you do this, I promise you, your prospect is far more likely to read it. The "mutilation principle" is covered very thoroughly in Chapter 15.

2. Instead of sending a handwritten note, only write what you can put on the back of your business card. Take your business card, flip it around, upside down and backward, and write on the back, "Here's the information I promised." And sign only your *first* name. Then, using a paper clip, attach the card to the *upper-right-hand corner* of the mutilated material.

When the information arrives, the prospect will open the envelope, see your first name on the back of the card, won't have a clue as to who you are, will then have to take the card off, read it, and then, staring him in the face in his other hand, is your written material with phrases like "Read This" or "See Page 9" in orange or some other prominent color.

The prospect will now read what you've highlighted and perhaps the rest. Plus, by forcing your prospect to get physically involved with your business card, you've had the opportunity again to let him or her know who you are.

Remember, you didn't send the prospect information because you care if he or she reads it. You needed to send it in order to establish who you are and to prove *through your actions* that you're not a high-pressure salesperson.

3. When you make your cherry callback, *bypass* whether the prospect received or read your material. Never ask, "Did you get it? Did you read it?" Instead say: "I sent you that material last week, but before I recommend you get involved, there are two or three questions I would like to check with you. Do you have a moment or two?"

Rewriting the Cherry Callback Script

Like the qualification script, your Cherry Callback Appointment Script is made up of distinct parts. We'll go over them one at a time. I would recommend you sit down at your computer and get your *scripts.doc* and go to work. In case you've been a slug and haven't downloaded it yet, run, don't walk to billgood.com. The password, if you will recall, is: bretgood. Find the section labeled Cherry Callback Script and work with me step by step. When you're done, you will have a Cherry Callback Script tailored just to you. More important, you will have had even more practice in script rewriting.

Here goes with the Cherry Callback Script:

1. Intro and Bypass

By "bypass" I refer to the technique whereby we ignore completely whether the prospect received or read the material sent. Here's how you do it:

> May I speak with M/M_____, please? M/M_____ this is_____with (Company). I sent you that information last week but before I recommend you get involved, there are two or three points I would like to go over with you. Do you have a moment or two?

Please note: I didn't even remind the prospect what the information was on. And I really don't care if the prospect remembers getting it or not. All I care about is the fact that by accepting the material from me, the prospect is now obligated to discuss it. With the intro and bypass in place at the very beginning of the second call, you should hear a lot less of the "I didn't get it/I didn't read it."

A NOTE OF WARNING: Please don't expect everyone you qualified on first calls last week to make an appointment for this week. Here are some very broad rules of thumb that you can apply. About 20 percent of the people you talk to will be too busy right at the end of your intro. Another 20 to 30 percent will blow away before you get to your appointment close. And finally, if you do it right, you should be getting one or two appointments from last week's cherries. Another one or two prospects will require additional information (still cherries) and you'll wind up downgrading some to green and info lead status. As you develop and work your pipeline, you will get at least as many hot prospects from your pipeline as from fresh cherry callbacks.

ASSIGNMENT

In Section 1: Intro and Bypass, review this section of the script. You may wish to make some changes. I cannot imagine what they are as these lines are as close to perfection as you will see on this earth.

2. Sell Yourself or Your Company

If you work for a very well known company, an IBM, a Merrill Lynch, a Bank of America, you don't need to spend any time telling your prospect about your company. These companies do an extraordinary job of that for you. But suppose you work for Pterodactyl Computers. You've got a real problem.

We are going to solve *part* of that problem by sending some information about you and/or your company when you send out the requested literature. (We will cover that in detail in Chapter 15.) In the scripts below, I will give you several different ways to sell yourself or your company, depending on what information you sent out.

Here's the rule: If your company is unknown, sell it. If your company is known, but you aren't, sell yourself.

Frankly, I learned of this principle when I first started my business. My practice was to go out on a sales presentation, make the presentation, and then go directly to a coffee shop and sit down and analyze what I had done. A number of patterns began to emerge. One of them was that when I would get down near the close, the prospect would say, "Who are you again?" And I would have to present my credentials all over again. So I began experimenting with giving my credentials at different points in my sales presentation. Here's what I now believe: The best place to present your credentials or those of your company is close to the beginning of the second call and again at the very beginning of a sit-down sales presentation.

Seminar Sales

Mr. Jones, let me tell you just a little bit about who we are and what we do. The name of the company again is Bill Good Marketing, Inc. My name is Bill Good. We specialize in training salespeople to find new business by phone; and in your industry, we've worked with such people as_____, _____, and_____. I would imagine that if you did get interested in one of our seminars, you would want to check with some of the other people in your industry who have used us, is that correct?

They always want to check references. So I tell them they should. I even insist that they write down the names and phone numbers of the people who have given me their permission to use them as referrals. What kind of credibility do you think I earn with that?

Financial Services

Since we've never met, I'd like to tell you a little about myself and the kind of work I do. My name, again, is_____. I specialize in (Product Sent), tax-advantaged investments, and retirement planning. I'll answer any questions you have and stay in touch with new ideas and needed information. But I recognize that you're probably busy, and I'll respect that by keeping my calls brief and to the point. Does that sound fair enough to you, M/M_____?

Generic (Sent Company Info)

In the materials I sent you, I enclosed some information about (Company Name). I highlighted a couple of points, specifically _____ and_____(Offer Restated). Did you have any questions about us?

Example: In the materials I sent you, I enclosed some information about Pterodactyl Computer. I highlighted a couple of points, specifically the technical expertise of our staff and the fact that we've been right here helping people get more computer for their money for twelve years. Did you have any questions about us?

Remember: People like doing business with people they know. Since you have never been introduced, let's now take care of that. In reality, a salesperson with, say, one hundred accounts has one hundred part-time jobs. If you were in fact applying for a part-time job, you would, of course, tell something about yourself. So let's do it here as well. Its effect is unbelievable.

Also, the "sell yourself or company" step is very important to start establishing a professional image. You'll need this image to get your prospect to answer detailed and sometimes very personal questions. Part of qualifying the prospect is getting the prospect to give you true answers to detailed questions. If you are able to communicate a professionalism early in your contact with the prospect, you have a much better chance of getting your questions answered later.

I should point out that with the sell-yourself step, we are fading away from prospecting skills to selling skills. In this section, we've begun using a sales technique called assumptive selling. We are beginning to act as if the appointment has already occurred. Reread the financial services self-introduction on page 172. You'll see what I mean.

One Old Schooler wrote a book and said: "The sale begins when the customer says no." I would say: "The sale really begins with the sell-yourself step." While this is not a book on sales technique, we do need at least to begin using some sales ideas at this point in our presentation. It's from this point forward that we begin acting less like a prospector who is discarding dirt and more like a gold refiner who is making sure he or she doesn't lose a speck. This is not an open sesame to begin pit polishing. Just begin to shift your point of view from discard to keep.

ASSIGNMENT

In Section 2: Self-Introduction of Cherry Callback Script in *scripts.doc,* rewrite your own self-introduction or company introduction. When complete, it should not take more than thirty seconds to deliver. It should end with a question.

3. Bridge to Questionnaire

After your introduction, you'll need a transition to get smoothly into the questions you'll be asking. Here's a Bridge to Questionnaire, both a generic and a rewritten example. Please note once again the assumptive selling techniques.

> **Generic:** To make sure our (NAME OF PRODUCT) is exactly the right (TYPE OF PRODUCT) for you, there are a few questions I would like to run past you. We can do that in one of two ways. You can set up a time to come down to the showroom, or I can spend a few minutes by phone with you right now. Which way would you like to proceed?

> **Rewrite #1:** M/M_____, to make sure our new Thundermobile is exactly the right car for you, there are some questions I would like to run by you. We can do that in one of two ways. You can set up a time to come down to the showroom, or I can spend a few minutes by phone with you right now. Which way would you like to proceed?

Rewrite #2: For me to do a good job for you over time, I'll really need to know more about where you are financially, how you got that way, but most important, where you want to be in the future. We can do that one of two ways. We can set up a time to get together, or I can run some questions by you right now. How would you like to proceed?

ASSIGNMENT

In *scripts.doc*, Section 3: Bridge to Questionnaire, rewrite as necessary. As always, throw away those passages you won't use.

4. The Questionnaire

The guts of the Cherry Callback Script is a questionnaire. Since there are thousands of products that can be sold and tens of millions of questions that can be asked, it is very difficult in this section to do any more than give a list of the kinds of questions that should be asked, the broad rules that apply, and several examples of questionnaires.

Please note: One questionnaire may not be enough. You may need a different one for each product or market you work in.

- The first two or three questions should be null questions—that is, a question whose answer doesn't matter. It simply gets the prospect answering questions. For example:
  a. Let me just make sure I have your address correct. I have you down at 405 South Main Street, is that correct?
  b. And your position is: Vice-President, Materials Acquisition, correct?
  c. And normally, what's the best time of day to reach you?

None of these questions is critical, but each plays a role in getting the person into the *flow of question answering*. The pattern you want to establish is: You ask, they answer.

- Ask less personal, less confidential, or less sensitive questions first.

Call it the salami technique if you want. We just take a small slice at a time rather than going for the whole thing. If you try and grab the whole sausage, people will resist. Just ask for a little bit at a time. Here are some examples of questionnaires from financial services, insurance, and commercial real estate industries, and how I might design one for an automobile dealership. Please note that in question eight below I am qualifying *again*. I did it on the first call. Now I'm going to make certain my prospect has some MONEY. Sometimes prospects will tell you on the first call that they have money but it may not be available RIGHT NOW. That's why it never hurts to requalify.

FINANCIAL SERVICES

1. Normally would you prefer information sent to your home or office?

2. What is the best time of day to get hold of you?

3. How would you describe your investment philosophy?

4. Based on your past performance, on a scale of one to ten, how would you rate your abilities as an investor?

5. Have you ever had any outstanding investments?

6. Have you ever lost a lot of money on an investment before?

7. If you wanted to raise $_____for an investment, how long would it take?

8a. Occasionally, we get some extremely attractive prospectuses that require a minimum investment of $_____. If one of these came along, would that be a problem for you?

8b. *(If problem:)* If it were something you *really liked,* what is the *most* you could conceivably come up with?

9. How much do you expect to have available within the next twelve months in the way of new investable funds? Where is it coming from?

10. What about CDs? When will they be expiring in the next year?

11. Normally, what kind of balances do you keep in your money market funds and checking accounts?

12a. Have you ever bought (PRODUCT SENT)?

12b. *(If yes:)* What do you (LIKE, NOT LIKE) about it?

13. Just a couple of other questions here. How far are you from retirement age?

14a. *(If not retired:)* At what after-tax rate of return are your investments going to have to grow in order to meet your retirement needs?

14b. *(If retired:)* What after-tax rate of return do your investments have to yield in order to maintain your current lifestyle?

By the way, this questionnaire is not the longest I have ever designed. Probably just the best. Like most salespeople who have seen this for the first time, you probably don't think there is a chance in the world people would answer it. What can I say? You can die a disbeliever, or you can give it, or its equivalent for your industry, a try. Your success with a questionnaire such as this depends only on your having previously been accepted as a professional *and* on delivering the questionnaire in a relaxed, easy style.

Here's a much, much shorter questionnaire.

INSURANCE

1. What are your savings goals, say, twenty years from now?

2. Have you worked out how much you need to set aside in order to achieve that?

3. At what rate do your investments have to grow in order to meet your retirement objectives?

And if I were to get a call from GM, here's how I might design a second-call questionnaire form for Cadillac or any other high-end car.

AUTOMOBILE

1. What do you most want in a car?

2. How many in your family?

3. Who would be the main driver?

4a. Were you planning to trade in your current car?

4b. *(If no)* What kind of financing did you have in mind?

5. If you were really excited about, say, our_____model, what's the most you figure you could handle on a monthly payment?

HOW LONG SHOULD A QUESTIONNAIRE BE?

Too long.

Now, lest you think this is a flip answer, let me explain. When you first begin working on your questionnaire, make up more questions than you ever expect to use. As you start using your questionnaire, you will find that some of your questions just don't work. Throw them out. Your questionnaire will get shorter.

Keep running prospects (and clients) through your questionnaire. It will shorten up even more. The first questionnaire I did when I started my business was forty-five questions long. After some months of working with it, I had it down to just five questions. Each one usually generated an "I don't know" response.

The manager of an office should know the answers to the following questions. When he or she does not know, that just indicates the need to find out.

1. How many calls do your salespeople make per hour?

2. How many prospects are they finding per hour?

3. How many salespeople do you have who are less than two years in the business?

4. How many of them come in at least two evenings a week?

5. What kind of system do they have to keep track of their prospects?

6. How would a decision be made to give a seminar? Could you decide or would you need to check with a regional director?

What normally happens in the course of this questionnaire is that the sales managers would say, "What does it cost?"

If that question came too early in my questionnaire, my response was "I'll come to that." If it came later, say around question four or five, I would swing right into a close. So as you develop your questionnaire, ask questions that your prospect should know the answer to and doesn't. By the way, when you hear "I don't know," the correct answer is: "Hmmmm." Squeeze off two or three hmmmm's in the course of a questionnaire, and I promise you will own the account!

ASSIGNMENT

In Section 4: The Questionnaire, develop a questionnaire designed to discover need and requalify for interest, money, and time as necessary.

5. The Close

The close for the appointment is actually quite easy. If you really have a hot prospect, you just ask. If you've done a good questionnaire, the questions have worked some magic on the prospect's mind. They've actually created interest. And so we really don't need too many techniques for closing for an appointment. Generally, we just ask the prospect if he or she would like to get together and talk about it, and the answer will generally be "Sure."

We do, however, want to be just a little bit more elaborate than this. So we'll use a *closing formula* I call the ABC close. You can use this to close for anything. But our interest here is to get an appointment with a qualified and interested prospect. (By the way, some Old School sales trainers used the phrase ABC to indicate "Always Be Closing." I think this is junk. The close is simply that part of a presentation that asks for a commitment to act. The entire presentation is not made up of closing, as this statement indicates.) Here's what the ABC close is all about:

A IS FOR ACTION: A close always involves an action. You don't want the prospect to just *think* about anything. You want him or her to *do* *something.* So on the first step of our close, we'll recommend an action. Here are some examples of action steps:

> Mr. Jones, I think it would be an excellent idea if you brought your last two years' tax returns down to my office.

> Mrs. Smithers, why don't you pull together all of your insurance policies?

Or, to your teenage daughter,

> Nicci, I think it would be an excellent idea if you cleaned up your room now.

B is for Benefit: To make certain no good prospect gets away at this point, stress a benefit for taking the action you have just recommended. Even restate your original offer. Here are some benefits for taking the actions recommended above. I have put the benefits in italics.

> Mr. Jones, I think it would be an excellent idea if you brought your last two years' tax returns down to my office. I am sure I can show you a way to *cut your taxes significantly.*

> Mrs. Smithers, why don't you pull together all of your insurance policies? There's an excellent chance I can show you how to get *more coverage for the same amount you're now paying.*

> Nicci, I think it would be an excellent idea if you cleaned up your room now. By doing that now, you have a *faint chance of seeing daylight next weekend.*

C is for Commitment: After you've told the prospect what you want him or her to do and have given a good reason for doing it, go immediately, without pause, without passing go, without collecting $200, to the commitment question. Here are some complete closes with the commitment question in italics.

> Mr. Jones, I think it would be an excellent idea if you brought your last two years' tax returns down to my office. I am sure I can show you a way to cut your taxes significantly. *I have a spot on my calendar on Thursday at four and I'm also free Friday morning at ten. Which of those would be better for you?*

> Mrs. Smithers, why don't you pull together all of your insurance policies? There's an excellent chance I can show you how to get more coverage for the same amount you're now paying. *I have to be out your way next Wednesday evening. I have a time available at six-thirty and again at eight-thirty. Which looks best to you?*

> Nicci, I think it would be an excellent idea if you cleaned up your room now. By doing that now, you have a faint chance of seeing daylight next weekend. *Would you like to start now or in thirty seconds?*

ASSIGNMENT

In Section 5: The Close, fill in the blanks on the "Fill-in-the-Blanks Close." For the benefit of those who have not managed to bestir themselves, due no doubt to being riveted to this book, here is the exercise you would be looking at in *scripts.doc*.

> **Action:** M/M_____, I think it would be an excellent idea if you (SPELL OUT ACTION THE PROSPECT SHOULD DO).

> **Benefit:** I'm sure I can show you how (DESCRIBE BENEFIT FROM ACTING NOW).

> **Commitment:** I have a spot in my calendar on (DAY) at (TIME). How does that look to you?

REQUALIFY (PROSPECT IS NOT IN FACT HOT)

A definite minority of cherry callbacks will go straight through to the appointment. So if it becomes apparent during the call that you don't have a hot prospect, what are we going to do? Whine? Sniffle? Hardly.

If our cherry callback does not produce a hot prospect, we need to see what kind of prospect we do have. So here go some *requalification legs* to your script. As a rule, start the process by requalifying as a cherry. If it becomes apparent you don't have a cherry, requalify as a greenie. If no go as a greenie, see if you have an info lead. If you can't find any interest at all, well, you had what I call a "false cherry," which I'll define as a pit wearing a vinyl cherry skin.

Remember, when you "pit" the prospect, you basically just return him or her to the mass-mail list from whence he or she regrettably came.

> **Requalify as Cherry:** Is there any additional information I can send you, M/M_____, anything that might interest you enough to keep talking at this time?

> **Requalify as Greenie:** M/M_____, let me ask you this. Is there a time in the future when you would better be able to consider my offer? (RESPONSE) Terrific. Suppose I add your name to my mailing list. I will stay in touch until (MONTH). Meanwhile, if you have any questions, you let me know, OK?

> **Requalify as Info Lead:** Let me ask you this, M/M_____. Would you like to receive information from us from time to time? (RESPONSE) Great! Here is what we'll do. I will add your name to our mailing list and then every so often I'll touch base to see if conditions have changed—fair enough?

ASSIGNMENT

In Section 6: Requalify, review the three requalification paragraphs and revise if necessary.

6. After the Close

The appointment is closed. Now let's really firm it up. You can do this with a number of simple questions:

1. I have your address as 405 Bilgewater Lane, is that correct?

2. What is the nearest major cross street?

3. Do you have a pencil handy? My name again is Balph Burgher. My phone number is 333-4444. If there is any problem with three o'clock next Thursday, you'll give me a call, won't you?

4. Very good. I'll see you next Thursday, and you have a nice day, OK?

ASSIGNMENT

Almost done with your Cherry Callback Script. In Section 6: After the Close, rewrite Balph Burgher's "post close." It can be almost any three or four confirmation-type questions.

SAMPLE SCRIPT: REAL ESTATE INVESTOR

Intro and Bypass: Hi! This is_____over here at_____. I spoke to you last week and you wanted me to check out some properties for you in (NAME OF AREA). I found something I think you will be very interested in, but before I recommend we go ahead, there are two or three points I would like to check over with you. Do you have a second?

Sell Self: First of all, I would like to tell you just a bit more about myself and the kind of work I do. I specialize in only one kind of property, and that's apartment buildings. I don't sell houses. I don't sell raw land. And I don't sell office buildings. And I'm in no particular hurry to find a building for you, especially one that's not right for you. Does this sound like the kind of person you could conceivably do business with?

Bridge to Questionnaire: For me to do a good job for you over time, I will need to know exactly what you are looking for. I have a number of buildings in mind, but I need to check some points with you first. We can do that now or we can set up a time to get together and we'll do it while we're driving around to see several buildings currently on the market. Which way would you like to proceed?

QUESTIONNAIRE

1. If you did decide to buy a building, would your main motivation be tax advantages or income?

2. What income properties do you currently own? And when did you buy it/them?

3. I would imagine that you would want to manage these yourself rather than hire someone to do it for you, is that correct?

4. To raise a down payment in the area of $_____, would you need to liquidate another property or could you just write a check?

5. What is the most you could carry now in the way of a negative cash flow?

ABC Close: Very good. Here's how we work. We first get together here at the office and look over the photos, rents, prices, costs, and so forth. We also go over the tax and wealth-building implications of owning buildings and see if that is really the direction that is right for you at this time. If all systems are go, we drive by those you like. So, what would be the best time during the week for us to get together? (RESPONSE) Very good. I have a spot open on (DAY) at (TIME) or (TIME). Which of those would be better for you?

AFTER THE CLOSE

1. Do you have a pencil handy? My name again is_____. My phone number is_____.

2. Our office is located here at_____. Do you know where that is?

3. *(Give directions if necessary.)*

4. If there is any problem with (DAY) at (TIME), will you give me a call?

5. Very good. I'll see you then on (DAY). You have a good day.

SAMPLE SCRIPT: LIFE INSURANCE

Intro and Bypass: May I speak with M/M_____, please? Very good. M/M_____, this is_____with_____. I sent you that information last week, but before I recommend you get involved, there are two or three points I would like to go over with you. Do you have a moment or two?

Sell Self: Since we've never met, I would like to take a moment and tell you a little about myself and the kind of work I do. When we meet, you will notice I am in my twenties, early twenties. And you may certainly wonder why someone who looks like they just got out of high school should be making recommendations that could affect the rest of your life. Well, let me tell you this. I can promise you two things: The company has been here a lot longer than I have, and second, if I don't know the answer to something, I'll certainly find someone who will. Does that sound fair enough to you?

Bridge to Questionnaire: For me to do a good job for you over time, there are some things I need to know about where you are financially, how you got that way, but most important, where you want to be in the future. We can do that one of two ways: You can come down here to my office or I can come visit you. Which way would you like to proceed from here?

No Go on Appointment: Just one quick question and I'll let you go. Right now,_____is extremely competitive on our homeowner's insurance. Tell me, am I too early or too late to give you a quote? (RESPONSE) In what month does your policy expire?

Expires Soon: OK. M/M_____, what I would like to do is drop by, work up a quick quote for you, and just leave it with you. I have to be in (NAME OF AREA) on (DAY). I have a spot open at (TIME) and again at (TIME). Which of those would be better for you?

Expires Later: OK. Suppose I get back to you in (MONTH) and work up a quote for you then? By the way, when do you pay premiums on your auto insurance again? And who carries it currently?

Auto Expires Soon: OK. M/M_____, what I would like to do is drop by, work up a quick quote for you, and just leave it with you. I have to be in (NAME OF AREA) on (DAY). I have a spot open at (TIME) and again at (TIME). Which of those would be better for you?

Auto Expires Later: Very good. I will give you a call on your auto insurance in (MONTH). We'll get together then, OK?

Comment: This script was written for a salesman who, at the time, was twenty-three and looked about seventeen. When he went into people's homes, their jaws would hit the floor. The principle here is: Handle obvious liabilities as early as possible *and you bring them up first.* You will also note that I went directly for the appointment at the end of the Bridge to Questionnaire. Why? It felt right. Also note that I built a fallback into my second-call script. As you progress in your scriptwriting skills, you will see that you can definitely "mix and match" script parts.

Second-Call Appointment Script Development Form

Intro: May I speak with M/M_____, please? Very good. M/M _____, this is_____with (COMPANY). I sent you that information last week, but before I recommend you get involved, there are two or three points I would like to go over with you. Do you have a moment or two?

Sell Self/Company: Since we've never met, let me tell you a little bit about myself/my company and the kind of work we do. First of all, my/the company name again is_____. Basically, I/we specialize in

_____. I'll answer any questions you have and stay in touch with new ideas and needed information. But I recognize that you're probably busy, and I'll respect that by keeping my calls brief and to the point. Does that sound fair enough to you, M/M_____?

Bridge to Questionnaire: For me to do a good job for you over time, I'll really need to know more about (WHAT YOU NEED TO KNOW). We can do that one of two ways. We can set up a time to get together, or I can run some questions by you right now. *How would you like to proceed?*

QUESTIONNAIRE GOES HERE

CLOSE

Action: M/M_____, I think it would be an excellent idea if you (SPELL OUT ACTION THE PROSPECT SHOULD DO).

Benefit: I'm sure I can show you how (DESCRIBE BENEFIT FROM ACTING NOW).

Commitment: I have a spot in my calendar on (DAY) at (TIME). How does that look to you?

AFTER THE CLOSE

1. I have your address as_____, is that correct?
2. What is the nearest major cross street?
3. Do you have a pencil handy? My name again is_____. My phone number is_____. If there is any problem with (TIME) next (DAY), you'll give me a call, won't you?
4. Very good. I'll see you next (DAY), and you have a nice day, OK?

Phone-Only First-Call Appointment Scripts

One of our campaign styles is obviously Phone Only. In this style, you get on the phone, call people, and try to set up appointments. There are quite obviously some similarities between a Cherry Callback Script and a First-Call Appointment Script. However, I should point out that unless you are selling something truly unique, well known, or in great demand, you may find it difficult to set up appointments on first calls. This is certainly not to say it can't be done. It can. But do keep in mind that if you run into stiff resistance on your first call, drop back to the qualification script and run a two-call approach.

In this section, we'll walk through the parts of the First-Call Appointment Script, give examples of each, give some examples of completed scripts, and then provide you with a Script Development Form that will help you create your own script.

1. The Intro

(This section is identical to the intro in the qualification script.)

> May I speak with M/M _____, please? Very good. M/M _____,this is _____ with (COMPANY). You know who we are, don't you? (*Or,* Can you hear me OK on this phone? *Or,* Does the name ring a bell?)

ASSIGNMENT

On the Phone-Only Worksheet, copy the introduction you did for the Phone/Mail/Phone First-Call Script. You've already done it once. Why do it again?

2. Reason for the Call

Here's where you make or break your First-Call Appointment Script. You really *do* need a good reason to call. "I'm going to be in your neighborhood" doesn't cut it. Who cares where you're going to be? Instead, consider the following possibilities as reasons for your call.

PRICE CHANGE   If your price is going up, or has just come down, you can certainly call and tell them. For instance, you might be selling computers. A reason for the call, in the event of a price change, might go like this:

> M/M_____, I'm calling to let you know that the price of our Pterodactyl Computer is going to go up in two weeks.

Or, if prices have dropped, you can call and say:

> M/M_____, that Armadillo PC you've been thinking about has just come down in price.

NEW PRODUCT OR CHANGE OF PRODUCT INFORMATION: If there is any change in a feature or benefit of a product, call and tell people about it. For example, suppose you are a residential real estate agent. You may have a particularly desirable home that has just come on the market. Let's say the home sells for $145,000. You could call those people who presently live in homes worth about $120,000 and look for someone who might be in a position to make a 25 percent upward move.

Your call might go like this:

M/M_____, I'm calling to let you know that we have just brought a fantastic home onto the market. It's $145,000, has four bedrooms, and a beautiful view of the mountains.

Or, let's say you're in the seminars business and you just added a bit of material to a given seminar. Your call might go like this:

M/M_____, I'm calling to let you know that we have just added some material on gorilla hunting to our Basic Cold-Calling Seminar.

We've added an element here which we hope will excite some curiosity. My prospect has got to wonder, "What is a gorilla? And why do I want to hunt one in the first place?"

We use this approach a lot in the securities industry in helping account executives hunt for gorillas. (By the way, a gorilla is a prospect who can cut a check for $100,000 or at least raise it in a few days' time.) Gorillas generally are not motivated as much by greed as are people with less money. So to motivate a gorilla, you appeal to some other aspect. One of the most powerful is curiosity. A typical reason for the call on a gorilla hunt, using the curiosity approach, might go like this:

M/M_____, I'm looking for a very unusual investor this evening. This investor could raise $100,000 for an exceptional opportunity.

One of the oldest, and most effective, reasons for the call is an ability to save the prospect money. Regrettably, some organizations inflate a price and then offer a discount, and after a while no one believes them. And that, of course, makes it rougher going for the rest of us. Nevertheless, it is certainly the case that a legitimate opportunity to save someone some money is a highly effective reason to call. Here's an example from a script I wrote for a commercial real estate firm in Los Angeles:

If I could show you a first-class building at substantially less than market, would you consider a move when your lease expires?

Perhaps you don't want to have your prospects spend less money, but you can offer them more product for what they do spend. Here is an example of an approach I wrote for an insurance company to go after their competitors' whole life coverage.

M/M_____, if I could show you how to get two or three times as much insurance coverage for the money you are now spending, is this something you might want to hear about?

This is one of the most powerful motivations you can play with. Even if someone is not seriously considering buying something, they'll go on and grab it anyway just to make sure that it doesn't run out. Scarcity, of course, is also very powerful to use on a close. Here's how you might do it if you were a commercial real estate agent leasing an office building.

M/M_____, we've got only four prime retail spaces available in the Dumpview Mall.

Some companies build scarcity into their entire marketing approach. A health club, for example, will have so many memberships available at a certain price. Then the price goes up. Then it only has so many of those, and so forth. A phone call around that idea might go:

M/M_____, we only have thirty more places available at our introductory membership price. When they're gone, the price will go up $500.

This method is especially important if you are selling a service. For whatever reason, people seem to like "how-tos." Look at almost any self-help book jacket and you'll see the claim that the book will tell you how to get into a cold shower, how to stay there, how to get out of it with style, how to dry off quickly, how to get into your clothes, and how to look radiant and healthy. Here's an example that you could use if you were selling my seminar:

M/M_____, I'm calling to let you know that our seminar will show your salespeople how to find more business by phone and mail.

I am sure there are dozens more reasons that can be used for any one product or service. But these seven certainly should spark your imagination.

ASSIGNMENT

In Section 2: Reason for Call, rewrite any of the Reasons for Call given there that strike your fancy. Throw the rest of it away.

I trust you see that in each of these reasons there is a benefit. You don't call to offer yourself as a benefit. You call to offer your prospect some reason to be interested enough to listen to you.

3. The Leading Question

Immediately following your reason for the call, ask a leading question. It's called a leading question because it *leads* right into a short series of qualification questions. Its primary purpose is to test interest level.

Don't make the leading question too strong. If it sounds like a closing question people will back off because a positive response implies they've bought. It's therefore important to use words that don't grab for massive amounts of commitment. Sales is, of course, a seduction, not an assault. Some examples of good leading questions are:

- Is this the kind of thing you might want to find out more about?

- Would you be interested in hearing more about this?

As I've said, never ask directly, "Are you interested?" It sounds too much like a closing question.

Here is a complete call I might design for a high-end car. If I were a car salesman, every time I sold a car, I might just call everyone who lives on the same block as my new customer. Here goes my reason for the call and leading question (with apologies to GM):

> Mr. Jones, you may have seen the brand-new Cadillac the Barkingdogs, who live down the street from you, just bought. It's the one that looks so good I'm sure they'll want to lock it up at night because it might go cruising on its own. Tell me, did you hear him lay a trail of rubber when he took off for work this morning?

Assignment

In Section 3: Leading Question, pick a leading question and rewrite it to get one that will work for you.

4. Interest Building/Qualification Questions

Your questions in this section follow the same rules as the questionnaire you developed for your Second-Call Appointment Script. You can ask anywhere from three to ten questions in order to verify that the prospect is or is not worth seeing. One question should determine ability to make a decision. Another should check on how much money is available. And finally, you should obviously find out if the funds are available now!

Let's say you sell office furniture. Here are three key questions.

- "Fred, if you like our line, who else would be involved before a final decision is made?"

- "And how much, roughly, did you have budgeted for a redecoration?"

- "Are those funds available now?"

As you develop or refine your questions, keep in mind that the questionnaire accomplishes two goals: It lets you know whether the prospect is worth pursuing, and equally, if not more important, it provides the prospect with a way to evaluate you. The interest you show through your questions will be measured and, if genuine, returned.

ASSIGNMENT

In Section 4: The Questionnaire, copy in the questionnaire you developed for your cherry callback and most likely shorten it.

5. The Close

Here we use the ABC closing technique, which I have already discussed.

ASSIGNMENT

In Section 5: The Close, copy in your close from the cherry callback.

6. After the Close

The technique is the same as previously discussed.

ASSIGNMENT

Ditto.

First-Call Appointment Scripts

Here's a script we use to set up an appointment for one of my seminar presenters. When any one of my employees has any spare time in a city, I try to get him or her in front of a group. The script goes like this:

FREE MINI-SEMINAR SCRIPT

Intro: Good morning/afternoon. This is_____with Bill Good Marketing, Inc. You know who we are, don't you? *(In financial services, mostly they do know.)*

Reason for Call: How would you like a free mini-seminar on cold calling, something to pep up your brokers and get them back on the phone?

Questions: Just a couple of quick questions.

1. How many advisers in your office?
2. How many have been with you two years or less?
3. Of the remainder, how many would you say should be doing some cold calling and aren't?

ABC Close: Here's the plan. (NAME), the senior field trainer for Bill Good Marketing, Inc., will be in (CITY) on (DATE). He has some free time in the morning. I would like to arrange for him to spend about an hour with your troops. He'll give them some information they can use right then and there, and there is no cost or obligation. Our hope, naturally, is that they will get so excited they will want the full seminar. The only times (NAME) has available are (TIME) and (TIME). Which of those would be better for you?

AFTER THE CLOSE

1. For this to be worthwhile for us both, we will need about an hour. Your advisers will need to be on time and have an understanding with the receptionist to hold their calls. Any problems so far?

2. Let me ask you this. If you did like what (NAME) says at your free mini-seminar, and if your RR's like it too, do you have funds available now to buy the full seminar? (HE OR SHE WILL ASK PRICE). The price of the seminar is $_____plus expenses, which normally run about $_____. Would that amount pose a problem to you at this particular time?

3. Let me check your address. I have you down at_____. Is that correct?

4. *(Ask clarifying directions as necessary.)*

5. *(If free seminar is scheduled a week or more off:)* I will get a letter out to you right away. I will enclose a flyer that you can pass out to your brokers. The more you have attending, the more cold calling you'll get as an immediate result, OK?

6. Would you make a note in your calendar that (NAME) will be there about fifteen minutes early to visit with you and will start promptly at (TIME)?

7. I'll give you a call on (DAY) just to confirm, OK?

Comment: Sometimes I'll bury a very important question in "After the Close." I do that when I am almost certain I'll get the answer I want. This is the case with my "Money" question in this script. Also, as you can imagine by studying the "After the Close" section of this script, we had some trouble with earlier versions. The seminar wouldn't start on time and that would throw off the entire schedule. We have pretty much eliminated that problem with this "After the Close" script and with a confirmation letter that stresses timeliness.

CARPET CLEANING SCRIPT

Intro: May I speak with Mrs._____, please? (RESPONSE) M/M_____, this is_____. I am with Extra Dry Carpet Cleaning. Does the name Extra Dry Carpet Cleaning ring a bell?

> **If no:** We're the people who don't soak your carpets with water when we clean them.

Reason for Call: Since you have just put your home on the market, I'm sure you want it to look its very best. We can help you get your home looking absolutely wonderful with our dry, professional carpet cleaning. Have you considered how clean carpets might help you sell your home?

ABC Close: Here is what I suggest. I would like to drop by, measure your home, and show you how our method will make your carpets look fantastic. I will also tell you how much it would cost if you decided to let us clean them. Suppose I drop by on (DAY) at (TIME). How does that sound?

After the Close
1. I have your address as_____. Is that correct?
2. What is the nearest major cross street?
3. Do you have a pencil handy? My name again is_____. My phone number is_____. If there is any problem with (TIME) next (DAY), you'll give me a call, won't you?
4. Very good. I'll see you next (DAY), and you have a nice day, OK?

Comment: This approach quite obviously requires a list of people who have just put their homes on the market. A friendly realtor would provide such a list. Or you could call "for sale by owner" ads from the classified section of the newspaper.

GORILLA SCRIPT

Intro: May I speak with M/M_____, please? Very good. M/M _____, this is_____with (COMPANY), members of the New York Stock Exchange. You know who we are, don't you?

If no: We're the oldest, largest, friendliest firm in town. Ring a bell?

Reason for Call: M/M_____, I am looking for an unusual investor this evening. This investor could raise $100,000 for an exceptional opportunity. Am I talking with the right person or should we part company at this point?

ABC Close: Very good. The investment I have in mind has returned_____percent over the past_____years. Since you are not the kind of investor who is shocked by the idea of a $50,000 investment, I also know you are the type of investor who wants to see all the facts, figures, and arithmetic before you make up your mind. Tell me, when are you most likely to have some free time during the day? (RESPONSE) I have a spot open on (DAY) at (TIME). I am also free on (DAY) at (TIME). Would you prefer to come to our office or would you prefer I come to see you?

What Kind of Investment Is It?: That's exactly what I want to show you. If the idea of $100,000 doesn't blow you away, I know you are the kind of investor who wants to see all the information, and frankly, I can't do it justice over the phone. I tell you what. If I stay longer than fifteen minutes, it's because you have questions. Fair enough?

Comment: I broke some more rules on this one. My questionnaire, such as it is, is imbedded in my "Reason for Call" and my "Close." In the close, you really have to look carefully for the ABC steps. They're all mixed up, but they're there. Also, I have written in a response to the most common question this script elicits: What kind of investment is it? I am not going to tell the prospect because most of these investments require a detailed explanation. You might, with some justification, ask: Haven't you just violated every principle you set down about no-mystery leads? No, I haven't. It's not a mystery lead. The prospect knows I'm coming to talk investment. A stiff one. I am using the fact that gorillas are a curious bunch to keep the door open and to keep the interest level up until I arrive.

First-Call Appointment Script Development Form

Intro: May I speak with M/M_____? Very good. M/M_____, this is_____with (Company). You know who we are, don't you?

Reason for Call: I'm calling because _____.

Tell me, (Leading question goes here)

Questionnaire

1.

2.

3.

4.

Action: M/M_____, I think it would be an excellent idea if you (Spell out action the prospect should take).

Benefit: I'm sure I can show you how (Describe from acting now).

Commitment: I have a spot in my calendar on (Day) at (Time). How does that look to you?

AFTER THE CLOSE

1. I have your address as_____, is that correct?

2. What is the nearest major cross street?

3. Do you have a pencil handy? My name again is_____. My phone number is_____. If there is any problem with (TIME) next (DAY), you'll give me a call, won't you?

4. Very good. I'll see you next (DAY), and you have a nice day, OK?

Mail/Phone Scripts

One more set of Lead Generation Scripts.

One of the most powerful campaigns is our mail/phone campaign. You send out a letter and then follow it with a phone call. The follow-up call is made either by the salesperson or by a caller who simply runs interference for the salesperson.

Here are the business and residential versions. As with all the other scripts in this chapter, I have reproduced these in *scripts.doc.* By now, I think you've got the idea of script rewriting. So I will just present these to you with no further instructions.

Solicitor Follow-Up Call—Business to Business

FIND THE DECISION MAKER

To Receptionist: Good morning/afternoon. (PAUSE) This is_____. I need to speak with M/M_____'s assistant. Could you tell me his or her name, please?

To Screener: Good morning, (SCREENER'S NAME). This is_____. I'm with (FIRM) in (CITY). I am following up on a letter we sent to M/M _____about (OFFER). Could you connect me, please?

Decision Maker Available: *(Go to "Decision Maker Found" script on page 193.)*

Decision Maker Not Available: OK. This is regarding the letter about (OFFER). If you could put me through to his/her voice mail, I will leave a detailed message. If he/she is not interested, I'll just go on my way, but if he/she is interested, perhaps when I call back, you and I could arrange a time for my boss, the/a (TITLE) here at (FIRM), to speak with him/her. Would that work? (RESPONSE) Great. And with whom am I speaking? (RESPONSE)_____'s direct extension number is? (RESPONSE) (SCREENER'S NAME), could I have your fax number? (RESPONSE) And could you connect me to his/her voice mail?

Voice-Mail Message (if possible): Good (MORNING/AFTERNOON). This is _____with (FIRM). We are (PHRASE OR MORE IDENTIFYING FIRM). I sent you a fax/letter just recently headlined "_____." If you haven't seen it, definitely be on the lookout for it. I spoke with (SCREENER'S NAME)in your office and we agreed I would check back with him/her to see if this is the kind of thing you are interested in pursuing. If you are interested, I would like to set up a time my boss, the/a (TITLE) here at (FIRM), could spend a few minutes by phone with you. By making a telephone appointment like this, we don't have to start one of those endless games of voice-mail phone tag! If you have any questions, my name again is_____. My phone number is_____. Give me a call and I will be happy to set something up right away. Thank you for your time.

DECISION MAKER FOUND

To Decision Maker: Good (MORNING/AFTERNOON). This is_____'s office with (FIRM) calling. My boss,_____, sent you a letter recently headlined "_____." We realize you are very busy, which is why he/she asked me to call and see if you would like to speak with him/her about it.

(CONTINUE WITHOUT PAUSING.)

Boss Available Now: He/she is available now. Could you hold, please?

Boss Available Soon: He/she is just wrapping up another phone call. Will you be there in five minutes?

> **Decision Maker Will Be There:** Terrific. We'll give you a call right back.
>
> **Decision Maker Will Not Be There:** (Go to "Boss Not Available Soon," immediately below.)

Boss Not Available Soon: He/she asked if I would call and set up appointments for (TIME RANGE). By making a telephone appointment, we don't have to play voice-mail tag. I have a spot open on (DAY) at (TIME). Would that be good for you?

Decision Maker Did Not Receive Letter: Doggone it!

Let me ask you this: Are you interested in (OFFER)?

> **If no:** Oh well; the letter will probably still arrive anyway. If you change your mind, just give us a call—and thankyouverymuch for your time today.
>
> **If yes:** Let's go ahead and set up a time for you to talk to (BOSS). He/she's asked me to set up appointments for (TIME RANGE). By making a telephone appointment, we don't have to play voice-

mail tag. I have a spot open on (Day) at (Time). Would that be good for you?

Decision Maker Won't Set Appointment: OK. Is there a time of day that is normally best to reach you? (Response) In case we don't connect during normal business hours, is there a chance we can catch you early or late? (Response) *(If appropriate:)* And what is your direct extension number?

Solicitor Follow-Up Call—Business to Residence:

Combined Script

Two reminders:

- Don't leave messages with non–decision makers

- Don't leave callback information

To Any Adult Answering Phone: Is this M/M_____? (Response) M/M_____, this is_____. We sent (You/Addressee's Name) a letter recently headlined "_____." My boss,_____, would love to speak with (You/Addressee's Name) about it. Is he/she available?

Decision Maker Not In: I will call back.

Decision Maker In: Good!

Boss Available Now: (Boss) is available now. Could you hold, please?

Boss Available Soon: (Boss) is just wrapping up another phone call. Will you be there in five minutes?

Will Be There: Terrific. We'll give you a call right back.

Will Not Be There: *(Go to "Boss Not Available Soon," immediately below.)*

Boss Not Available Soon: He/she asked if I would call and set up appointments for (Time Range). By making a telephone appointment we don't have to play voice-mail tag. I have a spot open on (Day) at (Time). Would that be good for you?

Decision Maker Did Not Receive Letter: Doggone it! Let me ask you this: Are you interested in (Offer)?

If no: Oh, well; the letter will probably still arrive anyway. If you change your mind, just give us a call—and thankyouverymuch for your time today.

If yes: Let's go ahead and set up a time for you to talk to (Boss). He/she asked me to set up appointments for (Time Range). By making a telephone appointment, we don't have to play voice-mail tag. I have a spot open on (Day) at (Time). Would that be good for you?

Decision Maker Won't Set Appointment: OK. Is there a time of day that is normally best to reach you? (Response) In case we don't connect during normal business hours, is there a chance we can catch you early or late? (Response) *(If appropriate:)* And what is your direct extension number?

Salesperson Follow-Up Call—Business to Business or Residence: Decision Maker on Phone

To Decision Maker: Good morning/afternoon. This is_____with (Firm) calling. We sent you a letter recently headlined "_____." I realize you are very busy, which is why I sent a letter first. Before I recommend you get involved, there are two or three points I would like to check with you. Do you have a moment or two?

If Sales Rep/Firm/Product/Service Is Unknown: Since we've never met, first let me tell you a little bit about myself/our firm/what I'm offering you/our services:_____

I realize you're busy and so I will do everything possible to keep our calls and any meetings brief and to the point. Fair enough? Let me check over two or three additional points with you. Based on your answers, I'll know whether to send you additional information, whether we should set up an appointment, or just let it pass at this time.

1. First of all, let me verify your decision-making process. How exactly does it work?

   (Then ask two or three questions to determine need.)

2.

3.

4. One last question *(make this a question they cannot answer or to which they will generally give a nonoptimum answer):*_____ *(Give "Hmmmm" response.)*

Set Up Appointment (ABC Close): *(Action)* You know what, M/M_____? We really should get together. *(Benefit)* I will show you how (Stress What Major Benefit Does). *(Close)* I have a spot open on (Day) at (Time). I am also free on (Day) at (Time). Which of those would be better for you?

Requalify as Cherry: Is there any additional information I can send you, M/M_____, anything that might interest you enough to keep talking at this time?

Requalify as Greenie: M/M_____, let me ask you this. Is there a time in the future where you would be better able to consider my offer? (Response) Terrific. Suppose I add your name to my mailing list. I will stay in touch until (Month). Meantime, if you have any questions, you let me know, OK?

Requalify as Info Lead: Let me ask you this, M/M_____. Would you like to receive information from us from time to time? (Response) Great! Here's what we will do. I will add your name to our mailing list and then every so often I'll touch base to see if conditions have changed—fair enough?

Salesperson Follow-Up Call—Business to Business

Find the Decision Maker

To Receptionist: Good morning/afternoon. (Pause) This is_____. I need to speak with M/M_____'s assistant. Could you tell me his or her name, please?

To Screener: Good morning, (Screener's Name). This is_____. I'm with (Firm) in (City). I am following up on a letter we sent to M/M_____about (Offer). Could you connect me, please?

    Decision Maker Available: *(Go to suitable sales script [not provided here].)*

    Decision Maker Not Available: OK. This is regarding the letter about (Offer). If you could put me through to his/her voice mail, I will leave a detailed message. If he/she's not interested, I'll just go on my way, but if he/she is interested, perhaps when I call back, you and I could arrange a time for him/her and me to spend a few minutes by phone. Would that work? (Response) Great. And whom am I speaking with? (Response)_____'s direct extension number is? (Response) And how about your fax number, (Screener's Name)? (Response) And could you connect me to his/her voice mail?

    Voice-Mail Message: Good morning/afternoon. This is _____ with (Firm). We are (Phrase or More Identifying Firm). I sent you a fax/letter recently headlined "_____." If you haven't seen it, definitely be on the lookout for it. I spoke with (Screener's Name) in your office and we agreed I would check back with him/her to see if this is the kind of thing you are interested in pursuing. If you *are* interested, I would like to set up a time when you and I could talk for just a few minutes. By making a telephone appointment like this, we don't have to start one of those endless games of voice-mail tag. If you have any questions, my name is_____. My phone number is_____. I will be giving (Screener) a call back this afternoon/tomorrow/in a couple of days. Thank you for your time.

CHAPTER 14

Lead Processing Scripts and Voice Mail

Remember this well: Half of all your new clients will come from a properly managed prospect file system. "Properly managed" means:

1. Every prospect gets a letter every month about something the prospect is interested in. This is why we keep track of their interests, both on your prospect card and in the computer.

2. Every prospect gets a phone call at least four times a year. This is why we have set up the filing system so that your prospects who are not in active follow-up right now are filed ninety days after the last personal contacts. At that time, you will take out a deck of, say, info leads, and go through them with one of the scripts below.

Obviously, part of managing the file will involve sending letters, and part of it will involve phone contact. If you *only call,* you will not be able to maintain enough contact with your file, because it will get too big and you cannot contact it enough. If you *only mail,* you will also fail. You must have some degree of personal contact in order to build the right relationship.

The Lead Processing Scripts

Very broadly, there are two broad categories of lead processing scripts:

Follow-up

Drip

Follow-up scripts are specifically tailored to certain categories of leads and are used only in the situation to which they are obviously intended. Drip scripts are used to maintain phone contact. You can use any of the variations to keep your name in front of your prospects by phone.

These scripts, of course, will be on our home page at billgood.com. The password for those scripts is: jenny. (Jenny is my youngest daughter.) You will be downloading the Lead Processing Scripts. In the pages that follow, I will explain each of the scripts and give you a copy to study. In order to build a complete campaign, you should definitely download these scripts and rewrite them to fit your own products and markets.

Follow-Up Lead Processing Scripts

There are two Follow-Up Lead Processing Scripts. The first ensures that deadbeats don't clutter up your list. The second *processes* one of your most important categories of lead: the *dripped-on green cherry*.

Greenie Callback

Two or three weeks before the *funds due date* or *opportunity due date*, you should call back your green cherry prospect. By now, this prospect may have received several drip letters, as well as several phone calls. Ideally, with just a little nudge from you, you will find you have a hot prospect, and the appointment will be set without much effort.

Green cherries, managed as I have outlined, will be among your very best prospects.

Hopefully, you will find a sizzling-hot prospect when you make contact. But of course, if you find the prospect is still not hot, you may want to requalify it so that you know what track the prospect should be on. The choices, naturally, are: cherry, new green cherry, or downgrade to info lead status. For each of these new conditions, the computer operator will send an appropriate letter after consulting with his or her cheatsheet.

The Script for Greenie Callback

Hi! This is_____at_____. How are you?

We originally made contact last (Month 1), when *I/we/one of my assistants* called and talked to you about (Subject). I've been in touch by mail since. You mentioned back in (Month 1) that you would have the time/money to consider my offer in (Month 2). Do you have just a moment or two?

Requalify (Ask as Many of These as Necessary)

Interest: When we spoke in (Month 1), you indicated an interest in (Topic). Is this still a concern to you?

Decision: When making this kind of decision, are you the decision maker or do you consult a significant other? *(If an "other":)* Who else would be involved in the decision?

Money: When we spoke last (Month 1), I indicated you need to have available funds in the area of $_____. Will that be a problem?

Time: What's the time frame you feel comfortable with for making a decision of this magnitude?

Hot Prospect: Set Appointment

Action: M/M_____, my recommendation is that we get together.

Benefit: I'll be able to show you (Best Benefit).

Commitment: I have a couple of spots open this/next week. What looks good to you?

Wrap Up: *(Double check address and give or get directions as necessary.)*

Upgraded Cherry—Needs More Info: Let me put some information in the mail for you and I will give you a call, say on (Day). If you're still interested, we'll set a time to get together. Fair enough? *(On prospect card: Upgrade to A Cherry)*

Still Green—Money/Time Later: With your permission, I will leave you on my mailing list and stay in touch until (Month 3). I'll get back in touch with you then, OK? *(On prospect card: Just make a note. There is no status change.)*

Downgraded to Info Lead: Interested but No Firm Date: Let me ask you this: Do you want to continue receiving information from us? (Response) Do you foresee the possibility that we could do business in the future? (Response) Great. Then I'll be in touch. *(On prospect card: Up/Downgrade to B Greenie)*

Standard Conclusion: Thankyouverymuch for your time! *(Mark prospect card.)*

New Info Lead Requalification

A very important call is your info lead requalification call. As you will recall, an info lead is someone who has barely made it onto the food chain. He or she is only interested in receiving some information, and we have been unable to determine if or when money will be available.

An info lead, when acquired, will receive three letters, ten days apart, and then a requalification call. The purpose of the Info Lead Requalification Call is to make sure you aren't wasting your time and money on pits or jerks. So in order to remain in your lead box, in this script we will insist that the info lead specifically request to remain on your mailing list. Naturally, if this does not occur, you have a pit, not a prospect. So back to mass mail it goes.

The Script: Info Lead Requalification

May I speak with M/M_____, please? M/M_____, this is_____ with_____. How are you? You may recall we first made contact last (Month, Day), and I've been sending you information about who we are and what we do. Does this ring a bell? To make certain we are sending you the right kind of information, I would like to run some questions by you. Do you have a moment or two?

REQUALIFY (ASK AS MANY OF THESE AS NECESSARY)

Interest: When we spoke last (Month, Day) you indicated an interest in (Subject). Is this still a concern to you?

Decision: When making this kind of decision, are you the decision maker or do you consult a significant other? *(If an "other":)* Who else would be involved in the decision?

Money: When we spoke in (Month), I indicated your need to have available funds in the area of $_____. If this were something you were interested in, would that amount be a problem at this particular time?

Time: What's the time frame you feel comfortable with for making a decision of this magnitude?

HOT PROSPECT: SET APPOINTMENT

Action: M/M_____, my recommendation is that we get together.

Benefit: I'll be able to show you (BEST BENEFIT).

Commitment: I have a couple of spots open this/next week. What looks good to you?

Wrap Up: *(Double check address and give or get directions as necessary.)*

Upgraded Cherry—Needs More Info: Let me put some information in the mail for you and I will give you a call, say on (Day). If you're still interested, we'll set a time to get together. Fair enough? *(On prospect card: Upgrade to A Cherry.)*

Upgrade to Green—Money/Time Later: With your permission, I will leave you on my mailing list and stay in touch until (Month). I'll get back in touch with you then, OK? *(On prospect card: Up/Downgrade to B Greenie)*

Requalify as Info Lead: Interested but No Firm Date: Let me ask you this: Do you want to continue receiving information from us? (Response) Do you foresee the possibility that we could do business in the future? (Response) Great. Then I will be in touch. *(On prospect card: There is no status change so nothing to mark.)*

Phone Dripping: An Introduction

According to me, "There is more than one way to skin a cat." There is also more than one way to drip by phone. In the next few pages, you will learn four ways to phone drip. I will talk about "basic dripping." We will discuss what I call a "mini-profile" technique. We will take a look at "upgrade dripping." Finally, we'll cover "voice-mail dripping."

I guarantee that if you do not stay in touch by phone and mail with your prospect, when you do call there won't be even the faintest memory that you ever existed on planet earth. And that means, for you, more cold calling! It's rolling the rock up the hill . . . one more time.

So, once again, some of this contact *must be* by mail, some of it *must be* by phone. There is no way to accomplish our objective by phone *only* or by mail *only*.

Basic Drip

Basic dripping is simply a low-key, service-oriented phone call. It is highly appropriate for dripping on green cherries, and on just about anyone else who needs some dripping.

As you will see in the script, if the person you are calling is not available, just leave an informative voice-mail message, which you will learn shortly how to do. The point is not so much what you say but that you say something. And if you can't say something directly, leave an informative message.

May I speak with M/M_____, please? (Response) M/M_____, this is_____with_____. You have been getting my mail for a while. Does the name (Your Name/Company Name) ring a bell?

Not Available: Could you connect me with his/her voice mail, please?

Voice-Mail Message: Hi, this is_____with_____. You've been getting my mail for a while, and I am just calling to let you know (Provide Valuable Info). If you have any questions about this or if there is anything we can do for you, please call me. My name again is_____. My phone number is_____. Thankyouverymuch. Hope to hear from you soon.

Is Available: I am just calling to let you know that (Provide Valuable Info), and I wanted to touch base and see if there is anything we can do for you at this time. Would you like an appointment? Additional information? Anything like that?

No Appointment or Info: You have a great day, and if there is anything I can do for you, please call me. Thankyouverymuch for your time.

Hot Prospect: Set Appointment

Action: M/M_____, my recommendation is that we get together.

Benefit: I'll be able to show you (Best benefit).

Commitment: I have a couple of spots open this/next week. What looks good to you?

Wrap Up: (Double check address and give or get directions as necessary.)

Upgraded Cherry—Needs More Info: Let me put some information in the mail to you and I will give you a call, say on (Day). If you're still interested, we'll set a time to get together. Fair enough? (On prospect card: Upgrade to A Cherry)

Mini-Profile Drip

One way to develop a prospect into a client is to call and ask a series of questions. The more you know about the prospect, the better able you are to recommend the right thing at the right time.

On a mini-profile drip, you do not ask for appointments. With the exception of "Is there anything I can do for you?" you don't even ask for commitments. You just ask a few questions and add to your knowledge of the client in little bits instead of large chunks. If the prospect asks you a question or otherwise gives you a green light, well, naturally you do what any salesperson should do: Get the appointment or order.

Your questionnaire should have several questions designed to find out what the prospect is interested in. As you learn about new interests, you can add new color-coded dots to your prospect card. The computer operator, of course, will update your database so that you can then mail to the prospect based on what he or she is interested in.

If you feel your questionnaire is too long, don't worry. Just use the mini-profile technique and fill it out over a series of calls. No one said that a long questionnaire has to be filled out over a single call. As with basic dripping, if your prospect is not in, leave an informative voice-mail message.

> May I speak with M/M_____, please? (RESPONSE) M/M_____, this is_____with_____. You have been getting my mail for a while. Does the name (YOUR NAME/COMPANY NAME) ring a bell?
>
> **Not Available:** Could you connect me with his/her voice mail, please?
>
> **Voice-Mail Message:** Hi, this is_____with_____. You've been getting my mail for a while, and I am just calling to let you know (PROVIDE VALUABLE INFO). If you have any questions about this or if there is anything we can do for you, please call me. My name again is_____. My phone number is_____. Thankyouverymuch. Hope to hear from you soon.
>
> **Is Available—Choice 1: File Update:** I was reviewing my notes on (COMPANY), and a couple of questions popped into my mind. Do you have just a moment?
>
> **Is Available—Choice 2: Specification Review:** I was just reading over the specifications for our new (NAME OF PRODUCT), and it occurred to me there are a couple of things about (COMPANY NAME) that I just don't know. Can I run a couple of questions by you?
>
> **Go to Your Questionnaire** *(ask two or three questions):*
>
> **Wrap It Up:** Is there anything we can do for you at this time? Would you like an appointment? Additional information? Anything like that?
>
> **No Appointment or Info:** You have a great day, and if there is anything I can do for you, please call me. Thankyouverymuch for your time.
>
> **HOT PROSPECT: SET APPOINTMENT**
>
> **Action:** M/M_____, my recommendation is that we get together.
>
> **Benefit:** I'll be able to show you (BEST BENEFIT).

Commitment: I have a couple of spots open this/next week. What looks good to you?

Wrap Up: *(Double check address and give or get directions as necessary.)*

Upgraded Cherry—Needs More Info: Let me put some information in the mail to you and I will give you a call, say on (DAY). If you're still interested, we'll set a time to get together. Fair enough? *(On prospect card: Upgrade to A Cherry.)*

Upgrade Drip

As you make the various calls and send your various letters to your prospect file, remember your objective: Get appointments with hot prospects and move other prospects up the food chain or, if necessary, down or even off.

If you always call and try to sell something, your call will become unwelcome. But if you never call to get an appointment or sell something, you will starve. End of discussion. So some of your drip calls need to be more aggressive than others. Upgrade dripping, then, is designed to get appointments where appropriate or, failing that, move your Ds to Cs and your Cs to Bs.

As you can see when you read it, this is a tough script. Of the three drip scripts, this is by far the toughest.

Reminder: As you make these calls, keep good records. Lists of green cherries, info leads, or pitch and miss leads are, after all, just lists. We evaluate them by the same standards as other lists: How many cherries per hour? A well-dripped-on list of green cherries with funds or opportunity due in the next few weeks should generate several hot prospects per hour, while a well-maintained info lead list should generate at least four to seven cherries an hour. Where can you find cold calling lists like these? Answer: You can't! You have to make your own.

May I speak with M/M_____, please? (RESPONSE) M/M_____, this is_____with_____. You have been getting my mail for a while. Does the name (YOUR NAME/COMPANY NAME) ring a bell?

Not Available: Could you connect me with his/her voice mail, please?

Voice-Mail Message: Hi, this is_____with_____. You've been getting my mail for a while, and I am just calling to let you know (PROVIDE VALUABLE INFO). If you have any questions about this or if there is anything we can do for you, please call me. My name again is_____. My phone number is_____. Thankyouverymuch. Hope to hear from you soon.

Is Available: We have introduced a new (NAME THE FEATURE), which will enable you to (NAME THE BENEFIT). I can send you some information on it or, if you know this is something you are interested in, I'd be happy to set up an appointment and come out to see you. Would you like to make an appointment?

Upgrade to Cherry: OK. Would you like me to send you some information and then follow up in a week to see if you have any questions?

If Yes: Very good. I will get that out to you right away, and then give you a callback in a week. Meantime, if something comes up earlier than that, let me give you my direct extension. Do you have a pen handy? My name again is_____. My phone number is_____. You should get this by (DAY), and I will touch base on (DAY), OK? *(On prospect card: Upgrade to A Cherry.)*

Requalify as Green: OK. Hmmmm. Let me ask you this: When in the next six months or so do you expect to have the funds/time available to take a closer look?

Gives Time: Great! Suppose I give you a call a couple of weeks before and, in the meantime, I'll stay in touch by mail so that you know how to get hold of me if anything changes. OK? *(On prospect card: Up/Downgrade to B Greenie.)*

Requalify as Info Lead: One last question and I'll let you go. Would you like to continue receiving the kind of information I've been sending you?

If yes: Very good. I will keep you on the mailing list and stay in touch by phone from time to time.

If no: Not a problem. If things do change, you have my address. Thanks for your time. *(On prospect card: Downgrade to C Info Lead.)*

The Voice-Mail Drip

Some months, if time is short, you might just want to call and ask to be placed on your decision-maker's voice mail. Remember, what we are trying to do is build identity. To do that, we are dripping by mail and by phone. So why not just use voice mail to leave a message that your prospect will find interesting? The type of voice-mail message to leave is an informative mail message. So let's learn how to do it.

Early in the relationship, voice mail can be almost impossible to overcome. That is why we call it the voice-mail wall. It is imperative that you know how to deal with it.

There are at least three different kinds of voice mail:

1. The greeting

2. Informative voice mail

3. Persuasive voice mail

The Greeting

Sometimes, the very first contact people have with you is your voice-mail greeting. According to me, "You don't get a second chance to make a first impression." So let's make sure that your greeting serves you well. Here are the rules:

1. Keep it short.

2. Sound alive and well and not like you're working in a funeral home. (I had to tell one of my clients recently that his voice-mail message made him sound dead from the toes up.)

3. State when you will be available and when you will return your calls.

4. Tell people how to talk to a person now. It is a big annoyance to get five levels deep in someone's voice-mail system and then not be able to reach a person.

5. If appropriate, give people alternate-contact information, such as your pager number or another number where you can be reached.

Sample Greeting: Hi! This is Bill Good. I'm out of town giving a seminar today. I will be back in the office tomorrow. I will be picking up my messages several times today and will do my best to get back to you today or tomorrow for sure when I return to the office. If you need to talk to my assistant now, press 0. To leave a message, speak after the tone. Have a great day.

Words: 75

Time: 20 seconds

Informative Voice Mail

A word of caution: Informative voice mail is mostly for existing prospects and client relationships. You can waste an enormous amount of time leaving all kinds of voice-mail messages for people who have never heard of you and do not care. Since they only rarely call you back, you have wasted your most valuable resource. With that warning in mind, you can and should use informative voice mail to save a lot of time. Properly used, it's wonderful. Obvious occasions for this type of voice mail are:

- You called, and will call back
- Reschedule appointment
- New information about your product

Here are the rules that apply to informative voice-mail messages:

1. Don't talk too fast.

2. State your first and last name and company name clearly.

3. Always state your phone number twice. Otherwise, your prospect may have to replay the message. This is annoying at best.

4. Try very hard to keep your message thirty seconds or less. People have better things to do than listen to long-winded voice-mail messages.

5. Sound upbeat, not tired, bored, or sour. Who wants to call back a sour-puss?

Sample Informative Message: Terry, this is Bill Good with Bill Good Marketing. Sorry I missed you. Please call me at 801-572-1480. My assistant will schedule a telephone appointment for us when you call back. You can reach her almost any time. I will mostly be available afternoons. I'm in town until next Thursday. That number again is: 801-572-1480.

Words: 55

Time to speak: 25 seconds

PERSUASIVE VOICE MAIL

Greetings and informative voice mail are really just common sense. There is no particular art form on either. Persuasive voice mail, however, is another kettle of fish. Your choice of words is very important, and your message must be crafted to build interest or curiosity.

In its most advanced form, when combined with a good mail piece, it can get a decision maker to tell his or her assistant to put your call through when you call back. Persuasive voice mail, then, deals with getting someone we don't know to do something he or she would otherwise not do . . . take our call or return one. The question is: How do we do that? Answer: We stress our strongest benefit. We omit all features. We are trying to get someone interested; you don't create interest by what you say. Interest is created by what you mention and withhold.

If you can get the prospect interested, he or she will take the call. So, how do we do this? Well, here are the rules. Please understand, it's not just the words; how you sound may be even more important than what you say.

1. Be brief.

2. Be upbeat

3. Give your best benefit as to why someone should take your next call or return this one.

4. In prospecting the individual marketplace, don't leave messages with people you don't know. Also, don't take any callback information.

5. In leaving your phone number, always repeat it twice.

6. If possible, state your offer twice.

Here are two examples:

Persuade Decision Maker to Read Material and Take Next Call: Hi! This is Bill Good calling. I just spoke with your assistant, Mary. I'm sending you some material on how my company, Bill Good Marketing, can help your salespeople find more and better prospects. It will arrive by fax today. I will give Mary a call on Friday. We really can get you more and better prospects. If you are interested, just scribble the word "yes" on the fax and give it to Mary. She will set a time we can meet by phone. Thank you for your time.

Words: 89

Time: 30 seconds

Persuade Decision Maker to Return Call: Good morning! This is Bill Good calling. My company, Bill Good Marketing, produces seminars to help salespeople find more and better prospects. I have three questions for you, and I promise that if I take more than three minutes of your time, it is because you had some questions of your own about more and better prospects. Please call me at 801-572-1480. That number again is 801-572-1480. I look forward to hearing from you.

ASSIGNMENT

In *leadproc.doc*, which you have downloaded previously, create your own set of Lead Processing Scripts and put them in a notebook. Also, I've created some convenient forms to help you create voice-mail messages. Be sure and print those out and put them in a convenient place.

Lead Processing Letters

Mail

Virtually every campaign requires some form of written communication, even if it's only a "Here's the info I promised to send" letter. Today, these written communications may be transmitted by e-mail, fax, or letter. For convenience sake, we'll use the term "direct mail" to refer to the message and its appearance.

I am well aware that for some readers of this book, the very thought that you may have to prepare some letters is enough to inspire terror or, worse, blankness. However, before you sink into the swamp of despair, you absolutely must read the three chapters on letters.

In Chapter 15, I will cover Lead Processing Letters. These are the letters you need to follow up on the lead you generate and to send whenever something important with one of your leads changes. Since I know you have a hard time with letters, I have even done a first draft of the eleven letters you need to manage your leads. How's that for service?

But you also need some drip letters and some prospecting letters to use with mail/phone campaigns and standard direct-mail campaigns. In Chapter 16, I will show you some ways to get great copy without having to write a single thing yourself.

In Chapter 17, I will show you how to make your letters and faxes look great!

Now, what more could you want?

What Are Lead Processing Letters?

In managing a prospect file, the one constant is change. People who were less interested become more interested. Those almost ready to buy are now not interested or won't be interested for six more months. Your prospects move up and down the prospect food chain, and, of course, frequently bail out altogether. I have called these changes *interest changes*. Now that's not hard, is it?

An interest change is a change from a mass-mail name to one of the different kinds of prospects, or it is a change from one kind of prospect (cherry) to another (info lead). In most cases, an interest change is an occasion for a letter, phone call, and/or an appointment. Why do all this? Simple: We want to maintain contact and increase interest until a prospect is *hot,* meaning, of course, *willing to begin the selling process.*

Part of our strategy to maintain or increase interest is, of course, through dripping. But part of the strategy is also a series of routine or even etiquette letters that advises the prospect on what is going to happen as a result of a change in status. Once again, why? It's just another socially acceptable way to keep your name in front of your prospects.

By using impeccable manners and meticulous follow-up, the lists of prospects you develop—such as your green cherry list, your info lead list, and your pitch and miss list—will, when handled in the manner I am outlining, *produce more cherries per hour and hot prospects per hour than any other prospect list you will ever have.* By being able to generate more prospects in less time, you will be able to spend more time selling and less time prospecting.

I promised I would show you how to do that, right? Well, the *secret is in the filing system and the maintenance of the file.*

So, you would agree that Lead Processing Letters are important, and that you need to take some time to study and revise them as necessary, right? Then let's look at the New Lead Processing Letters and then we'll look at the Current Lead Processing Letters (designed, of course, for existing leads as opposed to new ones). But first, a very short lesson on how to send out information.

The Mutilation Principle: How to Send Out Information

The Old School says, "Don't send out information. It's just an excuse to get you off the phone." I say, "If someone wants information, send it and do it today!" I know that countless people have told you, "I didn't get it" (you know they did) or "I haven't had time to read it" (not true either—had they been interested, they would have read it). For all intents and purposes, when you hear these excuses you are shot out of the water on that call. You're beached. You can't say, "That's fine. Many of my clients don't receive the information but they set up appointments anyway. Let me just highlight what was in it. . . ." The name of the game is: Get the prospect at least to look at enough of your material to be able to feel she or he has read it. That's why we have the *mutilation principle.* The more you have mutilated the material you send, the more likely someone is to read it or at least look at it enough so that when you call back they won't say, "Didn't get it/didn't read it." Here are the steps:

1. With a pen or highlighter, mark important passages. On any page, write: "See page xx."

2. Add some sticky notes.

3. Clip your business card upside down and backward to the upper-left-hand corner of the material.

4. On the back of your business card write, "Here's the info," and then sign your first name only, "Joe."

Here's what happens: Prospect opens material. Sees your note. Asks himself, "Who's Joe?" Pulls card off pile, turns it over, thinks, "Oh, Acme Widget, I remember." Eye catches: "READ THIS!! THEN SEE PAGE 9." Browses through material for a moment. Sets it aside.

You call with your second-call script: "M/M Good, this is Joe Blow with Acme Widget. We sent you the information you requested on our widgets, and before I recommend you get involved, there are a few points I would like to go over with you. Do you have a moment or two?" Response: Sure.

By combining the mutilation principle with the exact wording of the second-call script, you can almost completely avoid the "I didn't get it/didn't read it" trap.

The Lead Processing Letters

For convenience sake, we'll break the Lead Processing Letters into two categories:

- *New Lead Processing Letters* (Obviously, these are for first responses.)

- *Current Lead Processing Letters* (Once someone has responded, he or she may or may not get hot enough to make an appointment. If it's someone you want to do business with, they stay in the prospect file and are moved down the appropriate track. When you get an interest change from a current prospect, it's an occasion for a letter.)

For each of the two categories, I will name the interest change and give you the file name of the letter as well as, perhaps, a bit of explanation. Your mission, should you choose to accept it, is to edit these letters so they fit your market.

By each letter is a recommended file name. Naturally, you can name them anything you want, but the file names used here are also used in the Salesperson's Cheatsheet and the Computer Operator's Cheatsheet. To save you some typing, you can download these letters from our home page at billgood.com.

The New Lead Processing Letters

These letters are designed for when prospects first respond. Please note: In the case of new cherry, green cherry, and info leads, there are two very slightly different versions of each letter. File names ending in *SP* mean that a salesperson made the initial contact. If the letter file name ends in *C*, that means a caller made the initial contact for the salesperson. If it ends in *M*, that means the initial response was by mail. All direct-mail responses requesting information are considered cherries. Referrals, when contacted, are either hot (in which case they get an appointment confirmation letter) or they are cherries, green cherries, or info leads, just like anyone else.

New A Cherry

FILE NAME: NuChrySP.doc (Salesperson Called)

Thanks for taking a moment to visit with me.
I am enclosing the information you requested as well as something about who I am and the kind of business I do.
I'll check back in a week to see if you have any questions. If anything comes up earlier, call me at 555-4444.

FILE NAME: NuChryC.doc (Initial Contact by a Caller)

Thanks for taking a moment with my assistant.
I am enclosing the information you requested as well as something about who I am and the kind of business I do.
I'll check back in a week to see if you have any questions. If anything comes up earlier, call me at 555-4444.

FILE NAME: NuChryM.doc (Direct-Mail Response)

Thanks for responding to my letter.
I am enclosing the information you requested as well as something about who I am and the kind of business I do.
I'll check back in a week to see if you have any questions. If anything comes up earlier, call me at 555-4444.

New B Green Cherry

* Reminder: New green cherries are not only sent one of the initial letters below, but they are also sent two additional letters: Info1.doc and Info2.doc. See these letters below. Current prospects who upgrade or downgrade to green are only sent one letter.

FILE NAME: NuGRNSP.DOC (SALESPERSON CALLED)

> Thanks for taking a moment to visit with me.
> I am enclosing the information you requested and, as we agreed, I will follow up down the road when your funds become available.
> Meantime, you will hear from me from time to time by phone and mail until then. I am also enclosing some information now about who I am and about our firm.
> If anything comes up before then, do give me a call at 555-4444.
> Sincerely,

FILE NAME: NuGRNC.DOC (INITIAL CONTACT BY A CALLER)

> Thanks for taking a moment to visit with my assistant by phone.
> I am enclosing the information you requested and, as we agreed, I will follow up down the road, which, I understand, will be a more appropriate time than right now.
> Meantime, you will hear from me from time to time by mail and occasionally by phone to see if anything in your situation has changed. I am also enclosing some information now about who I am and about our firm.
> If anything comes up before then, do give me a call at 555-4444.
> Sincerely,

New C Info Lead

FILE NAME: NuINFOSP.DOC (SALESPERSON CALLED)

> Thanks for taking a moment to visit with me by phone.
> I am enclosing the information you requested.
> In the next few weeks, I will send you some additional information about who we are and what we do. And as agreed, I will add you to my mailing list.
> From time to time, we will give you a call just to make sure the information we're sending is of continued interest to you.
> At no time will we pressure you to buy anything. If you ever find the information we send you to be of little or no value, please do request to have your name removed from my list.
> If you have any questions or if there is anything I can do for you, do give me a call at 555-4444.
> Sincerely,

FILE NAME: NUINFOC.DOC (INITIAL CONTACT BY A CALLER)

Thanks for taking a moment to visit with my assistant by phone. I am enclosing the information you requested.

In the next few weeks, I will send you some additional information about who we are and what we do. And as agreed, I will add you to my mailing list.

From time to time, we will give you a call just to make sure the information we're sending is of continued interest to you.

At no time will we pressure you to buy anything. If you ever find the information we send you to be of little or no value, please do request to have your name removed from my list.

If you have any questions or if there is anything I can do for you, do give me a call at 555-4444.

Sincerely,

Second and Third Letters for Green and Info Leads

The second and third letters received by both green and info leads are identical. Info1 is mailed ten days after the first letter the prospect receives. Info2 is mailed ten days after Info1.

FILE NAME: INFO1.DOC

Just recently, we sent you some information you had requested.

I do want to explain a little bit about how I work. Perhaps this will help set me apart from the others who call on you.

I realize you are busy, and I will try and respect that by keeping my calls brief and to the point.

I completely understand that my role is not to push you into making this or that decision. So in our future dealings, should they occur, you may rest assured that neither I nor anyone who works for me will ever pressure you to buy anything.

It is my hope that offering you timely information and good ideas will motivate you to give me an opportunity to compete for at least a portion of your business.

I am enclosing a résumé that will give you a better idea of my background.

If you have any questions, please call me at 555-4444. I'm here every day from 8:00 a.m. to 5:00 p.m.

Sincerely,

FILE NAME: INFO2.DOC

By way of reminder: In the last couple of weeks or so, I have sent you some investment information as well as my résumé.

In this note, I just want to enclose some information about Reliable Securities. I've highlighted some of the important points.

In making any investment decision, there are really three things to consider.

1. The investment choices
2. The person offering investment advice
3. The company with whom you're considering investing

Hopefully, the information I have already sent you weighs in my favor. Perhaps what I'm enclosing now on Reliable Securities will tip the scales further, toward some point in the future when you will favorably consider me as one of your financial advisers. Please, if you have any questions, call me at 555-4444.

Sincerely,

Thanks—New Client

Whenever someone buys something and becomes a client, thank them.

FILE NAME: TksNuCl.doc

Just a note to say thank you very much for placing your confidence in (COMPANY NAME) and me.

I just want you to know I will do everything possible to continue to earn your business.

If there is anything I can do for you, never hesitate to call.

If there are procedures that are followed when someone makes a purchase, these can be included in the thank-you letter.

Upgraded to A Cherry

The main reason we maintain a file of green cherries, info leads, and pitch and misses is very simple: These names, when called, yield more cherries and hot prospects per hour than any other lists. So when a greenie, info lead, or pitch and miss upgrades, we send a letter.

FILE NAME: UpChry.doc

I am delighted you are interested once again!

I am enclosing the information you requested.

I will be calling you back in about a week. As you look over the material, you might jot down any questions. We can go over your questions when I call.

Moreover, I'll have some questions for you, to make certain that this is right for you at this particular time.

If something comes up earlier, call me at 555-4444.

Changed to B Greenie

Green cherries are wonderful leads to have lots of. Some will come when a cherry downgrades. You'll find others in talking to info and pitch and miss leads. These will upgrade. The two letters below cover both scenarios.

FILE NAME: DOWNGRN.DOC (FORMER CHERRY)

I'm sorry we won't be doing any business in the immediate future, but I do want to thank you for giving me a chance to compete in the future.

Between now and then, I will periodically touch base by mail and phone with you.

Meantime, if you have questions or if there is anything I can do for you, please call me at 555-4444. I'm here every day from 8:00 a.m. to 5:00 p.m.

Sincerely,

FILE NAME: UPGRN.DOC (UPGRADED FROM INFO AND PITCH AND MISS)

Thanks for giving me a chance to compete for a portion of your business at a more appropriate time in the future.

Between now and then, I will periodically touch base with you by mail and phone.

Meantime, if you have questions or if there is anything I can do for you, please call me at 555-4444. I'm here every day from 8:00 a.m. to 5:00 p.m.

Sincerely,

Downgraded to C Info Lead

Some cherries and green cherries poop out. To qualify one as an info lead, you should speak with the prospects. Assuming there is nothing they are interested in now and nothing at a known future date, you should at least verify that they wish to continue on your mailing list.

FILE NAME: DOWNINFO.DOC (FORMER CHERRY OR GREEN CHERRY)

I'm sorry we won't be doing any business in the immediate future, but I am glad you've elected to stay on my mailing list.

I will periodically touch base with you by mail and phone.

Meantime, if you have questions or if there is anything I can do for you, please call me at 555-4444. I'm here every day from 8:00 a.m. to 5:00 p.m.

Sincerely,

D Pitch and Miss

FILE NAME: PITCH.DOC (A GOOD PROSPECT
DECIDED NO OR JUST WON'T RETURN CALLS)

Pitch and miss is mostly for people who have been previous hot prospects and then bought from someone else or just didn't buy from you. You can, however, use this category—with discretion, of course—for ending a prospecting cycle with an especially desirable cherry or green cherry who won't return your calls. In most cases, people early in the prospecting cycle who don't return calls are just pitted. But on occasion you may want to keep an especially desirable prospect. The correct category would be pitch and miss.

I do want to take a moment and say thank you very much for giving me the opportunity to compete for a portion of your business.

Though we won't be doing business now, please do keep me in mind for the future.

I will periodically touch base with you by mail and phone. Meantime, if you have questions or if there is anything I can do for you, please call me at 555-4444. I'm here every day from 8:00 a.m. to 5:00 p.m.

Sincerely,

F Won't Return Calls

FILE NAME: NOCALL.DOC

I've left several messages and, alas, have been unable to make contact.

Please remember:

- I'm not with the IRS.
- I'm not selling insurance.
- I'm not trying to borrow money.
- I'm not asking for a job (I already have a great one—helping people like you!).

Since I'm none of the above, I must be someone you need to talk to!

Please call me at 555-4444.

A Note on Your Résumé

Anyone selling financial services, insurance, banking, real estate, consulting services, or any other form of expertise should have a résumé out-

Sample Résumé

James Q. Sellers
Financial Adviser
Reliable Securities, Inc.
1234 Elm Street
Waterby, CA 90038
(714) 555-3333 (Office)
(714) 555-2222 (Auto)

Objective	To assist business owners in retiring well-off, even if they are not able to convert the equity in their businesses to equity in their retirement accounts.

Financial Experience 1987–1988	After graduating from Ditchwater State College, I worked for two years as a marketing assistant. During that time, I learned a great deal about the operations side of the securities industry.
1989–1996	In early 1989, Reliable Securities appointed me an Investment Executive, and I have worked for the firm ever since. I am interested in working with business owners partly because of my father. He owned Ditchwater Pumping, but when the time came for him to retire he was unable to sell the company, and essentially lost the life's savings he had tied up in his business. Currently, I work with the owners or partners of 211 area businesses, plus 103 of their executives and employees. I also serve 51 professional people. I very strongly believe that my clients need me, because making money and managing money are each full-time jobs.

Education 1983–1987	B.Sc. in finance from Ditchwater State College. My undergraduate work also carried a minor in economics.
1992	Received designation as a Certified Financial Planner (CFP).
1992–1996	Special training in portfolio management and estate planning. Have completed four courses toward my MBA.
1996–2000 and beyond	While there are minimal continuing education requirements in my industry, I am personally committed to lifetime learning. When I have completed my MBA, I will pursue designation as an Investment Management Consultant through a three-year course. (It requires three trips to the Wharton School of Finance in Philadelphia, PA.) After that? Perhaps advanced training in insurance.
Community Activities	Chair, Waterby Rotary Fund-Raising Committee Assistant Director, Ditchwater Light Opera Festival
Hobbies	Collecting celebrity tennis shoes and ancient Egyptian pectoral necklaces.
References	Excellent professional references will be provided upon request.

lining their qualifications to do the job. Frankly, if there is any chance that your qualifications may figure into a buying decision, you should have a résumé or even a personal brochure.

On our home page at billgood.com, you can download a copy of this résumé along with complete instructions for making your own look like it. As you can see, it's designed for someone in financial services. I'm sure, however, that you can easily adapt it to your own needs. (Password: resume.)

See sample résumé on the previous page.

CHAPTER 16

Direct-Mail Letters

How to Have Good Letters Even If You're Not a Good Letter Writer

I am not going to tell you that you will become a great letter writer as a result of reading this chapter. I will, however, tell you that if you take the time, you will become a good letter rewriter. So let's jump right in.

Lead Processing vs. Lead Generation Letters

In our last chapter, we discussed Lead Processing Letters. Now, we need to look at Lead Generation Letters. These are the one or two letters that we send in some campaigns to make initial contact. Or, they may be used—and should be used—as part of your drip campaign.

Rewriting One More Time

I want to stress one more time that I am not going to teach you to become a direct-mail letter writer. I cannot do that in a short chapter—or even a long one. But I certainly can teach you how to rewrite. As I have learned over and over, it is easier for an overwhelming majority of people to rewrite than it is to write. So that is our strategy.

Rules of the Road

Here we go with the rules.

1. Prefer long letters to short letters.

I will start with the most controversial of these rules.
Frequently, when I do prospecting seminars, I ask, "How long should a letter be?" The answer is always "One page." "Who says?" I ask.

There is either no answer or someone pipes up and says, "Well, it's just common sense."

Well, it may be common sense, but it is also not true.

About 1980, I decided to study the subject of direct mail. By that time, I had some years of professional writing experience, and it seemed a natural extension to my business. I poked around in various bookstores and came up with the bible on direct-response marketing. In that book— *Tested Advertising Methods* by John Caples—I found the advice that long letters work better than short letters.

It sounded ridiculous, absurd, and so I decided to try it out. As my staff and my prospects know, I now believe in long letters.

Why do long letters work better than short letters? Who knows? There are several theories, but there is no point in going over them now. You can believe or disbelieve all you want. But you better know this: The only way to find out for sure is to test the ideas in this book. So give it a shot.

2. ALWAYS use the name of the recipient at least twice in the body of a letter.

This is a really simple rule and it means exactly what it says. You may think the reader will know his or her name is inserted in the letter by a computer. Absolutely true! But so what?

What seems to happen is this: A prospect gets a letter, and as he or she is about to throw it out, his or her own name catches the eye and forces the person to read a little more. Once again, don't believe what I say. Try it for yourself.

With any decent database program, you can insert various fields into the body of letters. So this is how one accomplishes this goal.

3. Use a catchy headline to get people to read your letter.

Let's talk about headlines for just a moment. Why do newspapers and magazines use headlines to start an article? To capture your attention, of course! If a magazine, say *Reader's Digest,* just presented text with no headline, people would not have an easy way to decide what to read and what to skip. We want to do the same thing with our letters: Use a good headline to capture attention.

For now, don't worry about how your headline should look. We'll cover such things in the next chapter. Also, later in this chapter, we'll discuss how to get great headlines to rewrite and turn into your own great headlines.

4. Use short sentences; use short paragraphs; use subheads and boldfacing to break up long letters.

As you rewrite your own Lead Processing Letters, pay special attention to this rule. Long sentences are hard to read. Short sentences are easy to read. If you have long letters that do not get broken up by subheads, people will find it more difficult to get the information they are interested in. In a long letter, people tend to read a little here, jump to there, and, based on spot reading, will decide what to do. So as you review your letters, make certain you have followed this rule. It makes a big difference.

5. First paragraphs: no shortage.

Sometimes, in the course of rewriting a letter, you may get stuck on the first paragraph. So I want to pass on to you a piece of advice I got from my first writing teacher. I was working on what would become my first published article, which was published in *Barron's Business and Financial Weekly.* At some point I realized I was stuck on the first paragraph. I told this to my teacher, and she said, "That's ridiculous! There is no shortage of first paragraphs. There are billions of first paragraphs. What I want you to do is sit down and write ten first paragraphs right now. Start!" So that's what I did.

The first several paragraphs I wrote were junk. Then, at number 6, I nailed it.

So if you get stuck on a first paragraph, just sit down and write one right after the other. The first few may be completely worthless. Not a problem. Just keep going. You'll get it right.

If you're still stuck, just go get some first paragraphs from a newspaper or magazine, and start rewriting them.

What to Rewrite

OK. Let's get down to work rewriting. The first question is: What are we going to rewrite? We will focus on four sources:

1. Letter formats: These are fill-in-the-blank letters that will provide three different styles of letter for you to rewrite. I will go over one of these formats in this chapter. You can download others from our home page at billgood.com. The password: niccole. (She is my oldest daughter.)

2. Brochure copy: One great advantage you have in creating Lead Generation Letters is various brochures that may have been written by your marketing department or by the companies that make the products you sell. It is always a mistake to send out brochures unaccompanied by a letter. They just get thrown away. I will show you how to take copy from a brochure and use it, word for word, in a letter.

3. Great direct-mail letters: In *Tested Advertising Methods,* there are lots of great ads and letters. In addition, there are books full of direct-mail letters. You can take any one of these letters and use its style and format to create your own. This method gets us closest to writing instead of rewriting. So you are better off mastering letter formats and rewriting brochure copy before you begin rewriting direct-mail letters.

4. Previous direct-mail letters: I'm not going to use precious pages in my book to reproduce some of my own letters; our home page gives you a series of letters I wrote that were basically rewrites of the first (and best) letter. You will enjoy these letters because they deal with "Monster Rabbits." No famous statements here, just good fun . . . and lots of money. (Password: monster.)

Letter Formats

The best way to show you how to develop a letter from a letter format is just to do one. So on the left-hand side of the page, you will get the copy of the letter format. On the right-hand side of the page, I will give you the letter. I have picked a completely absurd topic to show how easy it is.

In addition to the "Good News Letter Format" (named after myself, of course) there are two others. They are "Here's the Info Format" and "Feature/Benefit Format." You can download all three of these from my home page at billgood.com. (Password: dirmail.)

Good News Letter Format

Good News Letter from Bilgewater Pumps, Inc.

1. THE HEADING

Where an entire batch of letters is being printed for mailing over several days, omit the current date.

<Current Date>

<Full Name>

<Company>

<Address>

<City>, <State>, <Zip>

Your headline goes here, centered, occupying two lines if necessary:

1. The heading ►

August 31, 1997

Captain Joe Blow
Garbage Scow Unlimited
3309 East Main
Long Island, NY 33098

2. Your headline goes here ►

We Pump Bilges Faster

3. The salutation ►

Dear Captain Blow:

4. Announce you have good news ►

Captain Blow, how about some good news for a change?

5. Tell what the good news is ►

My company, Bilgewater Pumping, Inc., has done it again! In time trials, our SR90 Bilgewater Pump proved: **We pump more bilges faster than any other pump!**

6. Give three benefits the client ►
or prospect can expect from
ownership *or* from receiving
the free information

To you, Captain Blow, an SR90 Bilgewater Pump could mean:

- 50% more bilgewater pumped into the ocean than with any other pump.

- Less rot due to stagnant water because it gets pumped out faster.

- More time off in port because you won't have to be supervising your staff cleaning the bilges. It will be done before you dock!

7. Call for action ►

Captain Blow, ask yourself this question: Am I interested in less bilgewater and more time off in port?

If you answered yes, then send in the enclosed **Information Request Form**, and I will send you the details, fair enough?

Sincerely,

8. Signature ►

Balph Burgher
Senior V.P. - Bilge Pumps

9. Reinforce with PS ►

PS If you're thinking, "I don't know . . . ," just do it! Imagine, instead of pumping bilge when you hit an exotic port, you get to go ashore and enjoy! So go ahead and send in the Information Request, OK?

We Pump Bilges Faster

Dear <Salutation>:

Use a formal salutation for mass mail—*Mr. Ramirez:* Use familiar salutation for clients and prospects—*Steve and Edie:*

2. ANNOUNCE YOU HAVE GOOD NEWS

Choose one of the following

- I have some good news for you, <Salutation>.

- <Salutation>, how about some good news for a change?

- Most of the news you read in the papers these days is bad, isn't it, <Salutation>? Well, how about some good news?

- Last month I had some good news for you. This month? Surprise! More good news, <Salutation>.

- How about some more good news? <Firm Name> has just (announced/made available) <What It Is>.

- A major announcement from <Source> could be very, very important to you.

- Of all the possible places to put your (savings/speculative money/long-term funds/etc.) now, one in particular looks a lot more interesting than others.

3. **TELL WHAT THE GOOD NEWS IS, USING THE STRONGEST BENEFIT**

Use following prompts to stimulate your thinking

- The top . . .

- The best . . .

- One of the best . . .

- One of the newest . . .

- One of the top . . .

- <Well-known company or person> has done it again.

- <Well-known company or person> is still doing it.

- For the (third/seventh/etc.) (year/month/quarter) in a row . . .

4. **GIVE THREE BENEFITS THE CLIENT OR PROSPECT CAN EXPECT FROM OWNERSHIP *OR* FROM RECEIVING THE FREE INFORMATION**

Choose one of the following

- To you, <Salutation>, this means:

  <First Benefit>

  <Second Benefit>

  <Third Benefit>

- <Salutation>, you'll see how:

  <First Benefit>

  <Second Benefit>

  <Third Benefit>

5. Call for action

Choose one of the following

- <Salutation>, ask yourself this question:

  Am I interested in <Primary Benefit>?

  If you answered yes, then send in the enclosed Information Request Form and I will send you the details. Fair enough?

- To find out more about how you can <Get Primary Benefit Restated>, just put the enclosed Information Request in the enclosed envelope and send it back to me.

August 31, 1997

Captain Joe Blow
Garbage Scow Unlimited
3309 East Main
Long Island, NY 33098

> Here I have the offer in the headline

We Pump Bilges Faster

> Name used in body of the letter

Dear Captain Blow:

Captain Blow, how about some good news for a change?

My company, Bilgewater Pumping, Inc., has done it again! In time trials, our SR90 Bilgewater Pump proved: **We pump more bilges faster than any other pump!**

> Three benefits

To you, Captain Blow, an SR90 Bilgewater Pump could mean:

- 50% more bilgewater pumped into the ocean than with any other pump.

- Less rot due to stagnant water because it gets pumped out faster.

- More time off in port because you won't have to be supervising your staff cleaning the bilges. It will be done before you dock!

Captain Blow, ask yourself this question: Am I interested in less bilgewater and more time off in port?

If you answered yes, then send in the enclosed **Information Request Form**, and I will send you the details, fair enough?

> Call to action!

Sincerely,

Balph Burgher
Senior V.P. - Bilge Pumps

PS If you're thinking, "I don't know . . . ," just do it! Imagine, instead of pumping bilge when you hit an exotic port, you get to go ashore and enjoy! So go ahead and send in the Information Request, OK?

- If you have an interest in <Investment Type> with <Best Benefit>, call me, or just drop the Information Request at the end of this letter in the mail, and I will get additional details to you right away.

6. **SIGNATURE**

    Sincerely,

    (Susan A. Brokerman/whoever)

7. **REINFORCE WITH PS**

Choose one of the following

- PS If you're thinking, "I don't know . . . ," just do it. I promise you— no pressure, no obligation.

- PS If you're about to set this aside and think about it, I promise you, you will be better able to think about it if you have the information at hand that I will send you. So go ahead and put the Information Request in the envelope. OK?

- PS If you're thinking, "I don't know . . . ," just do it! Imagine, instead of pumping bilge when you hit some of the exotic ports, you get to go ashore and enjoy! So go ahead and send in the Information Request, OK?

Information Request

(FYI: Complete info on how to construct the Information Request is on the MS Word version of the Letter Format which is on our home page.)

1. **BODY OF INFO REQUEST**

Choose one of the following

  Dear <Initiator Name>:

___Sounds interesting. I want to see some additional information on <What It Is>. Please drop it in the mail for me.

___I'm not interested in <What It Is>, but I'd like information on:_____

_____

  Dear <Initiator Name>:

___I like hearing good news. Please send me additional information about <What It Is>.

___I'm not interested in anything now, but a friend might be. Please give me a call. Best time to call is: _____.

Dear <Initiator Name>:

___Yes! I did my part by rushing this to you. Now get with it and send me the information on <What It Is>.

___Well, maybe. Actually, why don't you give *me* a call! Best time to call is:_____.

2. **CLIENT/PROSPECT SIGNATURE SECTION ON INFO REQUEST FORM**

Sincerely,

  <Full Name>

  <Company>

> In writing the Information Request, you write yourself a letter you would like to receive if someone wrote a letter in response to yours. So address it to yourself.

INFORMATION REQUEST

Dear Balph:

___ Sounds interesting. I want to see some additional information on the SR90 Bilge Pump. Please drop it in the mail for me.

___ I'm not interested in the SR90, but I would like some information about _____.

___ I'm not interested in anything now, but a friend might be. Please give me a call. Best time to call is _____.

Sincerely,

> You will want to make your word processor insert the prospect's signature and other identifying information. This makes it easier for the prospect to respond, which means more response.

Captain Joe Blow
Captain
Garbage Towing, Inc.

Rewriting Brochures

Not too long ago, I was asked to design a mail/phone campaign for a client, American Skandia. (American Skandia packages variable annuities in the financial services industry.) In writing the letter, which was to be followed by a phone call, I decided to demonstrate how easy it is to use promotional copy in direct-mail letters.

The letter I wrote for Skandia is four pages, and therefore a very long letter. On our home page, you can download the entire letter and study it. I have highlighted the sections that I copied from a Skandia brochure.

Naturally, you will want to get permission from the company if there is any question about whether or not you can use someone else's material. But you can be assured that any company whose product you sell will be delighted if you use their material to make more sales.

So, check out our home page to download these letters.

Prize-Winning Direct-Mail Letters

The best (which means the most profitable) letter I have ever written was a rewrite of a 1938 letter I found in a book of great direct-mail letters. Unfortunately, that book grew legs and I cannot tell you how to get it, as I don't know where I got it myself. However, libraries and bookstores are filled with books that have lots of great direct-mail letters in them.

The particular letter I adapted was a letter about launching a longitudinal trip around the world. Whoever it was had put together an airplane trip that would fly over both poles. I took their concept and wrote a letter about the Bill Good Marketing System and how its purchase and implementation was like a journey, not around the poles of the earth but into outer space.

My mail room staff hated that letter because it was seven pages long. Ugly! It also made millions of dollars for my company. Today, that letter is part of the proposal we send to anyone who is interested in our system. If you want to see a seven-page letter, based on a rewrite, you can download "The Journey."

In adapting existing letters, you are coming very close to writing. So I repeat my warning: Learn to use the letter formats and learn to adapt brochure copy before you tackle rewriting great direct-mail letters.

Previous Direct-Mail Letters

One of the best sources of Lead Generation Letters is the letters you have already used. At my company, we have copies of every single letter we have sent out in the last eight years. So a good part of our preparation for sending new direct-mail letters is to study letters we have already sent.

One thing we do extremely well is to keep records on which letters produce sales. Such careful recordkeeping lessens our chances of sending out a letter that has failed at least once before.

Headline Writing: Where to Find Great Ones to Rewrite

Since headlines are such an important part of a Lead Generation Letter, I want to spend just a little time and tell you how to make sure you get good headlines.

More moons ago than I care to think about, I took a comedy writing class at UCLA. In this class, my teacher taught us how to do what he called Switching. This was where we learned how to keep the buildup of a joke and switch or change the punch line to something else. Then we learned how to keep the punch line and switch the buildup. Finally, he made us switch the buildup and switch the punch line, which, of course, gave us an entirely new joke! We had to write hundreds of jokes using this switching technique.

Well, with headlines, "same drill, different day."

If you want good headlines for your letters, the best thing to do is to get ten or twenty headlines that deal with your topic and then switch them. You'll get the headline you need in short order.

Where could you get headlines like this? Well, go directly to Electric Library. Search for articles that deal with your topic and copy down the headlines.

Here are some examples I switched. Obviously, these relate to financial services. Once you get the concept of switching, you can find a headline you like and make it work for you. The boldfaced headline is the original. My rewrites follow.

Earnings Reports Force Investors to Look Ahead

Population Statistics Force Business Owners to Look Ahead

Life Expectancy Statistics Force Business Owners to Plan Carefully

Hearts Pounding at Midyear, the Pros Take Pulse

Hearts Pounding as Retirement Looms, Business Owners Must Plan Carefully

Midyear a Good Time to Re-Evaluate 401K, Retirement Planning

Year-End a Good Time to Re-Evaluate Systems Upgrade Plans

These Are Bad News Days for Inveterate Bears

These Are Bad News Days for Slow-Moving MIS Managers

Soft-Landing Fans Wake Up to Hard Facts of Slowdown

Some Business Owners Wake Up to Hard Facts About Equity in Their Businesses

Money Matters: *Experts say the inability to manage assets effectively is a failing of millions of otherwise competent, knowledgeable and skillful American women*

Money Matters: Are you one of the millions of otherwise competent business owners who is making a major mistake in managing your retirement nest egg?

Coupon Design: The Secrets

One of the most important parts of a direct-mail letter is the Information Request. This is not just a form for someone to request information. It is a vital persuasive tool to get the prospect to act. No way should it be dull and boring. Here is the correct point of view to take when writing the coupon.

One of the first jobs I held when I left grad school was working as the assistant to the publisher of a small magazine. Part of my job was to type personalized renewal letters for the magazine. There were only about two thousand subscribers. But they each paid $700 per year to subscribe. So they were entitled to some special treatment. The publisher insisted that each letter be typed individually, with no mistakes. (This is one reason I now type 110 words per minute.)

Every renewal notice we sent out had a separate letter enclosed. To order his or her renewal, all the subscriber had to do was send back that letter in the reply envelope we had provided. The publisher told me many times, "When you design a coupon, always write yourself the letter you would like to receive if others wrote letters in response to yours."

That was the best advice I have ever seen on how to write coupons.

I do, however, want to add a few rules.

1. Unless there is a compelling reason not to use a separate sheet of paper for the coupon (also called Information Request), you should put it on a separate page. Your computer can be set up so that it prints the Information Request right along with the letter.

2. You may want to use a stand-alone business reply card instead of having the prospect enclose a piece of paper in a business reply envelope. If you do, you can print these three to a page using your laser printer. The other side of the card should be printed by a commercial printer, who will have all the postal service–approved artwork for the reply permit. The permit must be printed according to postal service requirements, or they will not accept it.

Caution: In some industries, stand-alone cards work fine, but not in financial services. The kind of person who will make a financial request through an open-mail system is not, necessarily, the kind of person you want to develop as a client. People who will send stand-alone cards are not, in my experience, very good prospects.

3. A very important point in designing a coupon is: How many choices should I use? You might think that you should have lots of choices in your coupons. If a prospect is not interested in your main offer, perhaps he or she would be interested in something else. If not that, what about this?

By following this logic, you could wind up with a laundry list instead of a coupon. I have found that when you have more than three choices on your coupon, your response rate goes down. So, what should the choices be?

    a.   In Choice 1, the prospect should have the ability to request information directly related to the offer in your letter. This choice can restate your offer, be humorous, urgent, but never boring.

    Example: Absolutely! Bill, I am very interested in your system. I have done my part by requesting information on how I can double my business or work half as much. Now it is time to do your part. Please rush me the information on "The Bill Good Marketing System."

    b.   In Choice 2, you should give the prospect the ability to request information on something else, and leave it up to the prospect what he or she wants.

    Example: Nope! I'm not interested in your system, but I am interested in_____.

c. In Choice 3, you provide a place for your prospect to refer you to someone he or she may know who could use information about your product or service.

There is nothing set in stone about these choices. You could certainly make a compelling case for one or two more choices or even fewer. Just know that *too many* will sink your letter.

4. Use your word processor to insert the prospect's name where the signature should go. The easier it is for your prospect to stick the Information Request in the mail without having to fill in name, address, and phone, the more people will respond. Make it easy by doing the work yourself.

Remember: The coupon or Information Request is a vital selling tool. Don't let it be dull or boring.

The Discipline: Introducing the "Rewriting a Direct-Mail Letter" Checklist

I have some good news and some bad news for you. Which would you like to hear first (age ten)? You want the good news? Great! I have made up a checklist to walk you through rewriting a letter. If you follow these steps, all will be well. The bad news is that the process of rewriting is a little more complicated than just picking up a letter format or brochure and rewriting it.

There is actually a discipline to the subject. By following this discipline in the same way over and over, you have an excellent chance of getting it right. So, in the next few pages, I will comment on the steps of this checklist, which I followed when I created the letter for American Skandia I previously mentioned. You can get the Microsoft Word file of the complete checklist, without any of my comments, from our home page at billgood.com.

By the way, can you skip some of these steps? Sure. But the first times you create a new letter, follow them, would you?

Creating a New Direct-Mail Letter: The Checklist

The Process

✓ **00.** What product do you want to sell?

American Skandia Variable Annuity

✓ **00.** Study all available literature on that product. List features and benefits on separate cards.

✓ **000.** What exactly is your offer?

By requesting the information, a business owner can better understand why he or she is unlikely to convert the equity in the business to equity in a retirement account.

✓ **1.** Who do you want to write to? Describe the list.

Men, probably early 50s. Professionals, self-employed, own their own business. Beginning to realize that the great spending years need to end and major accumulation needs to begin.

✓ **2.** Get a particular person in mind. Who is this person? Describe. Visualize.

Dr. K. He's a well-known plastic surgeon. Has invested enormous amount in a clinic. Spends a lot of money on equipment. Among the best in his field.

✓ **3.** What do you want this person to do after reading your letter? (Take phone call, return coupon, call and request info, call and ask for an appointment, call to discuss an investment?)

Slide the coupon in the enclosed envelope and return it to me.

✓ **4.** What broad area do you want to write about? (Retirement planning, investing in stocks, particular product?)

Accumulating enough money to live comfortably at retirement. (Will you really have enough money to live 25 years after you retire?)

✓ **5.** Identify the facts, quotes, benefits. Make stacks of note cards.

✓ **6.** Look up the key words and write down their definitions.

Done

✓ **7.** Why would you buy this product, request this information, etc.? List the benefits that appeal to you.

I would buy it to get tax-deferred compounding working for me.

✓ **8.** Choose a letter format, brochure, great direct-mail letter, or previous direct-mail letter to base the new letter upon.

Skandia has an excellent brochure that will do the trick. Lots of good ideas there.

✓ **9.** As they come to mind, write these. As appropriate, set it aside. Refer to letter formats as needed.

   ✓ **a.** Headline (Attention) Use switching!

   ✓ **b.** First paragraph (Interest) (Write a bunch of them)

   ✓ **c.** Body (Desire)

   ✓ **d.** Call to Action (Action)

   ✓ **e.** Coupon (Write the letter you would like to receive!)

   ✓ **f.** Re-enforce (PS)

✓ **10.** Set it aside.

✓ **11.** Put on your editor's hat. Read it aloud. Make sure it flows. Spell check and grammar check.

✓ **12.** Give it to someone who has not seen it and does not work for you. Get their impressions. Do this several times.

✓ **13.** More editing.

✓ **14.** Proof #1. Proof the letter. Circle anything that does not immediately make sense.

✓ **15.** Proof #2 Proof the letter. Circle anything that does not immediately make sense.

✓ **16.** Retype as necessary.

✓ **17.** If OK, submit for approval.

✓ **18.** Letter approved by: _____ on __/__/__.

✓ **19.** When approved, fill out Letter Printing Checklist.

Whoops. I didn't tell you about that, did I? I was going to slip it in the next chapter. I didn't want you overwhelmed by too many checklists all at once. Oh well, I guess you know. There is another one coming.

CHAPTER 17

Getting Letters
Out the Door

"You don't get a second chance to make a first impression."

—Bill Good, age eleven

One Sunday morning, I was spending a lot of time getting ready for church. My mother said, "Bill, hurry up." For some minutes, I did not show up as ordered. In a few minutes, she came up the stairs and saw me very carefully slicking down my hair. "What on earth is taking so long?" she asked.

"Mom, there's this really cute girl in our Sunday school class. Since you don't get a second chance to make a first impression, I thought I would look my best."

She thought that was clever and mentioned it to the ladies Bible class. Within days, one of the ladies mentioned it to her husband, who worked at one of the big cotton mills in Greensboro. They made a slogan of it. I never received credit.

Let's get right to the point.

1. No-nos, nevers, and don'ts:

Never use labels.

Never address a letter to "Occupant," "Owner," or any other unnamed title you can think of.

2. The look of a professional letter and envelope:

2" top margin

Headline: 24 pt. type, bold faced

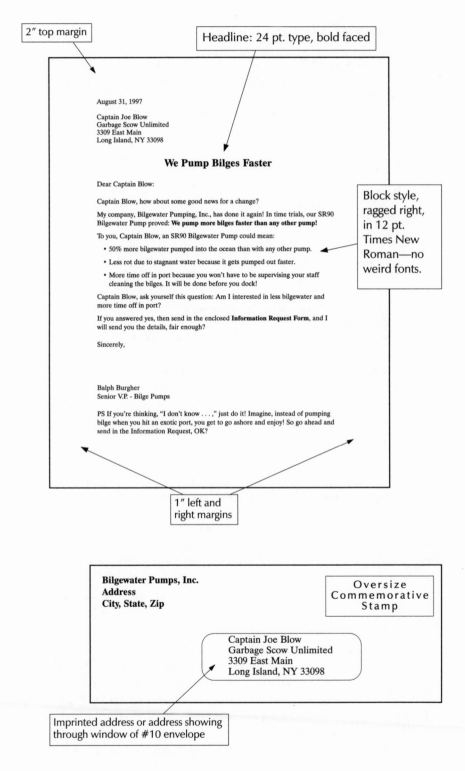

August 31, 1997

Captain Joe Blow
Garbage Scow Unlimited
3309 East Main
Long Island, NY 33098

We Pump Bilges Faster

Dear Captain Blow:

Captain Blow, how about some good news for a change?

My company, Bilgewater Pumping, Inc., has done it again! In time trials, our SR90 Bilgewater Pump proved: **We pump more bilges faster than any other pump!**

To you, Captain Blow, an SR90 Bilgewater Pump could mean:

- 50% more bilgewater pumped into the ocean than with any other pump.

- Less rot due to stagnant water because it gets pumped out faster.

- More time off in port because you won't have to be supervising your staff cleaning the bilges. It will be done before you dock!

Captain Blow, ask yourself this question: Am I interested in less bilgewater and more time off in port?

If you answered yes, then send in the enclosed **Information Request Form**, and I will send you the details, fair enough?

Sincerely,

Balph Burgher
Senior V.P. - Bilge Pumps

PS If you're thinking, "I don't know . . . ," just do it! Imagine, instead of pumping bilge when you hit an exotic port, you get to go ashore and enjoy! So go ahead and send in the Information Request, OK?

Block style, ragged right, in 12 pt. Times New Roman—no weird fonts.

1" left and right margins

Bilgewater Pumps, Inc.
Address
City, State, Zip

Oversize
Commemorative
Stamp

Captain Joe Blow
Garbage Scow Unlimited
3309 East Main
Long Island, NY 33098

Imprinted address or address showing through window of #10 envelope

A Comment About Stamps

Oversize commemorative stamps are best. And I don't mean the self-adhesive kind that you can just peel off. I mean the licking kind.

Why? It doesn't matter why. The facts are that letters with such stamps get higher rates of response. Here is your order of preference:

- Oversize commemorative
- Commemorative on self-adhesive paper
- First-class metered
- First-class presort
- Bulk-mail stamp
- Bulk-mail permit

Important Question: Which Stamps?

My advice is to avoid sicko topics like "Love," "Peace," "Children's Art," and other such politically correct topics.

The best topics? War and Sex! Try World War II commemoratives or Marilyn, Elvis, James Dean, and other Hollywood stars who will be featured on stamps. Madonna? OK, perhaps I got carried away. If you are promoting to a bunch of tree huggers, go ahead and use "Endangered Species" or some such.

Printing a Direct-Mail Letter Checklist

Part of looking great in print is making absolutely sure that your mail goes on the right stationery, in the right envelope, with the right stamp. Plus, it is mailed on the right day, and so on and so on. So, one more checklist.

I cannot tell you how important this one is in my company. We have been using a variation of it since 1982 to ensure that our letters go out the door on time, no mistakes, looking great!

In the sample below, I have filled one out for you and, where necessary, have added some explanations and comments. Please note that each step of this checklist is signed off by the person responsible for it. The first time I ever encountered such a checklist was when I got my student pilot's license. My instructor explained only once that my life depended on getting each step of that checklist right.

Your business life may well depend on getting these steps right.

Mine sure does.

Study it well, and when the time comes to send out your next (or first!) letter, use it. Naturally, you can pick up a copy of the MS Word file on our home page.

ORIGINATOR INSTRUCTIONS   The "originator" is whoever gets the ball rolling.

Special Instructions: _____

_____

_____

_____

_____

Name of Letter: ___Corpsem (Corporate Seminar)___

BG **1.** Describe in detail who should receive this letter.

___Purchased list of Sr VPs of Sales___

_____

_____

_____

_____

BG **2.** How many letters in this test? ___1,000___

BG **3.** ☑ Send them all at once on _10_ / _21_ / _97_.
☐ Send them _____ per day for _____ days beginning on ___ / ___ / ___ .

BG **4.** ☑ Use this oversize commemorative stamp ___Madonna Stamp___
☐ Use this regular-size first-class stamp _____
☐ Use first-class metered mail
☐ Use bulk-mail stamp
☐ Use metered bulk mail

BG **5.** Enclose this printed material: ___Corporate Seminar Brochure___

BG **6.** ☑ Use our usual printed envelope with laser-printed addressing
☐ Use our usual printed window envelope
☐ Use plain envelope with return address only
☐ Use other envelope: _____

BG **7.** ☑ Use digitized signature
☐ Do not use digitized signature

CO INSTRUCTIONS

_CΣ_ **8.** Print one letter and envelope as described above and deliver to originator.

ORIGINATOR APPROVAL

_CΣ_ **9.** If OK, sign it off. If not OK, repeat previous steps until it is.

CO INSTRUCTIONS

_CΣ_ **10.** Print all letters in one batch unless instructed otherwise.

_CΣ_ **11.** Stuff them and enclose printed material, if any. DO NOT SEAL.

ORIGINATOR APPROVAL

_BG_ **12.** Inspect one last time. Verify it's the right letter, correct enclosure.

CO INSTRUCTIONS

_CΣ_ **13.** Mail the letters according to the schedule above.

_CΣ_ **14.** Make a file for this letter. Insert this checklist, a copy of the letter, and any written material. As replies come in, copy all replies and file them here.

_CΣ_ **15.** Log date in originator's calendar 60 days from the date the last batch of letters went out to review this file.

CHAPTER 18

How You Sound

Writing about *sound* is a difficult task at best. That's why I am so excited about the capabilities that the World Wide Web has introduced. I can write about it here, and then by pointing your browser to our home page, you can *hear* about it. So first learn the *concepts,* which, taken together, make up a professional sound. Then pop over to our home page and *hear them.* Then follow the assignment at the end of this chapter. You're in business! (Password: howyousound.)

Some years ago I was doing a seminar for an insurance company in San Diego. As I walked around the room listening to everyone call, I couldn't help but notice one agent who, in all truth, sounded as if he were sucking on a lemon. And not only did he sound that way, his facial expression was curled into a sneer. He really sounded as if he didn't like the people he was talking to, and guess what? They didn't like him either. While everyone else in the room was getting excellent results, his results, like his sound, sucked lemons.

Our conversation went like this:

> BILL: Fred, I want you to smile when you talk.
>
> FRED: But I don't feel like smiling.
>
> BILL: I don't recall asking what you felt like.
>
> FRED: Well, I still don't feel like smiling.
>
> BILL: All right. Here's what I want you to do. I want you to smile anyway. It will change the sound of your voice whether you feel like it or not. And since people can't see you, who cares if you look like the cat from *Alice in Wonderland,* sitting on a limb just grinning?

After that exchange, I asked around and came up with an oversize makeup mirror. I propped it up on his desk and made him smile into the mirror. I really didn't care if he felt like smiling or not. I knew if he would physically put a smile on his face, it would change the way he sounded. And the response he would get from his improved sound would change the way he felt. If you want to prove this to yourself, simply read this paragraph into a tape recorder. Scowl as you read. Now paste on a smile. Read it again. Listen to them both. You will notice that putting a smile on your face puts one in your voice.

Our scowling insurance agent picked up several appointments that night . . . but not until he put a smile on his face.

Whether you are cold calling or following up on warm trade show leads, developing the "right sound" can mean the difference between success and failure. If you sound friendly, sound as though you know what you're talking about, speak at the right speed, and don't sound as if you're reading, you can succeed—especially if you have your list, script, and volume of calls under control. If you sound singsongy, bored, sour, too fast, too slow, or wishy-washy, you might as well go apply for a book-keeping job. When you get someone on the phone, all of your other good points—your good dress, your good looks, the way you sit and gesture—aren't worth a bucket of water in a rainstorm. They can't see you, they can't see your bright eyes, your nice dress, or your expressions. All they can do is hear you. So all you have going for you is what you say and how you say it.

So let's talk about the elements that make up the right sound: voice inflection, pacing, emphasis, speed, and enthusiasm. Perfecting these elements of speech will "un-can" any canned pitch. If you correctly use the five elements discussed in this chapter, your presentation can be read word for word but won't ever sound it.

Voice Inflection

Perhaps there should be a law in sales that says, "Certainty sells." For our purposes, let's define certainty as "sounding as if you know what you're talking about." If you are new in the business, you undoubtedly are *not certain* of many things. But your survival depends on sounding as if you are not only certain but are a veteran.

I could write pages on the people I have met who never made it because they didn't sound as if they had a clue whether they were in Mexico or whether it was Tuesday. One stockbroker I knew had an incredibly successful system of picking stocks. The few clients he had did extremely well. But he had such a severe case of stage fright that he couldn't tell his story without sounding like the new kid on the block. Consequently, he couldn't convince people he was telling the truth when he told them about his system. And he washed out of the business.

There are three elements involved in creating certainty. Perhaps most important is having a product to sell that you understand, can explain, and, most important, *believe in.* Second, you need to have a script that is effective. Third, you need to be able to deliver your script with the correct voice inflection. There's not much I can do for you here on your product. And we've already covered the subject of scripts. So let's talk about voice inflection as a very important element of developing certainty.

To give you a good idea of what voice inflection is, I want you to sing aloud the following lyric:

Twinkle, twinkle, little star, / How I wonder where you are . . .

If you're like most people, the word "star" was at a higher *pitch* than the word "are." Pitch simply refers to highness or lowness of the voice. A high C on the piano has a much higher pitch than a middle C.

Now that you know what pitch means, let's define "inflection." Inflection is the change in pitch that the voice makes in speaking a word, phrase, or sentence. A person speaking in a monotone would have no variation in pitch, no inflection. To get a good idea of the word "monotone," simply sing our little lyric here without changing pitch.

Inflection is very important as a speech element because of what pressure, fear, and anxiety do to it. People who normally sound like red-blooded human beings change their voice inflection when they are afraid or nervous. And not surprisingly, this change makes them sound afraid and nervous. As you read further, please keep in mind that you may *feel nervous* when you call. But I am going to try and help you *sound confident*. As people respond to your confident sound, your feelings of fear and anxiety will dissolve.

I am going to introduce some marks in your text here to indicate direction of voice inflection. An up arrow (↑) means that the voice goes up on that word. A down arrow (↓) means that the voice goes down on that word. Now, in the English language, when you make a statement of fact, your voice drops slightly at the end of the sentence. Please read aloud the sentence below. With a down arrow (↓) I have shown what should happen to the pitch of your voice.

My name is Fred Smithers (↓).

If you read that sentence correctly, your voice dropped slightly on the last syllable of the word "Smithers." If you walked up to a stranger and said, "My name is Fred Smithers (↓)," he would believe you. *Correct inflection creates belief.*

Now, let's take another example. If you ask a question, your pitch goes up on an important word in the sentence. Please read aloud the question below. (If you don't do these exercises aloud, it's very difficult for me to make the points I'm trying to make. So do follow along.)

Is your name Fred Smithers (↑)?

If you read this one correctly, your voice would have lilted up at the end of the sentence. The person you were addressing would have clearly recognized it as a question, and if his name was Fred Smithers, he would have said, "Yes, it is."

Let's take a final example. If you wish to issue a command, your voice drops sharply at the end of a sentence. I want you to imagine that you have a sixteen-year-old daughter. You've just inspected her room, and you find that it looks like the Russian army has only recently decamped. As you look closer, you see that what you thought was a pile of dirty clothes sipping a soda all by itself is actually your daughter. She's listening to a tape recorder, watching TV, and talking on the phone at the same time. Read aloud the command below. Emphasize the word "room" with a hard drop in your inflection.

Nicci, clean up your room (↓)!

If you read this one correctly, your voice would have dropped sharply on the word "room," and she would certainly have known that she had better do it right now.

Now let's take a look at some common inflection mistakes. Imagine the same situation with your daughter's room. Instead of inflecting down on the word "room," I want you to read it aloud and inflect up. Take what should be a command and make it a question with an up inflection. So here goes.

Nicci, clean up your room (↑)?

If you read this one as I indicated, there is little doubt that Nicci will respond,

Sure, Dad (↑). How about tomorrow (↑)?

And thus what should have come across as a command from parent to daughter comes across as a wimpish request and gets a mushy response. (And certainly no clean room!)

Let's take a look at a more common inflection mistake. Let's inflect what should come across as a statement of fact like a question. I want you to read the line below aloud with inflection marks as shown.

Good morning (↑). My name is Fred Smithers (↑). I work over here at Acme Company (↑).

If you read this one with the voice inflecting up as shown, you certainly sounded like a world-class wimp. And yet, without your being fully aware of it, the chances are at least fifty-fifty that this is how you sound on the phone. If you inflect up on the last syllable of your last name and your company name, it appears that you don't know who you are or where you work. And this lets people know right from the moment you open your mouth that you are brand new to the position *whether you are or not!* And who wants to have a new salesperson practice on them? Frankly, some people will take a minute out of their day to squash a wimpy salesperson just as they would an annoying bug.

If you want to conduct an interesting test, open the White Pages to the "Jones" or "Smith" or whatever section. Using your worst inflection, call the "Jones" column and read the script below. See if you can get anyone interested at all. Here's your script.

> May I speak to M/M_____Jones, please (↑)? M/M_____Jones (↑), this is Fred Smithers (↑). I work over here at Acme Company (↑). We are selling gold coins at half price (↑). Are you interested?

If you inflect the script as I've marked it, you will sound very hesitant and uncertain. You will find that not only won't people be interested in your offer, they will *act as if they didn't hear you.* Apparently, your own uncertainty is such that it clouds theirs, and they won't believe what they thought they heard because they aren't even sure they heard it. Evidently, *uncertainty creates disbelief.* To create belief, first believe it yourself, and then sound as if you believe it. If you let the anxiety of making the call force you into sounding like you don't know what you're talking about, you will cause your prospect to feel uncertain as well.

What I'd like you to do right now is read the script below into a tape recorder. Then listen to it. Did you get the correct inflection?

> Good morning (↑). This is (Your Name) (↓) with (Your Company Name) (↓). You know who we are (↓), don't you (↑)?

Avoid sounding wimpish. Use correct inflection (↓). (That was a command!)

If you have been following my directions so far, you will have already written yourself a script. What you should do now is go through that script and mark it up with up arrows and down arrows for correct voice inflection. Make absolutely certain that your name and company name are inflected correctly—that is, you'll want a (↓) on the last syllable of your last name and a (↓) on the last syllable of your company name.

Pacing

Let's add another speech element. We'll call it pacing and define it as simply the insertion of space between words. To dramatize this, read aloud the following passage:

Good morning. This is Fred Smithers. I'm calling to let you know
that you will receive a check in the mail for one million dollars.

Now that, certainly, would get someone's attention. Now read it
again. This time, make a slight pause everywhere you see a "/" mark.
This indicates a very slight amount of space. Keep playing with it until it
sounds natural.

Good morning. / This is Fred Smithers. / I'm calling to let you know
that you will receive a check in the mail / for one / million / dollars.

If you read it correctly this time, you would have added a lot of
impact to some already strong words. Marking your script for pacing is
the best way I know to force yourself to slow down. Can you guess which
newscaster has made exaggerated pacing his hallmark? Paul Harvey, of
course: "Good morning, Americans. / / / Stand by / / for / / news!" Paul
Harvey is one of the highest-paid broadcasters in radio. Next time you
hear him on the radio, listen to his pacing.

Below, I have taken some of the lines from the scripts I've used as
examples and shown how I would mark them both for inflection and pacing. To get a good idea of the flow and rhythm, you should read each of
them straight through with no pacing. And then read them through leaving some little pauses at the points indicated.

M/M _____, I have some very important information for you on a
guaranteed / investment. It's a bank CD and it's paying /_____/ percent. Could I send you some information on our terms and rates?

I have some important information on how you might get a higher
rate of return on your money than a CD. The interest compounds.
Uncle Sam doesn't touch it / at tax time. And if something should
happen to you, your family would get a whole / bunch / of money.
Could I send you some information on it?

M/M_____, I have some very interesting information for you on
how our cellular phone can save you time, / money, / and possibly /
keep you out of trouble with your (Husband/Wife) if you're going to
be late. Could I send it to you?

Emphasis

Let's define emphasis as stress on a particular word or phrase. By putting
emphasis on words, you communicate importance. Read aloud the paragraph below with no emphasis:

Good morning. This is Fred Smithers. I'm calling to let you know
that you will receive a check in the mail for one million dollars.

We'll use italics to indicate emphasis on a word. Now read the same passage again, this time with emphasis.

Good morning. This is Fred Smithers. I'm calling to let you know that you will receive a check in the mail for *one million* dollars.

Below, I have added an emphasis to some of our script lines that we used above but which previously only had pacing. Read each of them aloud with correct pacing and now emphasis:

M/M_____, I have some *very important* information for you on a guaranteed / investment. It's a bank CD and it's paying /_____/ percent. Could I send you some information on our terms and rates?

I have some important information on how you might get a *higher* rate of return on your money than a CD. The interest *compounds*. Uncle Sam doesn't *touch it* / at tax time. And if something should happen to you, your family would get a whole / *bunch* / of money. Could I send you some information on it?

M/M_____, I have some very interesting information for you on how our cellular phone can save you time, money, and *possibly* / keep you out of trouble with your (Husband/Wife) if you're going to be late. Could I send it to you?

Speed of Talking

Certainly one problem with a written script is that people tend to read too fast. And that is a big problem because a rapid-fire rate of speech is associated with HIGH PRESSURE. And we certainly don't want that.

So how fast should you talk? About the same rate as your prospect. If you call up someone who just moved to Texas from Manhattan, don't lay down a "good ole boy" Good Evening. Hedoesn'thavetime.

So concentrate on listening to rate of speech. And practice tracking with it. The best help you can get is to tape-record yourself and listen to your rate of speech and that of the prospect.

Enthusiasm

Since the beginning of time, sales trainers have preached enthusiasm as a surefire tool. In sales, after all, you are going to *motivate* someone to do something different from what he or she is now doing. And to motivate, you have to use energy.

By enthusiasm, I do not mean the phony, glad-handing, "welcome little goldfish to the shark bowl" so often associated with too many salespeople. I do mean an upbeat projection of energy.

I learned this lesson in my very first sales job, which, as I mentioned in the introduction, was selling dictionaries door-to-door for Southwest Publishing Company. My crew leader, an old family friend named Buzz, told me only two things about sales. The first one was: "Bill, I want you out there running from door to door." To which I responded, "Buzz, you've lost your mind. For twenty-three days in a row it's been over one hundred degrees. If I get out there and run from door to door, I'll die from dehydration and salt loss. I'll walk fast, but that's the best I'll do."

The second thing he told me about sales was "Good, I want you out there being enthusiastic." My response, never directly to him, was "Sure, Buzz. It's real easy to be enthusiastic to some of these 'blue hairs' that I meet at eight o'clock in the morning when I've just dragged my tail out of bed and thrown it out on the street."

Well, one day I was walking down the street, trying to be warm and friendly, and Buzz came tearing around the corner in his old brown Valiant that sounded as if it needed a muffler. He jumped out of the car, sprinted across the yard, grabbed me by the wrist, and we went running down the street to the next house. I knocked on the door, some lady answered, I went through my pitch, and she didn't buy anything.

> BUZZ: Good, you sound dead.
>
> GOOD: Buzz! I'm trying to sound warm and friendly.
>
> BUZZ: Warm and friendly? I never said anything to you about being warm and friendly. I said I wanted you out there being enthusiastic. I want you to wake these people up. They are asleep at the wheel.
>
> GOOD: Buzz, I don't feel enthusiastic.
>
> BUZZ (*scratching his head*):   I don't recall that I even asked you what you felt like. As a matter of fact, ask me how much I care. I don't care if you feel terrible. In my sales crew, you're not going to sound warm and friendly. You're going to sound enthusiastic. I want you out there being enthusiastic. As a matter of fact, if you'll just act enthusiastic, you'll start to feel that way.

I'd heard it before. To feel enthusiastic, *act* enthusiastic. On and on and on. That's all I ever heard from the guy. So, just to prove him wrong, I went to the next house, knocked, and some lady who looked as if she had just stuck her finger in a light socket answered the door.

"Hi!" I said in my most enthusiastic tone. She sort of shook her head, focused her eyes, saw me out there with a big smile on my face, and said,

"Oh, hi!" And I went right into my presentation with a big smile pasted on my face. "We're showing this new book in town. Have you heard about it?" And then I stuck out the book so that she had to grab it.

She said, "No, I haven't."

I said, "Let me tell you about it." And I sold her a book.

And then I tried it again, and very shortly I was selling two books an hour, which was up from one book every two hours. So my sales went up 400 percent as a result of moving quickly and being enthusiastic.

It's true. Genuine enthusiasm will almost wake the dead. If you don't have it genuinely, act as if you do and then you'll feel it.

ASSIGNMENT

1. Go visit billgood.com. Listen to the examples as much as you need. Then continue below.

2. Mark up your own script for inflection, pacing, and emphasis.

3. Read it aloud without any of these elements.

4. Read it into a tape recorder with correct inflection. Play it back. Keep working at it until you have the inflection right. It's not a bad idea to get someone to listen to you. Some people have a hard time hearing their own inflection mistakes.

5. Now read it with correct inflection *and* pacing. Use your tape recorder.

6. Add emphasis.

7. And finally, enthusiasm. Wake 'em up, tiger!

CHAPTER 19

How to Make More Calls

"Sales is a numbers game."

—Bill Good, age twelve

This was one of the last famous statements I made before I shut up. When I was in the sixth grade, I was selling subscriptions to raise money for the Cub Scouts. I sold more than anyone ever in the history of the Cub Scout movement. When all the dust settled (age ten), the company sent someone down to Greensboro, North Carolina, where I lived. He came into our living room, set up a tape recorder, got out his yellow pad, and settled in for what he thought would be a long interview. "Bill," he asked, "how did you do it?" I replied, "Sales is a numbers game. I just run door to door." He waited expectantly for me to say something else. But there was nothing else to say. "Is that all?" he asked. "That's all," I replied. After a while, he packed up and went home. Next year, guess what the slogan was? You got it. They ripped off "Sales is a numbers game." But by that time, I had already quit broadcasting my famous statements.

You cannot be a cherry picker on fifteen dials an hour. There is only one exception to this rule, and we can deal with it right now.

If you have an absolutely outstanding list, you don't have to, indeed can't, make the large volume of calls required on average or even better-than-average lists. I have seen lists in the securities industry, in real estate, computers, and long-distance telephone that are so good that the people you are calling take up a lot of time because they ask questions and otherwise get involved. They want to talk. You cannot, therefore, make lots of calls. But who cares *if you are getting three or even more cherries an hour?*

An outstanding list is the one exception: Without an outstanding list, you cannot cherry pick on just a few calls an hour. Why? Because there simply aren't enough cherries. The competition got there first and ate your lunch.

Sales Is a Numbers Game, But . . .

Anyone who has been around sales longer than one day has heard the statement, "Sales is a numbers game." This is very true. And the assumption is that sales is an "arithmetical numbers game." For those who don't remember what an "arithmetical progression" is, study the following graph.

What this graph says—if you double the number of calls, you double the number of prospects per hour—is just common sense.

It is also not true.

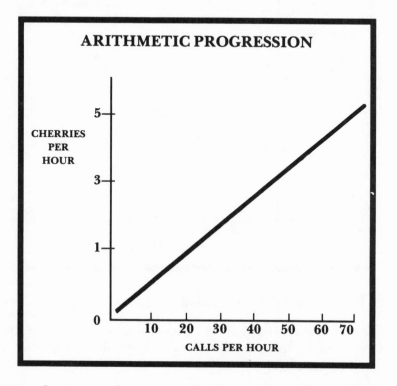

Yes, sales is a numbers game. But it is not an arithmetic game. It's geometric, and it's represented by a type of graph called a geometrical progression, pictured on page 252. This graph says that if you double your calls per hour from ten to twenty, don't expect much change in results. As a matter of fact, you will get more results *per hour* when you increase your dials from forty to sixty than you get if you double them from twenty to forty. As I said, sales *is a numbers game,* but most people don't push it far enough to reap the benefits.

Why such dramatic increases in results after about forty calls an hour? I think the reason has to do most of all with attitude. At fifteen dials an hour, you're not finding much. You're hungry. When you perceive even a flicker of interest in a prospect, you tend to hang on to it desperately. And I am sure you know, by not worrying about results, you will get them much more easily.

The name of the game, then, is to really crank out those calls.

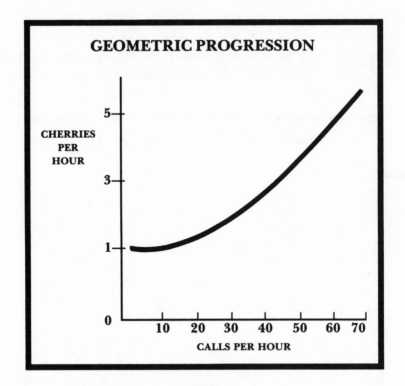

How to Make Lots of Calls

There are ten things to do or not do that will control how many calls you make. None of the principles outlined below will revolutionize your business if taken individually. Taken together, it's a different story.

Focus on Numbers, Not Results

The time to think about results is when you're planning or evaluating a campaign, not when you are executing it. To put it another way, while you are running the campaign, focus on numbers, not results. What I want you to do is to make a game out of hitting your goal in terms of call attempts per hour. These are the targets:

Residential calling: sixty to eighty call attempts per hour

Business calling: forty to sixty call attempts per hour

Let's call it the "twenty-twenty" game. Make twenty call attempts every twenty minutes.

There is some magic in focusing on numbers instead of results. As you increase the numbers, the value of any one call is diminished. It's worth less. As this occurs, somehow rejection matters less and this will have an enormous impact on the way you sound and therefore on your results. Right here is probably the explanation for why your results increase geometrically as the number of calls push past forty per hour.

So, while you're making calls, don't think about results: *Go for the numbers!*

Use a Headset

There are several reasons why you should use a headset. Two of them are: keeps your work flowing while you're on the phone, and you won't need surgery every three months to have the receiver removed from your head. Nor will you get frozen elbow. If you do not have a headset, get one. It is worth at least an extra five to ten call attempts per hour.

Always Use a Script

One of the many reasons to use a script: more calls. Without a script, the tendency is to wander all over the street. With a script, you will say what you need to say, you'll leave nothing out, and you'll get on to the next call. A script saves an enormous amount of time.

Put Your Lists on Cards or List Evaluation Sheets

I have already touched on this principle in Chapter 7. I need to restate it now. First, let me say that any card is better than no card. Once you get a lead, at least half of your time is spent writing down name, address, etc.

If you have placed your names on labels and then affixed the labels to cards, you have taken some big steps to speed up the process. However, the card I have designed enables you to cut down the time you spend taking notes even more. All you do with my card is check a box, make a brief note, and give it to the computer operator.

A very major reason you do not make as many calls as you should is that you spend too much time taking notes—or worse, typing stuff into the computer.

If you are calling a list that cannot be easily put on labels, and therefore cards, you want to copy the list and paste it on one of our List Evaluation Sheets. What you can do now is circle a name when they become a prospect, make a brief note as to what kind of information should be sent, and go to your next call. Your computer operator will then enter the name in the database, send the information, and make up a card for you.

BOX SCORE	
Date ___/___/___ Caller ___/___/___	**List**
Start : End : Elapsed :	**Evaluation**
Script	**Sheet**
Dials	
Contacts	List Description:
Appts	
Cherries	
Greenies	
Info Leads	
Cherries/Hr	
Comment:	Date List Acquired:___/___/___

Source: _____

BOX SCORE	
Date ___/___/___ Caller ___/___/___	
Start : End : Elapsed :	
Script	(Paste list here—or use space for
Dials	other notes.)
Contacts	
Appts	101 Jones, R.D. 555-2351
Cherries /	102 Smith, J.S. 555-3483
Greenies	103 Brown, K.W. 555-9132
Info Leads	104 King, M.J. 555-6159
Cherries/Hr	105 Doe, J.A. 555-2898
Comment:	106 Edwards, M.D. 565-5674

BOX SCORE
107 Thomas, G.K.   555-2782
Date ___/___/___ Caller ___/___/___
108 Simpson, F.R. 555-8352
Start   :   End   :   Elapsed   :
109 White, S.W.   555-4694
Script
110 Jones, C.T. 555-7138
Dials
Contacts
Appts
Cherries
Greenies
Info Leads
Cherries/Hr
Comment:

Yes, I know it takes time to do this work. That's why it should be done during nonoptimum calling times. So: *Put your list on cards or List Evaluation Sheets.*

Always Have the Next Number Ready to Call

In developing this set of principles to enable you to make more calls, I spent a lot of time just watching people work. I once watched some insurance agents. I simply stood around and watched them make calls. The typical work flow went like this:

Find the number of someone to call.

Call it.

Talk to the prospect.

Hang up the phone.

Find the next number.

Pick up the phone.

Dial the number.

This took forever. Anyone watching could see that a great deal of time was lost in the simple act of hanging up the phone between calls. Why were the agents hanging up between calls? Simple: They had to find their next number.

Therefore my first principle is: Always have your next number ready to call. To show you how to do this, we'll do a little exercise right here on the spot. Below, I have created a fictitious list from Main Street in Every City. Look it over and then continue reading; I'll tell you what to do.

South Street

101 Jones, R. D.	555-2351
102 Smith, J. S.	555-3483
103 Brown, K. W.	555-9132
104 King, M. J.	555-6159
105 Doe, J. A.	555-2898
106 Edwards, M. D.	555-5694
107 Thomas, G. K.	555-2782
108 Simpson, F. R.	555-8352
109 White, S. W.	555-4694
110 James, C. T.	555-7138

Get a business card or some other straightedge. Place it so you can read only the name of Jones, R. D., at 101 South Street.

Put your hand up by your ear as if you're making a phone call. Dial the number on an imaginary phone. The minute you imagine the phone starting to ring, move your straight edge down so you can see the next number. All the names except Jones and Smith should be covered by your straight edge.

101 Jones, R. D.	555-2351
102 Smith, J. S.	555-3483

So here is the principle when using a street address or similar list:

1. Put a straight edge under your first name and number.

2. Dial it.

3. The instant it starts to ring, pull your straightedge down so you can *see the next number.*

In our example above, you are talking to Jones. When Jones tells you he's not interested, you glance down just above your straightedge and see the name Smith, J. S. While leaving the phone at your ear, you disconnect Jones and immediately dial Smith. If Smith answers, you've got one hand to hold the phone and the other hand to take notes *while you're talking to Smith.* And if you're wearing a headset, you have two hands to manage the paper.

The instant Smith starts to ring, you pull your straightedge down so you can now see Brown. By following this simple procedure, you never have to put the phone down between calls. And by leaving the phone at your ear, you just bought yourself ten to twelve extra calls per hour.

If you keep your prospect names on note cards, the principle is slightly different. Here's how it works: Take a stack of cards and put them on your desk in front of you. With your hand at your ear as in the previous example, dial the top number on your imaginary phone. The instant that number starts to ring, pull the top card down in front of the pile so you can read the name and number of the next prospect.

As you attempt to implement this principle with either cards or lists, you may find you get confused and call the same person twice. If you do, don't worry. Rally with the cry of a cherry picker, thankyouverymuch, and disconnect.

Never Hang Up or Disconnect Except to Make Minimal Notes

Instead, hit *flash* and GO TO THE NEXT CALL. When salespeople hang up the phone or disconnect, they tend to do something else. I watched a financial adviser one day: He made a call. Hung up the phone. Put something on his stock quote terminal. Rummaged around on his desk for something. Took out a research report. Looked at that for a moment. Said something to the person next to him. And finally made another phone call.

When you're prospecting, you'll pick a lot of extra cherries by *never hanging up or disconnecting the phone.* If you followed my recommendations and pasted your cold-calling lists on List Evaluation Sheets or put them on cards, you won't have to stop to write down the prospect's name, address, and phone number. You'll just draw a circle around your cherry's name and jot down any other notes right there on the List Evaluation Sheet. You won't even stop to make up prospect cards or address envelopes. You'll do that at the end of an hour when you take a short break. By isolating similar actions into their own units of time, you develop speed and velocity at each.

Let the Phone Ring Four Times Before Disconnecting

Somewhere along the way I learned that 85 percent of the people who are home will answer on or before the fourth ring. So, what are the other 15 percent doing? Who knows. But we do know they don't want to come to the phone. If they had wanted to answer the phone, they would have gotten there earlier. So we can say with a fair amount of confidence that the people who do come to the phone after the fourth ring are not high-grade prospects.

There is, however, an exception. If you are calling a retirement community, allow up to six rings, since the people you are calling may not be as fast as younger people.

If you are calling businesses during the day, I can promise you that if you allow the phone to ring six times, and someone does finally answer, it will be some harried receptionist who will say to you, "Good morning, Acme Company, hold please." And you'll be listening to some easy listening station.

Don't Stay on Hold Forever

In most companies with more than ten employees, the first person who answers the phone is the receptionist. Normally, the receptionist does not screen calls. It's this person's job simply to route calls to the correct extension.

This brings us to the fact that there are two places you can get put on hold. The first is, of course, with the receptionist. You call for Ms. Jones, and in the process of being connected to her office, you get put on hold. I would not stay on this type of hold longer than about twenty seconds.

The second place you may get put on hold is after you have spoken to the screener, who is now going to put you through to the boss. Since in daytime calling it can be very difficult to reach people, you can afford to invest a bit more time in waiting to talk to the decision maker. I would give it about a minute. And then simply disconnect and go on to your next number.

Don't Write Down Negatives

We covered this principle in Chapter 7, but since it also affects speed of calling, let's look at it again.

Don't write down who's not in, who's not interested, or any other "NOTs." It's a waste of time. Simply recycle these lists again in six weeks. If you call the lists back today or tomorrow, and try to reach those same people, you'll be calling a list of people who, in the current time period, *are* "*NOTs*". Who cares what they are not being or doing? Right now they are just NOT. I know one salesman who literally went out of business because he violated this principle. He would call through a list and talk to those he could speak with. He would very carefully note down those who were not in, and so forth. Then he would turn around and call the list again. His contact rate on the second cycle through the list was worse than the first. However, he would still be able to reach some people. Not being one to quit, he would try a third time to reach those who had not been in on the second cycle through the list. By this time, he was really down to the hard core of people who are NOT. And he was wondering all along why he was having such trouble getting people to the phone. By writing down the negatives and then calling prospects back in the *current time frame,* he created a NOT list. Don't do it.

As I have already discussed, writing down negatives prejudices the list. Suppose you were given a list to call that said, "Not interested, not home, busy," and so on and so on. Would you want to call it? Writing down negatives prejudices the list when the time does come to call it back in six weeks or so.

Do Not Leave Written Messages or Get Callback Information from Non–Decision Makers

Before jumping into this, let me tell you that there is an exception to this rule that I will cover in "The Message Campaign" later in this chapter. Let me state clearly that I am talking about written messages left with family members or with someone *not the decision maker* at work. *I am not talking about voice-mail messages.* (They are governed by different rules.)

To make certain we both know what I'm talking about, let's define a couple of terms here. By "callback information," I mean information as to when Mr. Jones or Mrs. Smith will be in. By "non–decision maker" I mean kids, and wives or husbands, depending on who you are trying to reach. Here is what often happens when you try to get callback information from a non–decision maker at home.

YOU:	*(Ring, ring.)*
KID:	Hello.
YOU:	May I speak to your mom, please?
KID:	She's not in.
YOU:	When do you expect her?
KID:	I don't know. Talk to my sister. *(Puts phone down. Two minutes later:)*

OTHER KID: Hello.

YOU: Hi! I was just talking to your sister. . . .

OTHER KID: That was my brother. He just sounds like a girl.

YOU: I see. I'm trying to reach your mother. . . .

OTHER KID: She's out walking the dogs. You should talk to my dad. . . .

Here's how it should go:

YOU: *(Ring, ring.)*

KID: Hello.

YOU: May I speak to your mom, please?

KID: She's not in.

YOU: Thank you. I'll call back.

When someone asks, "May I leave a message?" your instant response should be: "No thank you. I'll call back." *Click. Dial tone.*

This is not just theory or stuff I made up. I spent a whole afternoon testing the "no callback information principle." One of my students and I called for several hours, and every time a screener would say that "So-and-So is not in," he would ask her when So-and-So would be expected. He would note down that time, then call back within five minutes of that time. If he couldn't place the call within the five minutes, he would just forget about it. In essence, what he was doing was developing a separate list of executives based on screener information. And obviously what I wanted to know was: Is this list any good?

While he was developing his list of people who were not in, I was calling and asking to speak with So-and-So. When I heard the word "not" as in "not in," "not available," "not on this planet," I cut and ran, going on to the next call.

When we tallied the results, it was clear that my student was developing a list of people who tended, in the current time frame, to be away from the office. Therefore, all the time spent in developing that list was wasted. And all time spent calling it was wasted.

Here's how these conversations (modified, as appropriate, by the rules for voice mail) should go:

YOU: *(Ring, ring.)*

SCREENER: Mr. Jones's office.

YOU: Hi, is he in?

SCREENER: He's not in right now. May I take a message?

YOU: No thanks. I'll call back. *(Click. Dial tone.)*

If you want to destroy your daytime rate, simply call and find out from screeners when Mr. or Ms. Jones will be in. Now write the answer down. Spend more time organizing it. And spend still more time calling it back. This will cut a decent daytime callback rate from forty or fifty calls per hour all the way down to twelve.

Don't Leave Messages

If you want to destroy your calling rate even further, leave written messages with screeners. That's good for an additional minute. Unless the boss knows you, or unless you are leaving an extremely persuasive voice-mail message, he or she won't call back. So the time you're spending with the screener is wasted. Don't do it.

Screener: The Rules

Surely screeners are the bone in the throat of most salespeople. They are the lion at the door. The dog at the gate. If only you could get past that screener and talk to Mr. or Ms. Jones, well, surely he or she would buy. But there sits the screener.

In some locations—Canada for one, small towns for another—the screener is not a particular problem. But in the major metropolitan markets with their high-powered, big-budget executives, there are thousands of salespeople banging away at the phones and doors. Very literally, if salespeople could all get through and talk to the boss, he or she would be unable to do anything else. Therefore, a screener, backed up by state-of-the-art voice mail, is planted at the door with instructions and technology to screen the calls.

You may wonder why I've included this section on screeners in the chapter on how to make more calls. The reason should be obvious. Screeners can waste a great deal of your time. Handling them correctly will enormously increase the number of calls you can make and therefore the number of contacts. Doing it right will get you through to more decision makers. So pay attention!

A broad principle for dealing with screeners is this: *Believe the screener when he or she tells you the boss is a pit. A screener knows the boss better than you.*

You can be sure that the Old School has infected this area, as it has others. A typical Old School conversation using these methods might go like this:

YOU:	*(Ring, ring.)*
SCREENER:	Good morning, Mr. Jones's office.
YOU:	Is he in?
SCREENER:	May I tell him who's calling?
YOU:	It's Fred Smithers. I'd like to speak with him. Is he in?
SCREENER:	May I tell him what the call is about?
YOU:	Yes, you can tell him it's Fred Smithers calling. I need to speak with him at once. Please connect me.

In other words, practitioners of this method try and intimidate the screener and shove their way past. And it will work. However, if you are successful in getting through to Mr. or Ms. Jones, please remember you will be calling back again—and the screener will remember. The hold button is a very long place to be.

In my office, practitioners of this method get put immediately on hold. In ten or fifteen minutes, my assistant will pick up and say, "Are you still there?" If yes, she will say, "He'll be right with you." We just leave them on hold until they give up. Occasionally, they will call back, at which point they get an apology and again get put on hold.

With this in mind, let's lay out seven different methods for handling screeners. I'm giving you these in order of preference. Please keep in mind that there is no way to tell which method will work best for which list in which city.

Method 1: Answer the Screener's Questions First

There *is* an old saying in sales, "The one who asks the questions controls the conversation." This may be a holdover from the Old School, but it's still true.

You can actually develop a method for handling the screener based on this principle. The way most salespeople commonly call for the decision maker leaves the screener in full control. The screener asks all the questions: your name, what company you're with, and what you want.

In Method 1, you take control by anticipating and answering all those questions first, and then asking one of your own, so you get some control. Here's how this method might work:

YOU:	*(Ring, ring.)*
SCREENER:	Good morning, Captain Price's office.
YOU:	Good morning, this is Balph Burgher. I'm with Bilgewater Pumping. I need to speak with him about getting those bilges cleaned out a lot faster. Could you connect me, please?

SCREENER *(uncertain)*:   Just a moment. I'll see if he's in.

CAPT. PRICE: Hello.

Now, granted, this method does not work all the time. Its primary benefits to you, the salesperson, are that it dislodges the screener a bit from the control position and it's very quick. Depending on your voicemail strategy, you will have to decide what to do if Captain Price is not in. Remember, if your decision maker does not want to talk to you, you don't want to talk to him or her.

Obviously, *the exact words you use to tell the screener what your call is about are critical.* Here's why: A vital function of a good screener is to relay communication. Method 1 uses this function, and your objective is to get the screener to relay a message that will strike the decision maker as important enough or interesting enough to come to the phone.

In financial services, I have found the best word to use is "money." If your call has anything to do with saving, investing, speculating, or even buying anything, your key word is "money." Here's the message the screener will relay to Mr. Jones:

SCREENER: Hey, Fred! There is some guy on the phone from Beam of Light Financial. He said it's about your money.

Now Fred has got to be wondering, "What money?" His money? The company's money? His wife's money? What's going on? So he may take the call to satisfy his curiosity. Always remember that curiosity is at least as powerful a motive for action as greed or interest.

If you can't use the word "money" when you tell the screener what your call concerns, simply experiment with different descriptions about why you want to talk to the boss. Try to find a combination of words that will get you through. If you aren't getting through, keep experimenting with a different message.

Here's a hint: Try the obvious. If you're a commercial real estate agent: "It's about the lease on your building at 404 Main Street." If you sell seminars: "It's about a seminar that can help your salespeople find lots of new business." If you sell cars: "It's about that old clunker you drive."

Method 2: Call When the Screener Is Not In

One of the very simplest ways to get in touch with hard to reach decision makers is to call before the screener gets in or after he or she goes home. The reality is: Bosses come in earlier and stay later than screeners. Therefore, when you first talk to a screener, if you cannot get through, do everything possible to get the decision maker's direct extension number.

Then call back before nine in the morning or after four or four-thirty in the afternoon.

Here is an excerpt from our script that shows you how to dig out the all-important direct extension number.

> **Decision Maker Not Available:** Let me ask you this. Do you think this is something he/she would be interested in? (Yes or Maybe) OK, I'm going to send this information to him/her and then check back with you. If he/she's not interested, I'll just go on my way, but if he/she *is* interested, perhaps you could relay back to me how to proceed further. Would that work? (Response) Great. Could I have/confirm your mailing address? (Response) Your fax number? (Response) Thankyouverymuch. I do want to leave a voice-mail message. But in case I get disconnected, what is his/her direct extension number? Could you connect me to his/her voice mail now?

Method 3: Slide By

This is a technique that will work on many screeners. The screener position is one with an enormously high turnover. Perhaps as many as 30 to 40 percent of the nation's screeners change jobs yearly. So the chances are pretty good that you'll speak with a screener who is not certain you don't have the right to talk to Captain Price.

As you prepare to test out this method, I should warn you that there is a type of screener we call the "office queen," although it naturally applies to both sexes. She is normally the screener to a high-level executive, has been there since Year One, and may in fact be one of the most powerful people in a major corporation. Undoubtedly she lives there, and the slide-by approach won't work with her. Further, if you try to slide by, she will sever your hand at the wrist, smile politely, and hand it back to you in a perfumed paper bag neatly wrapped.

With that warning in place, let's discuss how you can slide by many, if not most, screeners. The steps in this method are:

1. Know the name of the person you wish to speak to.

2. Get the screener's name from reception.

3. Slide by.

Here's how it works:

YOU:	*(Ring, ring.)*
RECEPTIONIST:	Good morning, Acme Company.
YOU:	Good morning. I need to speak to Mr. Jones's assistant. Could you tell me her name, please?

RECEPTIONIST:	Beverly Smith.
YOU:	Would you connect me, please?
RECEPTIONIST:	*(Ring, ring.)*
SCREENER:	Good morning, Mr. Jones's office.
YOU:	Hi, Bev! This is Fred. Is David in?
SCREENER:	*(Feeling terror at the possibility of insulting a friend of the boss):* Just a moment, please. *(Ring, ring.)*
CAPT. PRICE:	Hello.

Method 4: Preapproach Phone Call

Here's a theory for you. Behind the administrative screen of a well-defended list lies an undersolicited prospect. If you stop and think about it, you can see why. This executive has hired someone to screen his or her calls. Most calls, therefore, don't get through. The executive, then, does not receive his or her fair share of prospecting phone calls. Conclusion: If you can get hold of this person, you might have a very good prospect. So the name of the game becomes: penetrate the screen.

The method I'm going to outline for you should not be used on routine lists. It is best on a well-defended list. For example, you may want to use it on a list of senior executives for the Fortune 500 companies in your city. Use it if you've already tried Methods 1 and 2 and they didn't work.

Step 1 of this technique is a call in which you don't even try to speak to the boss. This is literally the preapproach phone call. It corresponds to and serves the same purpose as a preapproach letter. It paves the way. Here it goes:

YOU:	*(Ring, ring.)*
SCREENER:	Good morning, Ms. Jones's office.
YOU:	Good morning, this is Fred Smithers with the Acme Company. Please tell Ms. Jones I'll be calling her this afternoon between two o'clock and three o'clock. It's about an important idea that can substantially cut her computer supply costs, OK?
SCREENER:	Very good. I'll tell her.
YOU:	By the way, who am I speaking with?
SCREENER:	This is Beverly.
YOU:	Very good, Beverly. I'll give her a jingle this afternoon.

Write down the screener's name. As a matter of fact, any time you get a screener's name, write it down! And use it! Get the screener on your side.

Step 2 of the technique is the follow-up phone call in which you do try to get through to the boss. Here you're going to capitalize on the fact that you know the screener's name and that the boss is expecting the call. Here's how it goes:

YOU: *(Ring, ring.)*

SCREENER: Good afternoon, Ms. Jones's office.

YOU: Hi, Beverly, it's Fred over here at Acme. She should be expecting my call. Would you connect me, please?

This method was tested in one of the most highly resistant markets there is: New York City. A student of mine found that the time spent calling in the morning plus the time spent calling in the afternoon added up to better results than just calling and asking for Captain Price.

Remember, always evaluate a campaign or technique by results per units of time. Here the key factor to evaluate is the number of qualified prospects per unit of time and percentage of those which are cherries.

Method 5: The Message Campaign

There are some lists that are impossible to prospect by phone. Or should we say, are impossible to prospect by phone without the use of the message campaign. Take doctors, for instance. Cold calling doctors is like calling nowhere. They are always "with a patient." In fact, a new machine has been invented that only says, "Doctor's office" and "He's/She's with a patient." Other lists are nearly as impossible to call because the people have jobs that take them away from the office. You'll seldom reach sales managers or salespeople who work out of the office.

A relatively new market is developing that can be approached only through a message campaign or e-mail. I'm referring to *lone eagles.* These are independent consultants who almost don't have homes or offices. They work on contract here for a few weeks, there for a few months. Their home number may not be at a home but at a service. One solution, if you can find the numbers, is e-mail. The other solution for these hard-to-reach or hard-to-penetrate markets is: the message campaign. In a message campaign, you call up and very quickly leave a message with the screener or receptionist. If the prospect is interested, he or she may return the call.

This brings up a very important issue. Earlier I told you "don't leave messages." And yet here I am telling you to leave messages. What I'm really telling you is don't mix the two procedures. Either go after your decision makers and get 'em or forget 'em. Or, call up and *only* leave a message and *don't* try to get them to the phone. When running a message campaign, *always leave messages when you hit voice mail.*

Properly done, there is an actual rhythm to prospecting by phone. It seems to work best with a single limited objective. Where your approach has many legs to it, you will feel, at the end of an hour or two, utterly splattered and pulled apart. Your rhythm will be broken and it will cost you dearly in terms of number of calls that you make. However, see how the message campaign works with a single objective when calling a doctor.

YOU:	*(Ring, ring.)*
RECEPTIONIST:	Dr. Jones's office.
YOU:	Good morning, I have an important message for Dr. Jones. Will you write it down?
RECEPTIONIST:	Yes, I will.
YOU:	My name is Fred Smithers, I work at Beam of Light Financial. My phone number is 555-4821. The message is: "Pomona Sewer Bond; 5.5 percent triple tax-free. Call me." Did you get that?
RECEPTIONIST:	Yes, I did.
YOU:	Thankyouverymuch. *(Click. Dial tone.)*

There is a principle involved here. The principle is, don't tell everything in your message. Second, keep your message as short as possible. Seven words or less is the rule of thumb. Our message—"Pomona Sewer Bond; 5.5 percent triple tax free"—might certainly get the doctor to call back. If you're selling a financial product or service, don't name it. Name a benefit.

Method 6: Ask Them a Question They Can't Answer

This is a method designed for a well-defended, but reachable, list. It's not for a list like doctors, who are not reachable. In this method, you are simply going to act as if the screener is the decision maker and then ask the screener a question that he or she can't answer. If possible, you'll also appeal to the screener's own self-interest. The minute his or her feet are held slightly to the fire, if Ms. or Mr. Jones is in at all, the screener will probably transfer you.

I used this technique very effectively in a campaign I designed for a group of salespeople selling a credit collection service to comptrollers of Fortune 500 companies—small list, big prospects. Our call to the screener went like this:

YOU:	*(Ring, ring.)*
SCREENER:	Good morning, Mr. Jones's office.
YOU:	Good morning, this is Fred Smithers with XYZ. Are you Mr. Jones's assistant?
SCREENER:	Yes, I am. My name is Frank.
YOU:	Very good, Frank. I'm calling because we have developed a new method to help with your credit collection. Tell me, what percentage of your accounts go delinquent after ninety days!
SCREENER:	Ummmm. I'm not sure. Perhaps you'd better speak with Mr. Jones.

Again, *the key to this method is to ask a question the screener can't answer.* It should be a question that only the boss can answer.

Here is an example, using the same principle, for an insurance agent to call pension and profit-sharing plans. Note the way I have appealed to the screener's self-interest. Appropriate passages are in italics.

To screener: Good morning, this is Balph Burger with Acme Insurance. Are you Ms. Smith-Jones's assistant? With whom am I speaking? Great. Perhaps you can help me. I would like to send Ms. Smith-Jones some information on our pension fund management program that can very possibly increase the *amount of money Bilge Pump employees will get at retirement.* But I need to know exactly what kind of plan you have now. Is it a qualified corporate, HR-10, Super IRA, or 401K? (RESPONSE) Perhaps Ms. Smith-Jones has that info on the tip of her tongue. Could you connect me, please?

Method 7: The Mad Dog Method

Strictly speaking, the method I outline here will not help you increase the number of your calls. Rather, it is a humorous, and highly effective, way to get through to a single decision maker whom you want *very badly* to reach. The method was first used by a financial salesperson who is now a high executive at a major national firm. His nickname was Mad Dog Mike, and he first earned fame as one of the best cold-calling brokers around.

As Mike told the story to me, he read one day that a very wealthy man had sold a big piece of property for a substantial amount of money. Mike immediately called up and encountered the classic office queen. We'll call her Mildred. When Mike tried to get through to Mr. Jones, Mildred explained to him, "Mike, I assure you, he is very well taken care of. He has several brokers and does not require your services."

So over the next few days, Mike tried all the standard ploys to get through to Mr. Jones. He called at one minute before nine, at one minute after twelve, at ten in the morning, late in the afternoon, and so on, thinking Mildred would be on break. Nothing worked. She seemed to live there.

So one day Mike called Mildred up and he said to her, "Mildred, I just want to let you know that I'm now setting my clock."

> MILDRED: You're doing what?
>
> MIKE: I'm setting my clock. I'm setting it to go off at exactly nine o'clock, and every morning when it goes off at nine o'clock I'm going to call you. And Mildred, I'm going to call you every day until I die.

Mike began doing it. After a while, word got around the office, and each morning at nine, the office would gather around Mildred's desk for Mike's morning call. A typical call would go like this:

> MIKE: *(Ring, ring.)*
>
> MILDRED: Good morning, Mr. Jones's office.
>
> MIKE: Good morning, Mildred, it's me.
>
> MILDRED: Mike!
>
> MIKE: Is he in?
>
> MILDRED: You know you can't talk to him.
>
> MIKE: Thankyouverymuch. Call you tomorrow. *(Click. Dial tone.)*

This went on for several weeks. Finally one morning Mildred said, "I can't stand it anymore. I'm going to let you talk to him." So, Mike, at long last, got on the phone with Mr. Jones. Here's what he said.

> MIKE: Good morning. As I'm sure Mildred has told you, I've been calling quite a bit lately, and I just want to let you know, if you have any questions at all, you can give me a call, OK?
>
> MR. JONES: Ah, OK.
>
> MIKE: Very good. Thankyouverymuch. *(Click. Dial tone.)*

Shortly thereafter, Mr. Jones called back. "OK," he said. "You've got my attention."

Mike got the account.

Keeping Track

When I took my first sales job in 1974, I found out very quickly the truth of the "sales is a numbers game" principle. Very possibly my first inkling that the Old School was full of it was my observation that the more calls I could make the better results I would get. Right there, if I had really examined it, I would have seen the utter nonsense of the "Don't-believe-the-prospect-until-he-has-said-no-forty-two-times" school. The full insight was to come some years later.

What did become very clear to me was the importance of setting goals for the number of calls on *an hourly basis* and then tracking my goal by the hour. I found that any hour I didn't make my dial goal was an hour in which I didn't make my sales goal. I finally reached the point where the number of calls was far more important than pursuing a long-winded prospect who might, or most likely might not, buy. On pages 271 and 272, I am reproducing two charts that may help you keep track.

Chart 1 is designed to be used for each day's calling. Chart 2 is to be used to summarize weekly results. At the end of a day, simply tally up your results from Chart 1 and write them down on Chart 2. Managers would do well to require that Chart 2 be turned in every day. Part of your daily routine as manager is to inspect it, comment on it, and then return it. At the end of the week, file Chart 2 in each salesperson's folder. This gives you a running record of how your salespeople are doing.

File copies of both sheets are available at billgood.com. The password for this section is: joava. (She's my wife.)

Call Sheet

Here's how to use your Call Sheet:

Every time you make a call, put a slash mark through the number. If the call turns into a "contact with decision maker," put a / mark as shown.

1	2	3	4	5	6	7	8	9	10	11	12	13	14	15	16	17	18	19	20
∕	∕	—	—	—	—	—	—	—	—	—	—	—	—	—	—	—	—	—	—

When you make contact with a decision maker, turn the / mark into an X.

1	2	3	4	5	6	7	8	9	10	11	12	13	14	15	16	17	18	19	20
∕	∕	X	—	—	—	—	—	—	—	—	—	—	—	—	—	—	—	—	—

If your contact turns into a cherry, draw a circle around it.

1	2	3	4	5	6	7	8	9	10	11	12	13	14	15	16	17	18	19	20
∕	∕	X	⊗	—	—	—	—	—	—	—	—	—	—	—	—	—	—	—	—

If it's a green cherry, make a check mark in a box.

1	2	3	4	5	6	7	8	9	10	11	12	13	14	15	16	17	18	19	20
∠	∠	X	⊗	☑	_	_	_	_	_	_	_	_	_	_	_	_	_	_	_

If it's an info lead, put an "x" in a box.

1	2	3	4	5	6	7	8	9	10	11	12	13	14	15	16	17	18	19	20
∠	∠	X	⊗	☑	☒	_	_	_	_	_	_	_	_	_	_	_	_	_	_

Finally, when you download your copy, change my wording in the two boxes in the chart from "important number" to the number that is important to you.

For some companies, the "important number" for prospecting is leads. For others, it may be cherries. For calling prospects, it may be appointments. For others, it may be new accounts. And for some, it may be new account commissions. Just put what's important to you in that box.

How to Use Your Call Reports

The very first thing to check when you are not getting three cherries per hour is the number of calls you are making. If you are keeping a Call Sheet, glance over it. If you are making more than forty calls an hour and not averaging three cherries an hour, the problem lies elsewhere.

If the number of calls is in order, but you're not getting results, do you sound sour? Are you sticking to a proven script?

The numbers will tell you what the problem is.

Voice-Mail Rules

We have covered, elsewhere, how to leave various types of voice-mail messages. Here are some rules that may help you decide *whether* to leave a message.

1. Residential calling: Unless a relationship exists, when you hit voice mail, disconnect.

2. Calling individuals at place of work on personal matters: Again, unless a relationship exists, when you hit voice mail, disconnect.

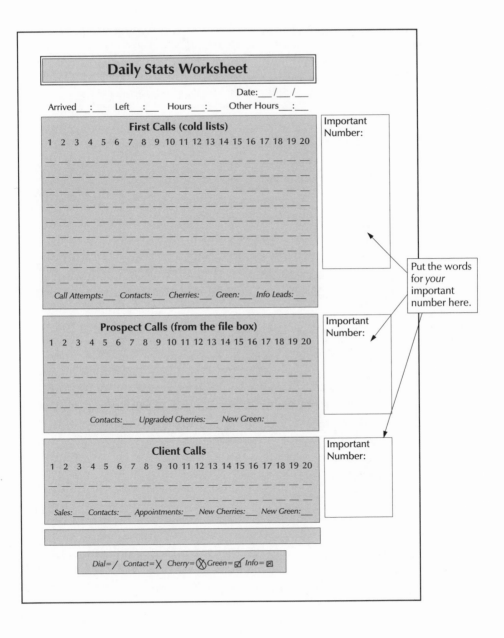

Daily Stats Worksheet

Date:___ /___ /___

Arrived___:___   Left___:___   Hours___:___   Other Hours___:___

First Calls (cold lists)

1 2 3 4 5 6 7 8 9 10 11 12 13 14 15 16 17 18 19 20

Important Number:

Call Attempts:___   Contacts:___   Cherries:___   Green:___   Info Leads:___

Prospect Calls (from the file box)

1 2 3 4 5 6 7 8 9 10 11 12 13 14 15 16 17 18 19 20

Important Number:

Contacts:___   Upgraded Cherries:___   New Green:___

Client Calls

1 2 3 4 5 6 7 8 9 10 11 12 13 14 15 16 17 18 19 20

Important Number:

Sales:___   Contacts:___   Appointments:___   New Cherries:___   New Green:___

Dial=/   Contact=X   Cherry=⊗Green=☑   Info=✉

Put the words for *your* important number here.

Daily/Weekly Report

For *statistical* week ending ___ / ___ / ___

Reminder: Fill in this sheet **daily**.

Prospecting

	List	Hours	Script	Call Attempts	Contacts	Cherries	Greenies	Info Leads
Monday								
Tuesday								
Wednesday								
Thursday								
Friday								
Weekly Totals								

Follow-up Calls to Prospects (may include various drip, requalification, 2nd call)

	Contacts	Appointments	Upgraded Cherries	New Green Cherries
Monday				
Tuesday				
Wednesday				
Thursday				
Friday				
Weekly Totals				

Note: These are calls from your prospect file box.

At the end of each day, results from the Call Sheet are transferred to the Daily/Weekly Report.

Follow-up Calls to Clients

	Contacts	Appointments	Upgraded Cherries	New Green Cherries
Monday				
Tuesday				
Wednesday				
Thursday				
Friday				
Weekly Totals				

Bottom Line

Primary Number:_____   Primary Number:_____

3. Business calling: If you first hit a decision maker's voice mail, disconnect.

4. Business calling: After securing agreement from an assistant to show the boss material that will be sent, you can ask to be connected to the boss's voice mail and leave a persuasive voice-mail message.

ASSIGNMENT

1. Download your call sheets and make any changes necessary to adapt them to the way you do business.

2. Make calls for two solid hours. Keep track on your call sheet. Transfer your records to your Daily/Weekly Report. You're on your way!

20

Breakout
Putting It All Together

The first part of this chapter is really for salespeople only. Managers have an entire chapter coming up just for them, and I want to talk for a moment to salespeople about getting a job in sales. A job is, after all, the first thing a salesperson needs if he or she is, as the title of this chapter suggests, going to "put it together." So you managers just go ahead and skip down to the next section, "The Breakout Plan."

For Salespeople Only

I frequently run into salespeople who ask me whether they should go and work for this company or that company. Over the years, I have developed a pretty good understanding that it really doesn't matter so much who you work for as long as you're working for a decent, honest company with a good product or service to sell. What matters a great deal, however, is which *manager* you work for. Whether he or she is called a branch manager, general agent, broker, sales manager, or supreme leader, your manager will be the most important person in your life for the next two years. (If you can survive the first two years, you can survive as long as you choose. By then, you're a professional.) I know many sales managers who almost never lose salespeople because of failure. And rarely do they ever lose salespeople to rival firms. These managers hire, train, manage, and motivate their sales crew to become winners.

So, if you are looking for a sales job, don't take the first offer. Conduct your own interview. You're interviewing for the most important person in your life for the next two years. Here are some things to look for as you interview for a manager.

1. Can the manager see into the sales room from his or her office?

This may sound like an odd requirement. Yet I've seen too many managers who get behind closed doors, crunch their numbers, and never become really involved with the day-to-day activities of the sales force. They are protected by iron maiden secretaries, intimidating offices, thronelike desks, and while they may be very successful as sales managers, it's more than likely they inherited an office with big hitters rather than grew their big hitters from scratch. You want an office where the manager is *involved*. If the manager can't *see* what's going on, in my experience, he or she is not involved.

2. Find out what the manager's turnover is.

Ask the manager, "If you hired ten people a year ago, how many of them are with you today?" And then ask, "How much money are the ones who are still with you today making?" And finally, "Do you mind if I talk to two or three of your one-year salespeople?"

In talking with those salespeople, find out what you get in the way of additional training. Does the sales manager himself or herself ever go and make sales calls? And of course find out how much money the one-year survivor is making by asking him or her as well as the manager.

3. Ask what the manager expects in the way of hours.

If you get a typical forty-hour-a-week answer, know that you are probably doomed to failure in that office. It takes a substantial commitment to get a new sales career off the ground, and if anybody tells you you can do it by seeing only the old customers in a territory, you can figure at best you're good for whatever the starting salary or draw is and not a whole lot more. If you exceed that, they may cut your territory. You will never enjoy the great potential of a sales career if you're offered a forty-hour-a-week job.

4. Find out if you can do the work.

If possible, ask to go out on a sales call with one of the one-year survivors and with someone who is established in the business. See if it's the kind of work you can do. I can tell you this for certain—if you don't like the work, or if you don't like the people to whom you sell, you are dooming yourself to a life of misery and frustration. What could be worse than getting up in the morning to go sell something you don't like to people you despise?

The Breakout Plan

Some time ago, I received a letter from a branch manager in the securities industry. He told me that six of his brokers had been following my system for a couple of months, were calling seven hours a week, ten hours a week, and they were getting really discouraged. These six brokers had, in two months, opened only thirty-five new accounts. That's an average of three per month per broker, which is certainly a free ticket to the food stamp line.

I gave this branch manager a call and in a few questions determined that they were all doing the right things. It just wasn't working . . . yet.

My advice to him was to keep the brokers' feet to the fire, because I could see an all-too-familiar pattern unfolding. And that is: Salesperson starts calling; salesperson gets middling or poor results, maybe even after hanging in there for a couple of months. Salesperson gives up. In reality, "the give up" almost always occurs at about the five-yard line, when you're almost there.

In the third month, this group of brokers "broke loose." The branch manager called to tell me that one of his brokers opened seven accounts in one week. The next week, another followed with five accounts. The others bounced out of the pits as well. And once again, I saw this almost magical phenomenon I have come to call breakout occur. And occur it does . . . especially if you don't give up at the five-yard line. Breakout is a sudden explosion of new business. Why does it occur? Let's compare the prospecting procedure we've developed to a pipeline. Pump oil in one end of a pipeline, and after a while it will come out the other end. Even pumping hard and fast, at first you'll only get a trickle *and then suddenly a torrent.*

Just like a real pipeline, if you stuff in lists, dials, cherries, second calls, appointments, closing calls, and closes, out the other end will come new accounts and commissions. And the new accounts seem to first trickle out, and then BANG! You've got breakout. In some industries, this pipeline is short, perhaps a matter of days. In other industries, like commercial real estate, it may be years. No matter what industry you're in, *it will occur.*

The Breakout Plan, then, is to stuff the pipeline with lots of prospects *and keep doing it for a period of weeks or months* until you get the explosion—breakout!

Creating Breakout

Let's first talk work habits.

Two hours of calling this week, a few letters next week that don't get followed up, four hours of prospecting the next week, a down week, and one hour the next week will create NOTHING. Just like an airplane taking off, a certain minimum amount of energy is required to create breakout. Less than that gets a pitiful dribble. And that leads you to believe the system is a failure. It isn't. *You just didn't pump enough energy into it!*

The energy for a prospecting system comes from letters and calls pushed out the door. Depending on your marketplace, you need a minimum of a hundred letters a week and seven to fourteen hours a week on the phone. When I say *seven to fourteen hours a week on the phone,* I'm talking about hours spent making *first calls.* They do not include time spent doing second calls, appointments, and so forth. We stuff the pipeline first with letters, hours, and dials. These generate cherries, which in turn create second calls. And so on through the pipeline. But with no letters, hours, and dials, there is nothing going in. *And therefore, nothing will come out.*

Why seven hours minimum? Because I have never seen anyone sustain a commitment when they started with less than that. Apparently, less produces so few prospects that the salesperson loses interest. But look at this: If you do seven hours a week for twelve weeks, if you average three cherries per hour, in twelve weeks you'll have 252 prospects in various stages of closing. You tell me that won't create a breakout!

When should you do your seven hours? If your prospects can be reached night or day, do one hour a day *every day* and then one evening of two hours. If your prospects can be reached only during the day, do an hour every morning, and then spend two hours late one afternoon (after the secretary has gone home!). And keep doing this for at least twelve weeks. Unless you are in a field like commercial real estate, you'll get breakout in twelve weeks.

So make the commitment now: a minimum of seven hours a week for twelve *consecutive* weeks. If you miss a week, you owe next week. This is a commitment with yourself to create your future. If you're brand new in business, just double everything and keep on that schedule until you cannot possibly follow up everyone you have developed as a cherry, green cherry, info lead, etc.

The One-Hour Test

Here's how you start. Grab a list. Any list. Write—or rewrite—a script, preferably phone/mail/phone style. As you write it, try and stay within one of the forms we've covered, but some script is better than none. Just make sure it's in writing.

Call the list using the script. Stick to that script for an hour. If it's obvious in midstream that it needs changing, make the changes in writing. Then start a new one-hour test. Chances are you will not get your three cherries an hour right off the bat. So what? Rome wasn't built in a day. (I guess you know who said that the first time, don't you?)

Now do another one-hour test. If you didn't get your three cherries in your first hour, work on your script. Or work on the number of dials per hour. Early on, you'll want to concentrate on your wording, your dials, and your list.

Upgrade Your List

Chances are excellent that the first list you grabbed for your first test is not the best list you could use. The important thing is this: The *FIRST THING* you do is call. THEN organize your lists. *Start calling first.* Keep calling, and as you do, upgrade your list and work on and improve your script. Frankly, I have seen too many salespeople in too many industries spend too much time on organization and never make the first dial. If the only thing in sight is the White Pages, grab 'em and start. And then, in your *nonoptimum calling time,* get to the library or wherever and start putting together your own specialized lists.

The First Call

Without a doubt, the hardest call to make is the first one. As you sit in front of your telephone with palms sweating and throat dry, you just know this isn't for you. And especially since this system is *different* from whatever you've done in the past, I know that you feel uncomfortable. You definitely felt uncomfortable the first time you passed an eighteen-wheeler after getting your driver's license. You undoubtedly felt uncomfortable the first time you made a sales presentation. And you were certainly uncomfortable the first time you ever stood up in front of a group of people to give a talk.

So what else is new? You'll feel uncomfortable the first time you do *anything* new; you certainly should not decide whether you're going to do something on the basis of whether it feels comfortable or not. Evaluate it on whether it makes sense to you or not, and then know that because it is new, you will feel uncomfortable. So what! You didn't let that stop you from passing the truck, making the sales presentation, or standing up in front of a group. Don't let it stop you now.

Keeping Going

It's very probable that you may be the only one in your company or group who is studying this system and implementing it. You may or may not get much help from your manager, and you probably won't get much help from the other salespeople in your group. So you'll need some techniques to keep your morale up and keep the ball rolling long enough for you to hit breakout.

Here are some suggestions:

1. Monitor your progress by the hour on first calls.

I've already given you a sample Call Sheet. This Call Sheet is built around the twenty-twenty plan. Twenty dials in twenty minutes. Yes, I know I've said forty dials an hour, but let's make it interesting and shoot for sixty. By putting your attention on the number of dials, you won't have time to think about whether you're succeeding with this person or that person. And that's the whole point.

Don't worry about how you're doing while you're doing it. That's why you're keeping records, so that later you can step back and look at them. If you're doing well, you'll feel good. If it's not working for you, you can begin to use the numbers you're generating to figure out why.

2. Keep to yourself.

This is a note of warning. I have observed in many cases that a group of salespeople will turn, almost savagely, on someone who threatens to move out and succeed on a grand scale. By succeeding, you'll be giving a slap in the face to those who have banded together at a low level of sales. And they don't like that. I have seen friendships dissolve, vicious rumors started, and things disappear off the desks of salespeople on the move. For whatever reason, the group you're in probably won't like it—or you—if you succeed.

So keep whatever plans you have for success to yourself. Don't make a big thing about what you're doing. Just quietly set out on your seven- or fourteen-hour-a-week plan, test your list, and so on. As success comes your way—which it must if you do all of the things outlined in this book—you might elect to share what you've been doing with a few select associates. But select them with care. If this sounds harsh, it's only because I have observed too many good people damaged by those who would remain in the mire of mediocrity.

3. Stick to your plan for at least twelve weeks.

It's too easy to quit at the five-yard line. Don't do it!

If It's Not Working

Dealing with ever-changing human beings as we do, there is certainly no guarantee that your first, or even tenth, approach is going to work and deliver the kind of results you want. Hopefully, by now you understand that I have not given you a ticket to success but rather the tools to build your own railroad. So in this section, let's pull it all together and learn how to use these tools to fix it if it's broke. Remember, however, *if it ain't broke, don't fix it.*

First, let's review the elements we have gone over to create a campaign. Then we'll look at them again, from a different point of view, and see how to use them to unstick a campaign that's stuck.

The Variables Revisited

Remember, we defined *variable* as anything over which the individual or company has control that can *change the outcome* of a prospecting or direct-marketing campaign. In prospecting or direct marketing, you need to learn to think with variables. We have spent virtually the entire book discussing them in detail. These variables are the analytical tools you'll use the most. You use them to plan a campaign, to correct it when it fails, and to lock it in when it succeeds.

Perhaps the concept can be grasped best from a story about a young man who didn't get the idea at all. In one of the very first classes I conducted in the securities industry, I had trained a stockbroker in Los Angeles (I'll call him Ernie). When Ernie went through my initial seminar, he seemed to be doing fine. He was bright, aggressive, and had a good voice; in short, he seemed to have everything going for him that it would take to succeed. At least, he had everything going that would help him succeed in opening new accounts. How he would manage those accounts, well, that can sometimes be a different story.

About two weeks after I first trained Ernie, I bumped into him in downtown Los Angeles. I remember our conversation well:

BILL: Ernie, how are you doing?

ERNIE: Not good.

BILL: What's happening?

ERNIE: Not much. I'm the only member of our class who hasn't sold anything yet.

BILL: Hmmmm. Sounds bad. Tell me what's going on?

ERNIE: They're just not buying.

BILL: Who's not buying?

ERNIE: The people I'm calling.

BILL: Who are you calling?

ERNIE: The Beverly Hills Yellow Pages.

BILL: Hmmmm. How long have you been calling the Beverly Hills Yellow Pages?

ERNIE: For the last two weeks. It's terrible. I can't even get anyone to talk to me.

BILL: You dough ball. You sat through my seminar and you've been calling the same list of jerks for an entire two weeks. Come with me.

I literally grabbed Ernie by the ear, hauled him into the office, and grabbed the North Long Beach Yellow Pages. "Here," I said. "Call these. At least in North Long Beach, the businesspeople are not in hock up to their eyebrows to the landlords. Plus you should know that practically any stockbroker, insurance agent, lightbulb salesperson is going to call the poor slobs in Beverly Hills because they are the first and most obvious people to have money. Their resistance is unbelievable. Throw them away."

Within an hour, Ernie had found a prospect who three days later bought $70,000 worth of bonds. As he reported to me, the difference in calling North Long Beach versus calling Beverly Hills was like calling a place where there were people versus some uninhabited wasteland of robots that answered the phone and were programmed to act like jerks.

So what was it Ernie missed? He missed the fact that *you can change your results by changing a variable!* I changed his list, and he went from poor results to excellent results!

A variable is something you control that affects the results of what you do. As we have seen, some of these variables affect the structure of the campaign. Some affect the execution. In Ernie's case, he could never get it off the ground because of a bad list. No matter how well he did the other things, the list would drag it down to defeat.

With that idea firmly in mind, let's take another look at the variables. We've studied them in detail. Now let's look at them in summary form. They are also embedded in your Campaign Development Checklist. The first five variables deal with creation of the campaign.

1. Who you call

This is your list of prospective customers. Some of your most dramatic changes in results will come from a change in your list.

2. Your campaign objective

This is what you are looking for. It's hot prospect, appointment, cherry, or someone willing to talk. Set it too high, and you'll get discouraged at how long it takes to find what you're looking for. Set it too low, and you can bury yourself with too many people with too low a qualification.

3. The style

This, of course, refers to the combination of media that describe how a campaign is run. While there are no hard-and-fast rules, by the time you have decided on your list and your campaign objective, you have a good idea of which style to use.

4. The offer

This is what you'll use to find interest. It's a desired end result someone might enjoy from owning your product or service. You use the offer in your letters, scripts, and sales presentations. Changes in the offer affect virtually every single letter and script in the campaign.

5. The message

This is your sales message, the exact words of your letters, and the exact wording of your scripts. Ideally, these embody your offer. If you want a fully developed campaign, I assure you there may be several letters and several scripts. Change your words on letters or scripts and I guarantee you'll change results, sometimes for the better, sometimes for the worse.

Once you have created your campaign, it's time to run it. This brings us to the two primary *execution* variables:

6. The numbers

How many letters and how many calls can you or should you stuff into your pipeline? The number of letters is related to your postage budget and, in the case of mail/phone, your ability to follow up. The number of calls is obviously related to the length of your message as well as your work flow. If you are making a long-winded call, you can't make very many of them. This is not necessarily to say that you shouldn't make long-winded calls, but your ability to do so effectively is governed by the quality of your list. If your list is just an average list, you really have to move through it quickly to find those cherries. But if it is a superb, well-researched list, not only can you spend a bit more time but you can achieve more per call.

The thing to be most concerned about is: how many calls per hour. Keep it at or above forty, and some magic will begin to happen.

7. Your sound

In telephone contact, where "sound" and "words" are the only means of communication, "sound" is very important. I have proven over and over again that you can have everything else right but miss on sound and all your good work elsewhere is a waste of time. Within just a very few seconds of picking up the phone, a prospect has made a snap judgment about whether to continue the call or not. That snap judgment, in my opinion, is based on *sound*.

Using Variables to Create a Campaign

Variables one through five are the ones you focus on when you're developing the campaign. Numbers six and seven are the variables you try and lock in to professional standards when you execute a campaign. With Sound and Numbers under control, you roll it out watching at all times for the number of prospects you generate per hour.

If you can't get two or three cherries an hour, change a variable. If, after several attempts, you can't bring in two at a minimum, go through the Basic Skills Checklist below. If you still can't get your three an hour, throw away your list—it just may be the worst list you have. Always weed your lists from the bottom up.

Basic Skills Checklist

If you can't make it work, take each of the points below and do whatever it takes to turn a no answer into a yes.

1. Are you able to get through to people and talk to them?

I've seen some people bog down right here. They've got a list that is unreachable. If you can't reach the people on your list, try the steps given below. If these don't work, try a direct-mail campaign to the list. It's for certain no one else is calling the list either.

a. Review the portion of your script that deals with secretaries. If you've been trying a standard method, switch and try the pre-approach phone call, message campaign, or buddy-buddy.

b. If none of these works, try simply asking for the direct extension number when the secretary says, "He's not interested," "not in," or whatever. Say, "That's fine. I'll call him first thing in the morning. What's his direct extension number?" And then try the prospect early in the morning.

c. Try alternate times during the day to get through.

2. Do you have a written script?

Please note that the question is not: Do you have a script? If you are making repetitive calls, you have one. But have you written it down? If you haven't, changes will begin to creep into your call, and before long, what may have started out as a tight, disciplined, one-minute phone call is now a blubbering, bloated call. If it's not written down, write it down.

3. Are you asking for "just the right amount of commitment" on your script?

Here we get into the difference between going for an appointment on the first call and going for a qualified prospect. It may be that you are asking too much. If you are, revise your script and use a multicall approach as outlined in Chapters 12 and 13.

4. Does your script offer a benefit?

I can't tell you how many scripts I've heard that offer the prospect absolutely nothing. People want a benefit! If they are going to give you some time or a commitment, you've got to give them something in return. Give them a benefit.

5. Does your script offer the *right* benefit?

If your script offers a benefit, and if you're finding people are still not interested, switch the benefit. There is no way to know on any one product which benefit is most likely to attract and hold immediate attention. So try several.

6. Are you sticking to the script?

Or are you getting off the script so much you might as well not have it? If you have made a long-winded first call, you can certainly expect that you will have difficulty making that second call. So make certain your first call is less than a minute and a half long.

7. Do you *qualify* for money now?

One of the first things people drop out of their first call is the "money question." For whatever reason, people are shy or embarrassed about qualifying for money. You have to do it. If you don't, you're going to fill up your callback file with pits and green cherries. Nothing against the poor, and quite frankly the poor may be your market, but they at least have to have enough money to buy your product. So if they don't have it, you don't want to talk to them.

8. Are you making at least forty dials of the phone an hour?

An important thing to understand here is that if you're getting three cherries an hour, you're doing it right. Sometimes you might make fewer calls than that and have lots of prospects. No problem. If you're getting three an hour, you're doing it right. But if you're not getting three an hour and are making fewer than forty calls an hour, that ain't right. Press for dials. Implement the twenty-twenty plan.

9. Do you sound good?

If the answer to this is yes, great! But you should go at least a step further and check these separate points of your sound:

- Do you sound sour, as if you've been sucking a lemon?
- Is your inflection such that you sound uncertain and hesitant?
- Are you talking faster than your prospect?
- Are you talking more slowly than your prospect?
- Do you sound bored?
- Does your presentation sound canned?

To get an objective opinion, tape-record your calls and play them for someone you trust. You might even play them for people who are not in sales and ask what they think. Remember, most of these problems can be cured simply by rehearsal.

If you're unable to handle these problems on your own, I recommend very strongly that you take some voice lessons. I would actually call the drama department of a local school, college, or university. Get a good drama coach. Speech therapists are for those with severe handicaps. In the late 1960s, I took a few lessons from a drama coach to help me overcome some of the heavier sounds in my southern accent. I still have parts of it, but it was so heavy that people would ask me, "What part of the South are you from?" That got very old, and as a professional public speaker, I did not want people sitting there trying to figure out where I was from instead of listening to what I was saying. The drama coach cured it in no time.

10. Are you using a good list?

The only way to know if your list is good or bad is to isolate it as a variable. First, be sure that you have a good script for it, that you're making enough calls to it, that you sound good, and are calling and can get through. If you're getting two cherries an hour, you won't throw the list out. You'll work to replace it. Go spend more time on list development while keeping your calling campaign going. As soon as you've developed a list that can produce three cherries an hour, package up the one that will do two an hour and shoot it over to your competitor.

11. Are you setting appointments on your second call?

You should be getting 40 to 50 percent of your cherries to set up appointments with you. If not, check the following points:

- Are you calling back within five business days?
- Are you mutilating your material?
- Are you using your bypass principle as the introduction to your second call?
- Have you even written a second-call script?
- Does it contain an ABC close, and is the benefit in the close an actual benefit or just a feature?
- Are you setting your appointments as close as possible to right now?
- If they are set more than five business days away, do you confirm each appointment in writing and then with a phone call the day before?

The sale begins when the salesperson says yes.

Elmer Letterman wrote one of the classics of the Old School, called *The Sale Begins When the Customer Says No.* If you have followed me this far, you know what I think of this idea. But the question Letterman answered in his book is a valid one: Where does the sale begin?

If you have fully understood prospecting *primarily as an act of discarding,* then you know the answer intuitively. The sale begins when you have attempted to discard and cannot. To put it another way, the sale begins when you, the salesperson, say, "Yes, you're worth spending my selling time with." This will exist only when the prospect has the interest, the money, and the capability to buy NOW. You then switch from prospecting mode to selling mode.

As I mentioned earlier, this switch from prospecting to selling mode can easily occur after you introduce yourself. But it may not occur until after several in-person meetings. While you're prospecting, you're asking in all their dozens of forms the three basic prospecting questions: Are you interested enough? Can you afford it? Can you buy it? When you have answered these questions with a *yes,* you can start to sell the product.

What Is Selling?

Let's define selling as showing your product or service to qualified prospects in such a way that you increase their desire for it to the point they want it badly enough to part with their money. Quite obviously, then, selling skills are very different from prospecting skills, which have been the subject of this book. Among them are:

- Interviewing skills

(Some trainers use the phrase "probing skills," but I reject that on personal grounds because I don't like to be "probed." And I don't think anyone else does either.) As a professional salesperson, you will need to interview your prospects to find out exactly which of your products or services they should buy first.

- Personal presentation skills

By this I mean your dress, style, and personal mannerisms, which can go a long way toward making—or blowing—a sale.

- People watching skills

These are skills you learn by calling or seeing in person *hundreds or thousands of people.* When I'm talking with someone by phone, I can see them. And I know when to close for the order.

- Product presentation skills

These are the skills you use to further increase interest and involvement. Most specifically, you'll want to concentrate on presenting the benefits of your product or service that most closely align with the prospect's goals.

- Closing skills

These are the skills that enable the salesperson to get the prospect to make up his or her mind. Very literally, the word "close" means "to bring to a conclusion." It does not mean "sell" or "cause to buy." After you have done your very best in your presentation, you want the prospect to make up his or her mind, one way or the other. It's not the word "no" that kills off countless thousands of salespeople. It's "maybe." Closing skills enable you to convert some of the "maybes" into "yes" and the rest into "no." No more "maybe."

- Objection handling skills

Once you have decided that someone is a qualified prospect, you are no longer trying to discard them as you do when you prospect. Your entire frame of mind changes to one of "keep 'em." So you will need to answer objections in order to keep the sale going. In prospecting, when someone tells you, "I'm not interested," with the exceptions already noted, you let them go. But in selling, when they say, "I don't think I'm interested now," you don't just get up and leave. You find out why, attempt to handle the problem, and thereby rekindle interest and your sale.

Some Final Thoughts

Well, I've given it my best shot. If you want, you can go on and read the last chapter. You might learn a thing or two if you're just in sales itself. You might even decide that management is a place you'd like to be.

I would like to say this as a final observation. This system is definitely designed to generate too many prospects. Here's why. There are only three possibilities regarding the number of prospects:

1. You can have too many.

2. You can have too few.

3. You can have just the right number.

Needless to say, you'll never have just the right number. It's not going to happen. Having too few prospects is starvation for a salesperson. So my program is designed to generate too many. If the number you're generating literally overwhelms you, rejoice. But don't cut back on the number of hours you're calling. Instead, you may want to increase the qualification level. If you're an insurance salesman, instead of qualifying for ability to handle a $100-a-month premium, go for $200. Since all you have is your time, ultimately, the only way to make more money is to spend it better. And for a salesperson that means spending it, first with more prospects and then with more highly qualified prospects. Otherwise, you'll top out before you get rich. And after all, isn't getting rich why we all came into this business?

So, as we say on my end, Thankyouverymuch for reading this book. I hope you enjoyed it. I hope you use it. *(Click. Dial tone.)*

CHAPTER 21

For Managers Only

How to Work Magic with Your Sales Force

In this chapter I'll go over some ways a manager can help salespeople. As a salesperson, you can quite obviously learn something from this chapter. But it is designed primarily for the manager.

Most of the following techniques evolved over the two years before I started my own company. This period was my training ground. It all started while I was sitting in my car in a four-and-a-half-hour gas line during the second Arab oil boycott. At the time, I was the editor of a small magazine that catered to the restaurant trade. We were so undercapitalized that in order to pay the printing bill, we literally had to collect the money for our advertising in advance.

Now, I don't know if you know much about restaurant owners, but they are an odd lot at best. Most of them are broke, and the only time you can really talk to them is during lunch and dinner. But then they've got customers and problems in the kitchen, and so forth. So to sell our ads and get our money, we had to grab the owners during meals and sit 'em down. Then we at least had a chance to sell and get the check.

When the oil boycott began, we were in deep trouble and knew it. In Los Angeles at that time, you could only get gas every other day. And then you had to wait for hours. Given the distances one had to drive to get anywhere in Los Angeles, if you had one of the big old clunkers, a tank of gas would be gone in an afternoon.

So there I was, just off Franklin Avenue, sitting in a gas line and watching my job swirl down the drain. As I sat there, the thought in my mind was "There's got to be something else I can do." And then, like some kind of flash, I had it! I saw the gasoline problems getting worse. I saw prices going out of sight. And somehow I saw a lot of changes were in store for marketing and sales.

Within a very few days I had decided it was time for a change. I didn't see my writing career going anywhere. I had been able to survive, but I spent more time writing about people making and enjoying their money than I did making it myself.

So I quit my job at the magazine, pulled out the classified ads of the *Los Angeles Times,* and got a job in telephone sales. And what I know today about managing and training large numbers of telephone sales-people really began with that first job.

In the pages that follow, I'm going to share with you some of the ideas that enabled me to go from nowhere to a position of considerable influence in several industries. First, of course, I had to develop the technique—and we have talked about that at length in this book. But I also had to learn the *management* of the technique. That's what we'll talk about now.

As you read, try to separate style from substance. As a manager, I have my own style. It's fairly loose, upbeat, and with a good measure of theatrics thrown in. But beneath the style, there is substance. Perhaps the style makes the substance more palatable. But it is the substance that made it all work.

Not the Company Way

My first sales job was with a little company that has long ceased to exist. Perhaps their training program had something to do with their disappearance. It was all of an hour long. It consisted of a sales manager telling me, "Bill, here's the price list. There's your desk. That's the telephone. And here's where we keep all the Yellow Pages. Here is a copy of the script. If you have any questions, come and see me. You get paid every two weeks." I am sure there were a couple of other things thrown in, but this I can tell you for certain: After I was trained, I didn't know any more than when I started.

So I stood in my little office for a few moments, and then I went back to my manager. I asked him if it was OK if I didn't start making calls that day. "Steve," I said, "I'd like to listen to a few of the people around here before I get started and see if I can learn what they're doing. Who around here is making some money?"

Steve pointed to a man sitting not far from where my desk was. So I went over and introduced myself. He said his name was Don. I asked if it was all right if I spent an hour or two just listening to what he was doing. He said, "No problem."

So for two or three hours I listened to what Don said and did. I made a lot of notes. And it didn't take long to discover that what Don was doing was not the "official company way." Don had developed something quite different, and as I listened to him and wrote down what he was saying, I figured that instead of doing it the company way, I would do it Don's way. My assumption was that if I did what Don was doing, I would probably make a lot of money.

That assumption was right on the money. As I got to work over the next few days, I shot past all of the other new salespeople. From my first teacher, Don, I learned what may be the most important principle of all:

☞ *Find out what's working now and do that.*

If It Works, Make 'Em Do It

After about six months at that job, I decided to make a move into management. So I scouted around for a company where I might launch a "takeover." I found one with a lot of empty space, a good product, a decent management, but no sales management. I began telling people how much money I was making and very quickly I got a flow of people coming in the door asking for jobs. All of a sudden, the general manager was flooded with people and was getting quite overworked. So I went to him, told him he had a problem, and suggested that he promote me to sales manager to solve the problem of what to do with all these people. He agreed. I had the job.

At this time, my new company was largely an order-desk operation with a backroom telephone crew added on as an afterthought. As I recall, there were thirteen scruffy salespeople when I arrived. When I left, about two and a half years later to start Telephone Marketing Association (later renamed Bill Good Marketing), there were over eighty in a brand-new building that the owner had been forced to build in order to house this monster I created.

One of the early things I learned in my sales management career was actually taught to me by a young lady I had hired. Her name was Carey. As I began building my crew, I would write up various product descriptions and closes. With eighty to a hundred products, I soon had quite a pile of paper.

Carey was a promising saleswoman. But her production tended to fluctuate wildly week by week. I didn't know the cause, nor did she. One day as I passed her desk, I noticed her with a pile of 4×6 note cards, a pair of scissors, my product descriptions, and a pot of rubber cement. She was pasting the product descriptions and closes on cards.

"Carey, what are you doing?" I asked her.

She replied that she had noticed that whenever she stuck to the scripts, she made more money. But, she told me, "It's impossible to use all these scraps of paper you've written. So I'm pasting them up on some cue cards." I found that *very* interesting. So I kept a close eye on what she was doing.

Very shortly after getting her cue cards together, Carey's sales graph began to climb off the chart.

Up to this time, I had not really fully learned my lesson from Don. To be sure, I had learned it as a salesman. But I had not seen its full application as a manager. In my own sales, I would not consider ad-libbing or winging a sales talk, but I had taken a laissez-faire attitude toward my salespeople and assumed that they would adapt what I had written to their style. Everyone, I thought, should have his or her own style. Today, I know that idea to be rubbish, and it was really Carey who made me see it.

Not long after her sales began to climb off the chart, I sat down in my office with cards, paper, rubber cement, and scissors and put together five sets of cue cards. I brought in five of my lower-performing salespeople and told them that we had a new way of doing things. And for two or three hours, I rehearsed them on the cue cards and then sent them off to see what they could do. Without exception, their sales increased. And before long, everyone but my top performers had their own set of cue cards. And sales went up substantially.

Don had taught me something very important as a salesman. Carey taught me something as a manager. Added together the principle became:

☞ *Find out what's working now and do that. Then get everyone who is not making enough money to do it also.*

To put it another way, I no longer believe a salesperson is entitled to do it his or her own way. As a manager, your job is to get people making money. So I would tell them:

☞ *If you're in the bottom 80 percent, you do it my way. Not until you're in the top 20 percent can you afford your own style.*

How to Stay in Touch with Your Sales Crew

To know if they're doing it your way, you have to stay in touch. You have to know what your top performers are doing, what your new people are doing, and even what your old mossback sluggards are doing. How else can you improve performance? And perhaps even more important, your crew has to know that you know and know that you care. Here's how I learned that lesson.

Very early, when there were fewer than twenty of us, it was no big deal for me to get around and talk to each person several times a day. I thus had a good feeling for who was doing well and who wasn't. And at the beginning of each week, I would sit down and make a list of all my salespeople, look at what they had done the previous week, estimate what they could do the current week, and set a goal for making more sales than the previous week.

But as we grew past twenty, there were too many people. I could not necessarily talk to each person each day, and that began to present a problem. My planning fell apart because I didn't know who was doing what and who needed what when. So I established a daily report system. I decided on a daily report since by Friday the week is already gone and there is nothing you can do about it. I liked to know by the day, and in some cases by the hour, how people were doing.

So I came up with a simple form (similar to the chart in Chapter 19), which each member of my crew would fill out daily. It was to be labeled Daily/Weekly Report and put in a basket on my desk. Each day I would review it and hand it back. At the end of the week, I would file it in the person's personnel folder. Everyone would cooperate and no problem. Right? (A sample copy of the form is shown on page 271.) Easier said than done.

It took me about six weeks of cajoling, threatening, cutting off sources of lead cards, and attempts of bribery and coercion to establish the habit that people were going to keep their statistics and turn them in to me daily.

Once I got them doing it, this simple Daily/Weekly Report became very important to me, and perhaps even more important to my sales crew. It enabled me to know where to spend my management time, and it served to alert me to problems before they became disasters. To my sales crew, it seemed to be a way of letting them know someone cared.

One week, for whatever reason, I got a bit lazy and didn't turn the reports back on time. There was a storm of protest. People came up to me and asked, "Didn't you see how I did yesterday?" And that question came from people who had done well and wanted me to know it and from those who did poorly and needed help. That was the last time I failed to turn back the reports.

Looking back, my Daily/Weekly Report was just one of many channels with which my crew and I delivered and received communication. Some were formal, such as the Daily/Weekly Report. But others were informal and were perhaps even more important than the formal channels. One of the most important channels was the simple act of handing out lead cards.

In my office I had a giant file cabinet that would hold probably twenty-five thousand prospect names printed on 3×5 cards. I had access to more than three-quarters of a million such names stored in our computer. One of my jobs as sales manager was to make certain that people had enough names to call but not so many that they could hoard and thereby deprive others of good prospects. So I would typically give out twenty-five to fifty cards at a time. With eighty people doing at least some cold calling all the time, there would be days I couldn't even leave my office for a break without someone shouting at me, "Hey, Bill, don't go yet. I need some more cards." As you can well imagine, it was very difficult to get other work done.

One day, I got the bright idea to take my big filing cabinet and move it to my assistant's office and let her give out the lead cards. So I got two or three big strapping guys, a dolly, and we moved the cabinet into her office. And the trek of salespeople wearing holes in the carpet to my office was diverted to her office. At last I had some peace and could get some work done.

Just as I required all of my salespeople to post their commissions on a graph, I posted two graphs in my office, one on new accounts and the other on commissions. That week both graphs dropped. I didn't think too much about that because I was always able to get the graph up again. As a matter of fact, for one six-month period there were only two two-week periods where either graph dropped two weeks in a row. This was one of those times. The other was when I was out sick.

So I was beating my brains to figure out what I had changed that would cause those graphs to go down. I had the same number of salespeople. We were selling the same products. To the same types of companies. Using the same script. The number of calls made was in line. The only thing I could think of was that . . . I had moved the lead file into my assistant's office!

So I moved it back. Sales promptly went up. I concluded that the "lead line" where salespeople came to me personally to get new lead cards had been an important source of information on how they were doing. As they came into my office, I would read smiles, frowns, and other subtle signs and quite frequently send one back with a tape recorder to make a tape of his calls. When I moved the lead file, that line fell out, and with it I lost a significant amount of "touch" with my sales force.

From then on, the lead file stayed with me.

The principle I gleaned from this experience was:

☞ *There should be as many channels of communication between sales-people and manager as possible. The informal channels are just as important as the formal ones.*

Check the Whites of Their Eyes

There are four major problems that can wipe out otherwise good sales-people. I got on the trail of one of them in an effort to track down what I came to call the one-bad-day-a-week phenomenon. I noticed that almost everyone in my sales crew would have one bad day a week—sometimes two. When I gave it a bit more thought, I realized that those bad days were costing me about 20 percent of my sales. So I began to try to find out why a person would have a bad day.

To do this, I did everything I could think of. When one of my sales-people would hit a bad day, I would put him or her on tape. I would sit in their offices with them. I would work on their list, their presentation, their sound, and all the other variables we have discussed in this book.

Some of these bad days disappeared, but there was a hard core I couldn't crack. One day I was sitting in my office talking to a chap who had had two bad days in a row. He sounded good, was making lots of calls, his list was fine; in short, I didn't have a clue as to why he was hav-ing a bad day. As I looked at him, I noticed his eyes were a bit bloodshot, so I asked him, "Mike, how much sleep did you get last night?"

"Plenty."

"That's not what I asked. What time did you go to bed?"

"About two o'clock."

"And what time did you get up?"

"About five-thirty."

"Mike, get out of here. And don't come back until you've had a good night's rest." And I threw him out.

The next day he came back and I performed what later came to be called the white-of-the-eyes check. I grabbed him, jerked his head back, pulled his eyelids open, and he looked OK. I then asked him how much sleep he had had, and he said, "ten hours." I put him back on the phone, and he did fine.

Was I ever interested in this!

So I prowled around the sales halls looking for people not doing well. I found five. One of them I sorted out, and the other four got sent home for exhaustion. It took one of them two days to come back. They all did as well or better than they had been doing before the bad day.

Conclusion:

☞ *Lack of sleep kills salespeople. If you can't find any other explanation for a bad day, find out about sleep.*

There is another, perhaps related, phenomenon you should know about. If your business is generated through inside sales or just inside lead generation, this situation could well apply to you. In analyzing when our sales occurred, I would find in many cases that 30 to 40 percent would occur in the first hour of the day and the balance in the last five to six hours. Now, that just didn't make a lot of sense to me. So in checking it out, I found that people were not taking breaks. So I simply made it a policy that you could take your breaks in one of two ways: either ten minutes every hour, or after the second sale (or lead if your team is focusing on generating leads). I learned this from one of the best salesmen I ever knew. Very early in my own sales career, he took me aside and told me, "Bill, let me tell you how you can double your income. Whenever you make the first sale, don't put down the phone. Keep calling. You're hot then. Take your break after the second one. In many cases, sales come in pairs."

Truer words were never spoken, and to this day, this is a principle I try to apply in my own sales. When I'm hot, I keep at it.

The objective is to have several "first hours" during the day.

☞ *Make certain your crew takes frequent breaks. Try to encourage them to stay on the phone just after they find a prospect, set up an appointment, or close a sale. There's another one where that one came from.*

Here's another important point: Very early in my own selling career, I noticed that when I was hungry, I didn't seem to do as well. Evidently, actual physical hunger translates into a sound that prospects identify as a "hungry salesman." Rather than gorge on pizza and beer, I recommend that a salesperson eat something before spending a couple of hours on the phone, and then if you feel your energy level begin to drop, get a snack.

☞ *Don't let 'em prospect hungry. Keep the blood sugar up and avoid the "hungry salesman sound."*

Finally, one of the worst killers of salespeople is domestic strife. I can't tell you how many salespeople I have seen go down the chute in the midst of quarrelsome bickering at home. My only solution to this is to get both warring parties into your office and negotiate a truce. I had one salesman whom I had nurtured and cultured and trained to prove I could train anyone. And then all of a sudden he and his young wife went at each other. I called them both in my office and when they were both seated I turned to my salesman and told him, "Mike, you're fired." His face turned white, his wife drew her lips together, and I just sat there and shut up. She finally broke the silence and asked, "Why?"

And I told them: "You guys are at each other's throat and it's got Mike so upset that he can't sell. And he's no use to me. So he's fired." And I again shut up.

Finally, she said, "We'll stop fighting."

"That's what I hoped you'd say," I replied.

And so I pulled out an agreement I had already typed up and presented it to them for their signature. The agreement said that they would only fight from 5:00 p.m. on Friday to 6:00 p.m. on Sunday and would not fight during the week. I told them if they didn't sign it and if his sales didn't recover, he was looking for a job. They signed the agreement and stopped the shooting. Mike's sales recovered quite well.

Hiring New Salespeople

In telemarketing, whether in direct sales or prospecting, there is a notoriously high turnover. As far as I can tell, the reasons for it is that people don't make the kind of money they're promised or they just can't do the job. So they leave (or get asked to leave) and look elsewhere.

Turnover varies from industry to industry. I've heard that in some of the lead companies in the securities industry it's about 60 percent of new hires. In insurance it's well over 80 percent. In real estate it's probably over 80 percent. And so management is constantly faced with the need to recruit.

Early in my sales management career, I had the false idea that I somehow had the ability to spot the people who would succeed and those who would fail . . . all on the basis of an interview. Once my boss told me to hire a friend of his. After I had interviewed him, I went back to my boss and told him I didn't want to hire him. I said, "The guy's been out of work for two years, is demoralized, and the only thing I see happening is that he's going to get in here and demoralize the rest of the crew. I don't want to hire him."

"It's my company," he said, "hire him."

"Yes, sir."

Within a matter of days, it was obvious he would be a screaming success. So I decided then and there that I didn't know how to detect in advance whether a person had the ability to do this job, and quite frankly I don't think anyone else does either. A lot of people, mostly shrinks, make a lot of money testing recruits to see if they are suited for sales. Frankly, I don't think they have a clue as to who will succeed and who won't. They may be screening out as many successes as failures.

Make no mistake. This is a very real problem for sales management. In the securities industry, it may cost from $40,000 to $60,000 to train one recruit. Certainly you want to know whether that person has a reasonable chance for success. To be sure, in many industries a person has to have a certain intelligence level in order to comprehend a sometimes bewildering amount of technical material. Intelligence tests do seem to be able to screen for this. But the ability to handle the rough-and-tumble and rejection of a prospecting and selling career cannot, to my knowledge, be adequately tested. I know too many people who literally failed the test, had a branch manager go to bat for them, and then became wildly successful. The test misses some X factor. There is something the shrinks cannot test for.

So how do you decide to hire someone? The solution I came to, and which I have been recommending for several years now, is what I call the audition. Why not give potential salespeople a chance to audition for the job? Give them a short training course and let them prospect for an established salesperson. It does not follow that a person who can find new business can then close it. But it is certainly the case that if prospective salespersons *cannot* find new business, they cannot succeed in most sales careers unless assigned a territory that has established accounts.

So, as part of your hiring procedure, you need at least enough time to train the prospective employee enough to prospect. Explain that you want them to have a chance to find out what the work is actually like and that if they don't succeed in this part of it, they won't succeed elsewhere. I would recommend you pay them for their time, and at the end of their probationary period, you have a second interview and review what they think as well as let them know what you think of their chances for success.

How to Keep Them Down on the Farm (or the Phones Dialing)

One important tool for managers is certainly exhortation. By this I mean the manager needs to constantly urge his or her sales force to keep the phones dialing. But after days, weeks, or months of exhortation, it gets old and tiresome. So here are two methods you can use that will supplement or replace the simple need for continuous cheerleading.

If you yourself have gathered a good supply of lists, you can use the "list test." You take fifty names from a list, go by one of your salesperson's desks, plop them down, and say, "Fred, I want you to call these names, keep track of them, and let me know the results. It's a new list. Have the results in my office in a couple of hours. Thanks." Then you walk away. Needless to say, Fred has to make the calls in order to do the test.

Or try the tape ploy: When you see one of your salespeople gazing out the window with a far-off and glazed look, grab a tape recorder and go over to the desk. (All the phones in a salesroom should be wired to record calls. Depending on the nature of your phone system, you may be able to do this with an inexpensive device from Radio Shack called an inline tap. Or you may have to call your telephone system vendor and have them wire one or more telephones with a little pigtail that can be plugged into the mic socket of a tape recorder. For inside salespeople, there is no better training device than to be able to hear how they sound. Naturally, you should check with your in-house lawyer regarding the legality to do this in your area.)

Start hooking up the phone and tell the salesperson you're a little concerned, and that you'd like him or her to make a tape of the calls. Put a two-hour cassette in the recorder and ask him or her to please bring it to your office when it's done. Then walk away. To make a tape, they've got to make the calls.

Some sales managers have figured out that you can use a tape recorder as a time clock. Let's say you've told several of your salespeople to come in to make calls at night and you have other engagements. Give each of them a two-hour tape, and tell them that you'd like the tape on your desk the next morning. You don't have to tell them, of course, that you're using this as a way to check on their work. Your attitude should be that you want to help them, and the only way you can do that is if you have a tape. But you also know, in your heart of hearts, that the real objective is to get them making the calls.

Magic

Some of the principles we've talked about so far would come under the heading of good management. They are really routine actions. And certainly a lot of routine actions can create a wonderful sales force. But to create a legend, a place that's fun and exciting to work, well, you need something more than routine actions. You need some magic. What's magic? Theater, perhaps. Games. Surprises. Toughness. You need constant elements of unpredictability inserted into the humdrumness of routine. And magic creates money.

Contests

You can really work some magic with a good contest. Let's face it, no matter what you say or preach, a certain monotony can set in for any workforce that must do repetitive actions (cold calling, for example) on a daily basis. The monotony can and will be offset by success, but even so, it is important that the manager introduce change so as to control it. Certain things, of course, we don't want to change. So we better have change elsewhere.

Contests can be one of the best elements of controlled change, and it's for this reason that I have never really liked long ones. To be an effective change element, a contest cannot last long. When a contest goes on for a long period of time, it becomes part of the landscape. It is, therefore, no change. And unless the prize is substantial, a contest really doesn't offer much incentive to do something that you would not do anyway. A contest, then, can just cost money instead of make money.

Short-term contests, however, can definitely sweeten things up. For maximum effectiveness, the prize should generally not be cash but still something your people want. Every salesperson knows that if he or she gets just some extra money, taxes will get a bite and the rest of it will go to pay the overdue utility bill. And so he or she really doesn't have anything extra. Cash, interestingly, does not provide the best motivation available.

As I am in the process of rewriting this book, I can report on the overwhelming success of a noncash-prize contest. December for us has always been a hard month to deal with. We're always looking for something that will excite and motivate the troops. Well, I took the cover off the ball on our most recent December. Here's what happened.

On December 1, at a meeting for the entire company, I told the staff that if we made our sales target for the month by December 24, I would give everyone two days off after Christmas. Boom! I have never seen an effect like that. I frankly had no idea they would make it, but on the twenty-fourth, they sailed past the target by many thousands of dollars. And then, just to prove it wasn't a fluke, in the two remaining days before the end of the month, we had our second highest day ever and a record December.

What did it cost me? Nothing, really, because I absolutely know we would not have hit that target had not everyone been looking over my sales crew's shoulder asking, "How are we doing?"

So how do you find out what they want? Simple. Guess, as I did. Or ask. My old boss, who was as tightfisted as they come, told me one time that I could have $200 to spend on a prize. Big deal. I gave a lot of thought to what prize to offer, and when I didn't come up with anything that really rang my bell, I sent out a memo to all my salespeople asking them to write down a prize they'd like to have that cost around $200.

Lots of answers came back. I went through them all and wrote down any answer that was mentioned more than once. There were six or eight of them. On another memo, I asked my crew to vote on which of those items they would most like to have as a prize. When I tabulated their answers, the one that came out on top was a racing bicycle. It was a prize I would never have guessed. But it seemed to be what the people wanted. So I bought one, put it in the salesroom, and announced the contest. I then witnessed one of the most amazing phenomenon I have ever seen. After a while, the contest was down to just a few people. They were working more hours, coming in earlier, staying later, messing around less. Some were making far more money than they ever had before, and any one of them could certainly have bought the blasted bicycle with their increased earnings. Winning may not be everything, but it was certainly the only thing that counted for this bunch. As we rolled into the last week, it was a slugfest. Some people were working twelve to fourteen hours a day to win the bike.

Certainly, part of the magic of contests is the prize. But the other part seems to be the possibility of winning. To make certain I got as many players as possible, I handicapped my top performers by making everyone compete against his or her own previous best effort. This gave the new kids on the block a chance to make a run at the old kids. And it was a new kid who took the prize.

☞ *The first magic principle: You can buy a lot of sales for a little money if everyone gets a chance to win and if you offer something that people really want.*

Magic Cards

Very soon after I took over as sales manager, I put a box by the door to my office so salespeople could throw in lead cards they didn't want. Before long it became known as the junk card box. Every once in a while I would go through it, sort it out, and give them out again. No one ever knew the difference.

One day, for no apparent reason, I got an idea. I wanted to see if I could turn junk cards into "magic cards." So I closed the door to my office, dumped the cards out on the floor, sorted through them, and pulled out certain types of cards in certain geographical areas that I felt were probably OK. I then took those cards, put them in a file box that had a lock on it, and put the box on my desk. I took a black marker, and I wrote the words "Magic Cards" on the file box and just left it sitting on my desk.

It was only a few days before someone asked, "Bill, what on earth are those?"

My reply was "Don't you touch my cards. They're my solution to you. If you all decide to fail in this business, I'll take that box of cards and go and make some money with it. As a matter of fact, you shouldn't even be allowed to be in the same room with these cards. They are magic. Now get out of here."

Needless to say, he went out immediately to the other salespeople and told them I had slipped mentally again. Before long, someone else came into my office on some pretext or other and made some crack about the magic cards. I threw him out as well. Over the next two or three days, several people made unkind comments. I just smiled, grabbed the box, and stuffed it in the drawer, making a big show of throwing each person out of the office because they had referred to my magic cards in an unpleasant manner.

I let this run for several days. Then one day I was having a talk with one of my salespeople who was having a run of bad luck. All of a sudden I looked over at him and asked, "Tom, would you like to try some of my magic cards?"

He brightened up and said yes.

"All right," I said, "down on your knees and beg." And I made him beg for some magic cards. While he was still down on his knees, I very carefully counted out twenty-five cards, had him place his hands on the cards, and close his eyes. I then proceeded to bless the cards. I asked him, "All the bad vibes gone?"

"Oh, yes," he replied.

"All right," I said, "get the hell out of here and go make some sales."

He came back in fifteen minutes or so with a great big smile on his face and said, "It worked!" He showed me the order he had just written. And so the parade started. Everyone wanted some magic cards. But I would give them out maybe only once or twice a day to someone who was having some serious problems. And usually they worked. All of which brings us to the definition of a "great list."

☞ *A great list is simply a good list in which people believe. And belief must be created and sustained by the manager.*

Certainly I am not the only one to have identified this principle. I have never seen it written anywhere, but many good sales managers have grasped it almost instinctively. One of my very good friends in the brokerage industry is a former training director of one of the major firms. He had the concept of magic down cold. When he was a branch manager in Milwaukee, he used to hire high school students to come into the office on Saturday mornings. They would copy names and phone numbers onto note cards from the street address directory. During the week, when brokers would be having a bad day, they would come and ask for some of Hank's "special lists." Everyone agreed that his cards were much better than the street address directory. He was often accused of using the street address directory as his source but he would never confess to where the names came from. He just told everyone that if he let them know where the names came from, everyone would go and get them and he would lose control of his source.

☞ *The second magic principle:* *Actions that build belief are magic.*

If you wish people to believe something is valuable, act as if it is. I know one sales manager who keeps his list locked in a big file cabinet with a steel reinforcing bar bolted to the cabinet.

The Magic Tape Recorder

I forget exactly when I discovered the principle of the magic tape recorder. Nor do I recall who my guinea pig was, but I do remember very distinctly telling someone to make me a tape of his calls, and then having him run right back in and tell me he just got a sale.

That happened a few more times. So I went out and bought five tape recorders and whenever anyone was having a bad day, I would have them make a tape. In many cases I would never even listen to the tape, because once they started making the tape, they would quit doing things that they had been doing and do it the correct way—my way!

For the magic tape recorder to work, you must first have a prospecting and sales method that works. You also need to have demonstrated that you will crawl down the throat of salespeople who stray from the successful method. Given those two ingredients, when someone is having a bad day you simply tell them to make a tape. And they'll quit doing those things that they know you'll crawl down their throat for and start doing things correctly. After a while, especially if you make a few comments about your magic tape recorders, your crew will make remarks about your sanity. But when they're not doing well, they'll come and ask if they can borrow your recorder. And they'll do this even if they have one of their own right in their office.

☞ *The third magic principle:* *A little magic goes a long way.*

The Magic of Average

Nobody wants to be average. Not even the people who are. Or those who are below average. But there is some magic in "the average" that a sales manager can use to raise it. Here's how it works:

A few weeks after I was appointed sales manager, I asked the computer operator to give me a production run of my salespeople's previous couple of months. As I studied it, I realized it was quite a miserable, scruffy bunch. The average worker was making about $175 a week. When I divided that by five and did a little rounding, I concluded that the average salesperson was making less than $35 a day. Without giving it much thought, I decided that anyone making less than that was in serious need of retraining. My average became *the minimum acceptable.* So I announced that anyone who made less than $35 on any given day would attend an obligatory meeting the next day at 9:45 in the morning. And that was that. No questions about it. This later became known as the *bornyak* meeting. I came to define a "bornyak" as the lowest known form of human life that had only recently been discovered because it had such a short life expectancy. And lo and behold, there were some bornyaks working for me and they could be identified because they made less than $35 a day and were in danger of imminent starvation.

In their efforts to avoid the stigma of being called bornyaks and being forced to attend a bornyak meeting, those below average began to achieve the minimum. And arithmetically, of course, the average shot up.

Every manager knows that salespeople need individual goals to achieve. Very few know how to help the salesperson set the goal. It's absolutely senseless to speak to someone about "shooting for a goal of $3,000 a week" if the most he or she has ever made is $12,000 a year. You might as well talk about eliminating the national debt.

To be achievable, a goal has to be real. And it is my belief that to those below average, the average of the group *is very real.* And so in my first efforts at goal setting, I happened upon a highly successful formula that was to set a *minimum* for those below average to achieve. And that minimum was the average of the group.

What about those above average? Take the production of the above-average group and average it. The new minimum acceptable for this group is roughly 25 percent higher than the average for those below. And so on with your top 25 percent. The two or three salespeople on top are given a *minimum* of their previous best efforts. As each works to achieve the minimum, you'll see the average of the entire group go up dramatically. And, presto chango, you have an entirely new set of minimums. It's magic.

☞ *The fourth magic principle: Give the individual members of a group a minimum acceptable level. Hold a torch under them, and then get out of the way.*

Building Stars

I once hired a young man I didn't really want to hire. He kept coming around pestering me for a job, and so I finally decided to let him have a try at it just to get him off my back. He was sensational. I made a tape of his calls one day, just for my own education, and shortly thereafter, a new trainee asked me if he could listen to someone. So I gave him "Bill Loman's" tape. (My new salesman had a last name that was fairly hard to pronounce and decided to invent his own name. In a flash of inspiration, he first called himself Willy Loman, after the character in *Death of a Salesman*. Too many people were familiar with that, and he changed it to Bill Loman. Throughout tens of thousands of calls, only one person, to my knowledge, ever called him on it.)

After the new salesperson listened to Bill's tape and heard him rack up several hundred dollars in commissions in just a few calls, he was, understandably, excited about coming to work. So I got him signed up and started on his training. Later that afternoon, he came up to me and pointed to someone in the hall and said, "Is that Bill Loman?" I said it was, and took him over and introduced him.

There was a little magic that happened there. Bill was more than flattered, and my new salesperson was in awe. And over a period of many months thereafter, the Bill Loman tape was a very important part of my training program. Not only did it serve to train the new people, but it gave me a tool to constantly enhance and reinforce the "great salesman image" that Bill quite rightly deserved.

Yes, rewards and plaques and trips and special badges and corner offices are all important to the sometimes all-too-fragile ego of salespeople. But if you really want to help build a solid self-image for a salesperson, deliberately use your better salespeople as role models for your up-and-comers.

☞ *The fifth magic principle: Once held up as a role model and preserved on audio- or videocassette, no salesperson will ever fall back to a point where the honor is no longer deserved.*

The Magic of Product Knowledge

The question about product knowledge is: How much is enough? This really brings us to the question: Why do you need to know? In my experience, salespeople need product training for one reason: to build belief and certainty that the product is good. If the salesperson believes in the product, and if he or she is also secure in the knowledge that the product will solve the customer's problem, then he or she really doesn't need to know very much more. All he needs is to *believe*.

Let me give a very simple example. One of my very first clients was a company that sold central air-conditioning to homeowners. It was a pretty hard-sell outfit and has since gone by the boards. My job was to work with and train the soliciting crew that made the appointment for the salespeople. The sales manager had a hard-and-fast rule that you didn't teach salespeople about product. He was afraid they would get into conversations about air conditioners. All he wanted them to do was set up appointments. Some of them didn't even know what they were making the appointment for.

So I convinced him to let two or three of his best salespeople come in and give product demonstrations to the soliciting crew. One of the products this particular company offered was an electrostatic air purifier. They had developed a pretty dramatic demonstration for it by enclosing the thing in a Plexiglas box. Someone would light a cigarette, blow smoke into the Plexiglas box, flip on the electrostatic purifier, and the smoke would disappear in an instant. It happened to be a very good product, and was especially suited for people who had allergies to airborne particles.

When the soliciting crew saw the demonstration, it was as if magic had been done. They got excited. They wanted to see it again. And no sooner were they back on the phone than they were hammering away to discover if people had any allergy-related problems or any other problem for which the air purifier would be a solution. In the next few weeks, more electrostatic air purifiers were sold than in the previous few months. And it was done for one reason only: The salespeople believed in the product. And yet, how many product coordinators or product trainers make the presentation of the product as dull as a bucket of old mud water!

☞ *The sixth magic principle: Get a crack salesperson who believes in the product to teach it. Have him demonstrate it as if he's trying to sell it.*

Building Loyalty

While it's true that any sales manager is motivated, at least in part, by his or her own desire to make money, it certainly helps if you are motivated by a genuine desire to help others live better.

It is the ability actually to help people improve their lot in life that creates a loyalty among salespeople for a manager. I remember very well a young man named Mike. He was nineteen years old and had a terrible voice—he sounded as if he were speaking through a three-foot-long nose. He also had a seventeen-year-old, equally frightened, pregnant wife. (It was Mike I mentioned earlier whom I had forced to sign the agreement that he wouldn't fight with his wife.) I had hired him for two reasons. Number one, he really wanted and needed the job. And number two, I guess I wanted to prove to myself that I could train anyone, and he was as good a representative of "anyone" as I expected to find.

For weeks I invested a lot more of my time in him than one would have thought he was worth, but finally he began to come around. His sales began creeping up. And over the next several months, he got up to where he was making $300 to $400 a week, which for those times, and especially for him, was not all that bad. He was at least surviving.

Though it's many years since then, I believe to this day that I could call Mike up and tell him, "Mike, I want you to go stand down on the end of the Venice Pier and wait for a little green man. I don't have time to explain right now but I'll call you back later." *Click. Dial tone.* Now, Mike might think that I had fused a circuit board, but he would know that at the bottom of everything, he owes me one. I picked him up when he was down and helped him survive better.

Good managers can really do that. In reality, most of the salespeople you hire will have been failures somewhere else. Had they not failed elsewhere, perhaps even had high-level failure, they probably wouldn't be knocking on your door. And it is out of these failures that a great manager can build spectacular successes.

My hope for you as a manager is that you will help. Sales can be a wonderful and rewarding career. With help, many more can succeed than do.

Thankyouverymuch.

Index

A-B-C callback file system, *see* file system
advertising, 29, 50
    classified, 10, 25, 70, 83, 290
    newspaper, 10, 25, 31, 43, 70, 83, 290
    slogans, 54, 139
    television, 29
American Express, 29
American Skandia, 229, 233
appointments, 38
    confirmation of, 33–34, 104, 109, 110
    face-to-face, 167
    mystery, 168–69
    phone-only scripts for, 127, 183–92
    prequalified, 118, 167
    rules for, 33–34, 109
    setting up of, 21, 33–34, 73, 109,
        118–20, 167–69, 177–96, 202,
        203–4, 285–86
    telephone, 118–20, 124, 207
    timing of, 33–34
AT&T, 139, 145
automobile insurance, 9
automobile sales, 9, 18, 29, 83, 130–31

banking, 9, 78
Bank of America, 171
bankruptcy, 9
Barron's Business and Financial Weekly,
    222
Bartlett's Familiar Quotations, 15, 74
Basic Skills Checklist, 283–86
best practices lists, 64
Big Book, 71
Big Yellow, 71
Bill Good Marketing, Inc., 9, 11, 25–28,
    51, 126, 291
Bill Good Marketing System, 151, 229
    see also training seminars, author's
birth announcements, 80
books, 9–10, 11–12, 20
branch managers, 18, 64, 90, 275–76, 303
brochures, 126, 219, 222, 229

business cards, 169–70, 210
businesses:
    buying and selling of, 9, 82
    classification of, 62
    closing of, 9
    creation of, 9
    expansion and contraction of, 9
    lists of, 62, 64, 66–72
    needs of, 8, 9
    publications of, 11, 77–79, 81, 82
    see also corporations
    Business Week, 81

California, University of, at Los Angeles
    (UCLA), 230
Caller ID, 59
Call Sheets, 269–70, 271–72, 279
    Daily Stats Worksheet, 271
    Daily/Weekly Report, 272, 273, 293
Campaign Development Checklist, 51–55
    checking off steps on, 51, 53
    sample of, 52–53
    step-by-step process of, 49, 50–51, 55,
        122, 144, 281–83
campaigns, 43–54
    adjustment and change of, 43, 45, 46,
        47–48, 51, 279–86
    definition of, 43
    designing of, 11, 44–45, 49
    development of, 44, 45, 49–54, 62,
        129
    ditching of, 46, 47, 51
    dominance of, 43, 50–51
    evaluation of, 45–47, 51
    failure of, 37, 45, 46–48, 307
    focus of, 128
    four basic mistakes in, 46–48, 51
    importance of sound in, *see* vocal
        delivery
    low-key, 32, 36, 41, 87, 89, 125–26,
        198, 201–8, 210
    messages of, 45, 60, 133, 282

campaigns (*cont.*)
  no-key, 89, 91
  numbers considerations in, 45, 47, 61
  objectives of, 44, 52, 116–21, 122, 123,
    281
  offers made in, *see* offers
  producing predictable results in, 43,
    51
  profitability of, 37, 43, 45–46, 51, 127
  reevaluation of, 279–86
  repeating steps of, 43
  requests for orders in, 37
  scripts for, *see* scripts
  staying with, 47–48, 278–79
  styles of, 44, 52, 122–27, 146, 282
  summary on, 48
  testing of, 46, 62, 131, 277–78
  variables in, *see* variables
  weekly objectives in, 73, 272, 273, 293
  written proposals in, 37
  see also specific campaigns
Capples, John, 221, 223
cards:
  business, 169–70, 210
  business-reply, 231
  cue, 291–92
  lead, 294, 301–3
  "magic," 301–2
  see also Prospect Record Cards
cassette tapes, 17, 25–27, 28, 154, 299,
    303
casualty insurance, 66
CDs, 61, 66, 69–70
Chamber of Commerce Directory, 28
change-of-address notices lists, 81–82
Change Principle, 61, 75–85, 91
  corporate market and, 77–79
  examples of, 75, 76–77
  individual daytime market and, 77,
    81–82
  individual markets and, 77, 79–84
  individual nighttime market and, 77,
    82–84
checklists, 51
  see also specific checklists
cherries, 34–35, 41, 90
  callbacks to, 119, 167, 169–83
  clarification of, 34–35
  definitions of, 32, 34, 118
  finding of, 57, 58, 149
  grading of, 34, 93
  letters to, 212, 215
  lists yielding generation of, 57–58,
    59–61, 210, 250

  qualification of, 34–35, 52, 99, 119, 154
  requalification of, 37, 109, 118–19,
    167, 179, 195, 202, 215
  rules for, 35
  sending information to, 33, 34, 35, 118,
    126, 149, 167, 169–70, 171, 202,
    212
  setting up appointments with, 167–69,
    177–92, 285–86
  track of, 35, 99, 105, 108, 109, 110–11
Cherry Callback Scripts, 169–83
  after the close in, 180, 183
  Bridge to Questionnaire in, 173–74,
    180, 181–82, 183
  close in, 177–81, 183, 286
  form for, 182–83
  intro and bypass in, 170–71, 180, 181,
    182
  questionnaire in, 174–77, 180–81, 183
  samples of, 180–82
  selling salespersons and companies in,
    171–73, 180, 181, 182–83
cherry picking, 32–42, 250
  don't-care attitude and, 40–41
  method of, 41
  as way of life, 42
chimney cleaning, 10
Christian Science Monitor, 43
churches, new members for, 10
civil rights movement, 18
classified ads, 10, 290
  electronic, 83
  phone numbers in, 25, 83
clients, 64
  lists of, 92, 96, 99, 108–9
  mailing to, 99, 215
  new, 108–9, 114, 126, 197, 215
Coca-Cola, 29
cold calls, 30, 69, 87, 300
  aversion to, 75
  definition of, 18
  humor in, 68
  lists for, 85, 94, 256
  Old School style of, 18–20
  response to, 19–20
  service approach to, 90–91
  starting campaigns with, 87
  time spent on, 18, 116
Coldwell Banker, 88
color printing, 126
Commerce Department, U.S., 62
commercial real estate, 9, 60
  lists for, 29, 67, 82
  making offers in, 151, 153, 164

qualifying prospects for, 34, 155, 164–65
scripts for, 151, 153, 164–65
commissions, 12, 43, 294, 305
common law system, 66
computer-based marketing system, 151, 154, 156, 165–66
computer operators (COs), 74, 95, 101, 103–4, 253, 304
salespersons vs., 93–94, 96, 117
Computer Operator's Cheatsheet, 99, 102, 103, 107–10, 212
computers, 50
see also computer operators; personal computers
computer sales, 8, 35, 64, 128, 129
concept, 140–41
see also products
condo developments, 65
Connection Principle, 86–91
connections, 86–91
business, 86, 88
creating new perceptions with, 87, 88–90
delaying use of, 87, 88
family, 86, 87–88, 141
industries built on, 86–87
mailing to, 89, 90
personal and educational, 88
reluctant use of, 86, 87
service approach to, 90–91, 141
social, 86, 87–88, 141
telephone calls to, 90–91
core lists, 61–67
adding names to, 63–65
business sources for, 62, 64
development of, 61–62
improvement of, 62, 63–65
likely prospects for, 61–62, 64–67
residential sources for, 62, 65
corporations, 55, 60, 69
"best practices" shared by, 64
change and promotions in, 77–79, 80, 81–82
chief legal counsels of, 64
decision makers at, 157–66, 192–96, 208, 258–60
Fortune 500, 81
home pages of, 21, 64, 71, 72, 78
house organs or newsletters of, 77–78, 80, 81
information about, 67, 71, 72
marketing expenditures of, 44, 167
profiles of, 67, 70, 72, 80

publicly traded, 67
public relations and press releases of, 78–79, 89
TV ads of, 29
see also businesses
county courthouses, 80, 85
coupons, 227–28, 231–33
Creating a New Direct-Mail Letter Checklist, 53, 234–35
credit cards, 10, 70, 78
credit collection account sales, 9
Current Lead Processing Letters, 210, 211, 214–17

Daily Stats Worksheet, 271
Daily/Weekly Report, 272, 273, 293
Dean Witter, 31
death notices, 80, 84
Death of a Salesman (Miller), 305
Dejanews.com, 71
demographics, 62, 92, 302
dentistry, 9
Direct-Mail Letter Checklist, 238–40
direct-mail letters, 7, 80, 209–40
checklists for, 53, 233, 234–35, 238–40
computer processing of, 21, 89, 104, 114
downloading and printing of, 33, 36, 212, 223, 229
examples of, 33, 36, 89
follow-up to, 36, 37, 38, 90, 124–25
frequency of contact by, 111, 112
including résumés in, 217–19
Information Request form in, 227–28, 231–33
mailing of, 78, 89, 90, 236–40
offers included in, 44, 131
previous, 223, 230
prize-winning, 229
standard, 126–27, 132
techniques of, 9, 89
testing of, 62
volume of, 282
writing and rewriting of, 53, 220, 222–23
see also Lead Generation Letters; Lead Processing Letters; *specific mail campaigns*
Directory of Directories, 62, 68
divorce records, 80, 82
Dodge Reports, The, 82
dripping, 103
basic, 201–2
definitions of, 95, 111, 125

dripping (*cont.*)
    letter, 95, 104, 111, 114, 125–26, 132,
        209, 220
    mini-profile, 202–4
    samples of, 202–8
    scripts for, 197–98, 201–8
    telephone, 95, 111, 114, 125–26, 197,
        201–8
    upgrade, 204–5
    voice-mail, 202–8
Dun's Million Dollar Directory, 67

Edwards, J. Douglas, 17, 19–20
E. F. Hutton, 31, 64, 139
Electric Library, 72, 79, 81, 230
e-mail, 7, 21, 79, 209
Employee Relocation Council, 9
employment agencies, 80
    temporary, 10, 125
empty nest syndrome, 66
Encyclopedia of Associations, 62, 68, 69,
    78
envelopes:
    addressing of, 89, 236–37
    business reply, 125, 126, 231
    stamping of, 78, 90, 238
estate planning, 66
executive placement agencies, 10, 80
expendable supply items, 29

false cherries, 35, 37–38, 179
Farmers Insurance, 31, 64
faxes, 7, 21, 34, 209
Feature/Benefit Format, 223
file system, 94, 104–14
    categorical principles of, 110, 111, 112,
        113, 114
    cheatsheets for, 105, 107–14, 115
    cross-referencing in, 101
    date-ordering of, 94, 104, 197
    dividers in, 104, 115
    management of, 197–208, 210
    names used in, 212–17
    organization of, 34–38, 104–7, 211–17
    priorities in, 104
    use of color in, 104, 106, 107, 110, 115
financial advisers, 9, 15, 17, 76, 81, 116,
    138–39
financial services, 9, 11, 18–20, 60, 62, 64,
    76, 78, 81, 93, 107, 116, 148–49,
    153, 155, 163–64, 172, 175, 217–19
fire insurance, 66
First-Call Appointment Script
    Development Form, 191–92

First-Call Appointment Scripts, 183–92
    after the close in, 188, 189, 190, 191,
        192
    close in, 188–89, 190–91, 195
    interest building/qualification ques-
        tions in, 187–88
    intro in, 184, 188, 189, 190, 191
    leading questions in, 186–87, 188
    questionnaire in, 191
    reason for call in, 184–86, 188, 190,
        191
    samples of, 188–91
fishing, 63, 64
flyers, 17, 43
For Sale By Owner (FSBO), 83
Fortune 500 corporations, 81
fraternities, 88
funeral services, prepaid, 10
furniture, 10, 78

general agents (GAs), 86
General Motors (GM), 176
Godfather, The, 128
gold prospecting:
    discarding waste product in, 24, 42, 57
    extracting gold from ore in, 57
    risk taking and, 28–29
    staking of claims in, 28–29, 56, 58
    yields from, 28–29, 57
Good, Francis Williamson, 92
Good Filing Principle Cheatsheet, 105, 107
Good News Letter Format, 223–28
Good Prospecting Cards, 52
    see also Prospect Record Cards
green cherries, 35–36, 41, 75
    callbacks of, 198–99
    clarification of, 35
    definition of, 32, 35
    grading of, 35, 93
    letters to, 213, 214–15, 216
    low-key contacts with, 32, 36, 198, 210
    qualification of, 154
    requalification of, 35, 37, 99, 109, 179,
        196, 216
    track of, 36, 105, 108, 109, 111
Greensboro Daily News, 23
Greyhound Breeders Association direc-
    tory, 68
Guaranteed Good List, 59
Guinness Book of Records, 10

Harvard University, 138
heirs, 84
Here's the Info Format, 223

highlighters, 35, 36, 169–70, 210–11
high tech companies, 60
hobby clubs, 65, 68
homes, *see* residential real estate
Hoover Profiles, 72
hot prospects, 33–34, 41
    definitions of, 32, 33, 92, 118
    drip techniques with, 202, 203–4, 210
    measuring "heat" of, 118–20
    requalifying of, 35, 171, 198
    rules for, 33–34
    sources of, 33, 171
    track of, 33–34, 92, 105
    house organs, 77–78, 80, 81

Identify the Decision Maker Worksheet,
    162
info leads, 36–37, 41, 75, 93, 99, 210
    clarification of, 36–37
    definition of, 32, 36
    grading of, 93, 199
    letters to, 213–15, 216
    requalification of, 109, 179, 196,
        200–201
    rules for, 37
    track of, 37, 105, 108, 109, 112
information:
    change of product, 184–86
    mailing of, 7, 21, 28, 30, 32–37, 89,
        118, 149
    major free sources of, 58, 59, 65–67
    marking up and highlighting of, 35, 36,
        169–70, 210–11
    new product, 184–86
    public record, 65–67, 80, 82, 84
    request forms for, 227–28, 231–33
    on videotape, 126
Information Request, 227–28, 231–33
insurance agents, 60, 79, 85, 86–87
insurance industry, 10, 11, 17, 18, 29,
    60, 79
    prospect lists for, 29, 64, 66
    soliciting referrals from, 85, 86
    telephone questionnaires for, 176,
        181–82
    using connections in, 86–87
    see also specific insurance categories
Interest Table, 106, 107
Internet:
    corporate home pages on, 21, 64, 71,
        72, 78
    list-building resources on, 61, 71–72
    newsgroups on, 71
    search engines on, 66, 71

jerks, 32, 38, 39–40, 41, 59, 93
    clarification of, 39–40
    definition of, 39
    discarding of, 75, 114
    rules for, 40, 97
    track of, 40, 109
Journal of Record, 82
"Journey, The," 229

Kennel Club directories, 68

Labor Statistics Bureau, U.S., 80
lawyers, 59, 64, 82, 88
Lead Generation Letters, 220–35
    formats of, 222, 223–28, 237
    headlines of, 221, 230–31
    including coupons in, 231–33
    Lead Processing Letters vs., 220
    length of, 220–21, 229
    rules of, 220–22
Lead Generation Scripts, 144–96
    definitions of, 144, 167
    see also scripts; *specific telephone cam-*
        paigns
Lead Processing Letter Guidelines, 52
Lead Processing Letters, 99, 132,
    209–19
    examples of, 212–17
    Lead Generation Letters vs., 220
    Mutilation Principle and, 35, 36,
        169–70, 210–11
    rewriting and adapting of, 52, 210, 211
    see also Current Lead Processing
        Letters; New Lead Processing
        Letters
Lead Processing Scripts, 105, 123, 132,
    144, 197–208
    definition of, 167
    drip, 197, 201–8
    examples of, 202–8
    follow-up, 197, 198–99
lead tracking system, 33–41, 52
legal settlements, 82
Letter Format, 227
Letterman, Elmer, 286
Letter Printing Checklist, 235
librarians, 68, 78
libraries:
    business desks of, 68
    corporate information in, 78
    sources for lists in, 57, 61, 67–70,
        78, 82
licenses, 66, 82
liens, 82

life change lists, 79–80
life insurance, 9, 16, 17, 20, 30, 34, 35
Ling, Mona, 17
list brokers, 61, 62, 66, 70–71, 73, 80, 81, 95, 96
list development, 12, 28, 52, 55–91
    Change Principle and, 61, 75-85, 91
    improvement principles in, 55, 63–64, 74, 75–91, 285
    purpose of, 56–58
    resources for, 57, 61, 62, 65–72
    selection principles in, 61–65, 68, 71, 73
    three steps of, 55–56
    time and expense of, 58, 75, 85
    tips on, 85
    using nonoptimum time for, 57
List Evaluation Sheets, 94, 96, 98–99, 253–54
    attaching name lists to, 95, 96, 253, 254, 256
    making notes on, 256, 257–58
    recording activity on, 99, 253
    samples of, 98, 254
list management, 74, 92–115, 197–208
    cheatsheets for, 99, 102, 103, 105, 107–14
    computers and, 93–95, 99, 197
    definitions of, 92–93
    mass mail list, 95–99, 109, 110
    prospect list, 99–114
    rules of, 94–95
    see also specific lists
list replacement, 74–91, 97
    change lists for, 75–85
    connections lists for, 75, 86–91
    referral lists for, 75, 85–86
    three major sources of, 75, 91
    time involved in, 75, 85
Look-Alike Principle, 61–62, 63–64, 68, 71, 73, 77
Los Angeles City Library, 78
Los Angeles Times, 31, 290

McDonald's, 29
McGraw-Hill, 81, 82
magazines, 289
    ads in, 43, 289
    product articles in, 72, 89, 90
    subscribers to, 70, 231
mail, 7, 30, 34, 41, 67, 209–40
    see also direct-mail letters; mass mail lists; *specific mail campaigns*

mailing labels, 89, 90
mail/phone-style campaigns, 119, 124–25, 132, 167, 229
    follow-up calls in, 192–96
    prospecting letters for, 209–40
    scripts for, 192–96
manners, 40, 210
marketing:
    corporate spending on, 44, 167
    direct-response, 47, 48, 56, 221, 280
    mass, 29
    multilevel, 168
    prospecting as branch of, 39
MarketPlace, 62, 64, 70
MarketPlace Information Corp., 70
markets:
    business and corporate, 62, 77–79, 144, 156–66
    daytime, 77, 81–82
    domination of, 31, 74
    identifying prospects in, 8–10, 12, 62
    individual, 77–84
    limited, 8, 21, 29, 31, 74
    multiple approaches to, 12, 21, 30
    nighttime, 77, 82–84
    residential, 62, 144, 147–57
    resistance level of, 60, 120, 124, 150
    size and scope of, 8, 21
marriage announcements, 80, 82
Martin, Judith, 150
mass mail lists, 74, 92
    on database, 94, 95–96, 99
    management of, 95–99, 109, 110, 210
Mergenhagen, Paula, 79, 80
Merrill Lynch, 87–88, 171
microfiche records, 66
Microsoft.com, 71
millionaires, 67
money:
    availability of, 17, 21–22, 34, 35, 36, 57
    earning of, 7, 48, 128, 138–39, 291, 304
    lists and, 57, 60, 66, 67, 68, 82, 83–84
    pension fund, 60
    questioning prospects about, 34, 35, 45, 149, 155, 156, 174–76, 284
    return on, 15, 22
    saving of, 57
Monster Rabbit University letter, 47, 223
MS Word formats, 33, 96, 105, 227, 239
Multiple Listing Book, 83–84
Mutilation Principle, 35, 36, 169–70, 210–11
My Script Worksheet, 144–46, 149, 162

names, 147–48
   frequent use of, 150, 221
Netscape.com, 71
new-birth lists, 79, 80
new construction projects, 82
New Lead Processing Letters, 210,
      211–14
New School selling style, 21–40
   acceptance of negative responses in,
      22, 24, 26–27, 30–31, 42, 50
   Old School selling system vs., 21–22,
      24, 31–32, 38, 210
   persistence and, 30, 31–32, 90, 278–79
   principles of, 25–40
   two basic assumptions of, 21–22
NewsHound, 78–79, 81
newsletters, 77–78
newspapers, 72
   advertising in, 10, 25, 31, 43, 83, 290
   business pages in, 82
   daily, 81, 82, 83
   obituary notices in, 80, 84
   shopper, 81
   subscriptions to, 10
Newton, Isaac, 75–76
No Calls, 35, 37, 93
   filing of, 105, 115, 217
   letters to, 105, 110, 217
notebooks, 96, 97, 99

offers, 53
   changes in, 282
   concept approach to, 140, 141
   definitions of, 44, 128, 140, 145
   features vs. benefits in, 128–31, 145
   product approach in, 140–42
   scripting of, 44, 140–42, 145–46, 149,
      150–51
   service approach to, 140, 141, 142
   strength of, 52, 120
office equipment, 9, 78
"old boy" network, 8
Old School selling style, 17–22
   New School selling style vs., 21–22,
      24, 31–32, 38, 210
   persistence and, 19–20, 21, 24, 31
   principles of, 17, 18–20, 21–22, 56,
      177, 210, 269, 286
   rejection factor in, 116, 269
   training in, 17, 18, 19–20, 24, 177
   warlike beliefs of, 18
Olsen, Jill, 27–28
organizations:
   business and trade, 64, 69, 78, 88

hobby, 65
   lists of, 62, 64, 69
   membership directories of, 10, 62, 63,
      65, 68, 69

PaineWebber, 31
peddlers, 20
pension funds, 60
permits, 66, 82
personal computers:
   laptop, 128, 129
   letter processing with, 21, 89, 104, 114
   list management on, 93–95, 99, 197
   mass mail lists and, 94, 95–96, 99
   misuse of, 93–94
   record keeping with, 40, 50, 89, 92,
      93–94, 114
Persuasive Voice Mail, 162, 206, 207–8
phone/mail/phone-style campaigns, 72,
      119, 123–24, 126, 131
   first calls in, 124, 149–66, 278
   letters in, 209–40
   scripts for, 143–83, 277
   second calls in, 124, 149, 169–83,
      285–86
phone-only campaign scripts, 127, 183–92
photocopying, 10
pitch and miss, 37–38, 41, 93
   clarification of, 37–38
   definition of, 37
   letters to, 119, 210, 217
   rules for, 38
   track of, 38, 105, 110, 112–13
pits, 32, 38–39, 41, 57, 90
   clarification of, 38
   definitions of, 38, 143
   elimination of, 58, 152
   polishing of, 38, 152
   rules for, 39, 57, 97
   track of, 39
Polk's directories, 67
postage stamps, 78, 90, 238
Postal Service, U.S., 65
PR Newswire, 79
products:
   affordability of, 11, 16, 45, 145
   belief in, 11, 305–6
   benefits of, 36, 50, 53, 128–29, 130–31,
      145, 225, 284, 287
   creating interest in, 30–31, 36, 50,
      129–30
   definition of, 140
   demonstrations of, 306
   desire for, 50

products (*cont.*)
    features of, 36, 129–31, 145
    free offers for, 43, 45
    need for, 11, 31, 130, 145
    offers geared to, 140–42
    placement of orders for, 30
    prices of, 21, 60, 184
    recognition/familiarity factor and, 29,
        30, 120, 149, 150
    salesperson's knowledge of, 16, 29, 30,
        305–6
property insurance, 66
property tax records, 66–67
Prospect Definitions Cheatsheet, 33
Prospect Food Chain, 32–40, 92–93, 209
    see also cherries; green cherries; hot
        prospects; info leads; jerks; pitch
        and miss; pits
prospecting:
    attitude and, 41–42, 93, 251, 302–3
    aversion to, 7, 8, 12, 16, 20, 116
    campaign driven process of, 43, 50–51
    definitions of, 24, 49
    enjoyment of, 7, 8, 13, 42, 59
    financial factors in, 116–17
    gold, 24, 28–29, 42, 56, 57, 58
    group factor in, 39, 279
    hard work of, 13, 47
    hiring out and delegating portions of,
        85, 94, 117, 124–25, 303
    importance of discarding in, 49, 74–75,
        286
    important questions about, 45–46
    mistakes and waste in, 8, 11–12, 19–20,
        46–48, 51, 56, 85, 86, 93–94, 116,
        154
    problems of, 116–17
    risk taking and, 28–29
    selling vs., 50, 116–18, 124–25, 286
    tools of, 7, 21
    work habits and, 276–77, 278–79
prospect lists:
    adding names to, *see* list replacement
    basic laws of, 58
    business, 62, 64, 86, 88
    buying of, 44, 52, 55, 58, 69, 70, 81–82
    as campaign variables, 43, 44, 45
    common characteristics of individuals
        on, 58–59, 61–62, 63–64, 68, 71,
        73, 77
    concentration of cherries in, 57–58, 74
    core, 61–67
    creative thought on, 58
    on database, 40, 93–95, 99, 197

development of, *see* list development
evaluation of, 94, 96–99
generation of cherries from, 59–61, 62,
    74, 97
"good," 58–61, 72, 97, 302–3
improvement of, 55, 63–64, 74, 75–91
keeping names on, 32, 37, 38–39, 41
management of, *see* list management
mixing of, 97
money characteristics of, 57, 60, 66, 67,
    68, 82, 83–84
occupational characteristics of, 67, 69
profitability of, 39, 60, 73, 91
recycling of, 28–32, 56, 75, 97, 257–58
refreshment of, 56, 61, 97
removing names from, 37, 40, 74–75,
    90
residential, 57, 62, 65
responsiveness of, 44, 45–46, 65, 97
sources of, 28, 57, 61, 62, 65–72, 78
switching of, 57, 281
testing of, 44, 277–78, 279, 299
upgrading of, 278
volume of names on, 8, 21, 61, 72–73,
    74, 90
word of mouth possibilities in, 31, 61,
    63, 64, 65, 71
see also mass mail lists
Prospect Record Cards, 99–104, 107, 114,
    253–54
    affixing labels to, 74, 96, 99, 115, 253
    checking off options on, 96, 103, 106
    design of, 96, 104
    filing system for, 94, 104–14
    management of, 197
    sample of, 100–101
    showing changes of interest on,
        101–3
    starting of, 74
prospects:
    abundance vs. scarcity of, 8, 16–17, 41,
        145
    acquaintances and friends as, 86,
        87–88, 172
    assumptions about, 17–18, 21–22, 34,
        147–48, 150
    demographic analysis of, 62, 92, 302
    discarding of, 22, 24–25, 26–27, 37, 40,
        49, 74–75, 286
    grading of, 34, 35, 37, 92–93
    improving quantity and quality of, 12,
        288
    improving response from, 29–31
    interest changes of, 209–10, 211

interest of, 12, 21, 26–27, 32–37, 45,
99, 101–3, 106, 108, 110, 118–20,
149, 151–54, 197
keeping track of, 12, 34, 92–115
misclassification of, 32–33
multiple refusals from, 17, 19–20
prequalified, 21, 52, 118
qualification of, 21, 34–42, 45, 144,
154–57, 284
rejection by, 15–16, 17, 19–20, 21–22,
24–25, 26–27, 43, 152–53
requalification of, 32, 35, 36, 37, 38, 52,
101–3, 105, 109, 179, 195–96, 198,
199–201
searching for, 8, 41, 49, 74
sending information to, 7, 21, 28, 30,
32–37, 89, 118, 126, 149
subterfuge and lying by, 17–18, 21–22,
34
see also Prospect Food Chain; prospect
lists
Prospect Thermometer, 118–21
public record information, 65–67, 80, 82,
84

real estate, 11, 18, 78
fortunes made in, 67
1970s boom in, 84
onetime capital gains exclusion in, 84
value of, 29, 83–84
see also commercial real estate; residential real estate
real estate agents, 78, 80, 83–84
receptionists, 158–59, 192, 196, 257
record keeping, 44, 46–47, 50, 90
see also file system
references, checking of, 172
Referral Principle, 85–86
referrals, 33, 85–86, 212
lists of, 75, 86
promoting of, 85
soliciting of, 85, 86
Repetition Principle, 29–31
harassment and, 58, 75
Research Magazine, 11
residential real estate, 9, 80
equity in, 83–84
finding buyers and lists for, 15, 60, 66,
68, 72–73, 82–84
For Sale By Owner (FSBO), 83
qualifying prospects for, 29, 35, 77
recycling lists of prospects for, 29
résumés, 217–19
retirement, 80

Rewriting a Direct-Mail Letter checklist,
233–35

*Sale Begins When the Customer Says No,
The* (Letterman), 286
sales, selling:
closing of, 11, 16, 17, 21, 287
competition for, 16, 37, 58, 60, 120, 279
definitions of, 50, 286
door-to-door, 11–12, 20, 23
hunter/skinner partnerships in, 117
improvement in, 12, 279
as "numbers game," 12, 45, 96, 250–51,
268–69
overcoming objections to, 17, 18, 22,
287
prospecting vs., 50, 116–18, 124–25,
286
skills of, 286–87
starting the process of, 33
three steps to success in, 11
sales managers, 19, 25, 58, 73, 134, 269,
289–307
building of loyalty by, 306–7
contests created by, 300–301
expectations of, 18, 77, 275
hiring of sales-persons by, 297–98,
305
interviews with, 274–75
"magic" factor and, 299–306
motivation of sales crew by, 298–306
observation and creative thinking of,
290–92
staying in touch with sales crew by,
292–97
style vs. substance in, 290
training programs of, 19, 290, 305
sales meetings, 20
sales organizations, 20, 78
salespersons:
bad days of, 295–96, 303
breakout plan for, 275–87
communication with, 30, 31, 87
computer operators vs., 93–94, 96, 117
discouragement of, 20, 276
four basic mistakes of, 46–48, 51
high-pressure tactics of, 30, 31, 247
income of, 7, 48, 128, 138–39, 291, 304
motivation of, 298–306
optimal time use by, 57–58, 85, 93–94,
117, 121
personal problems of, 295–97
product knowledge of, 16, 29, 30,
305–6

salespersons (*cont.*)
 prospecting vs. selling by, 50, 116–18, 124–25, 286
 as role-models, 305
 sales management relations of, *see* sales managers
 selling of self by, 171–72
 "star," 10–11, 19, 121, 305
Salesperson's File System Cheatsheet, 107, 110–14, 212
sales trainers, 12, 17, 18, 19–20, 24, 40, 177
 see also training seminars
Salt Lake Tribune, 25
San Jose Mercury News, 78–79
screeners, 12, 125, 158, 192, 196, 259
 methods of dealing with, 261–68
 rules with, 260–61
scripts, 81, 97, 111–14, 125–26, 132–208
 analysis of, 283–84
 asking direct questions in, 143, 146–47, 149, 151–54, 155, 156–57, 170, 174–77, 186–88, 266–67
 changing of, 62, 97, 141
 covering important points in, 135
 definition of, 133
 delivery of, 45, 134–36, 241–49
 determining authority to buy in, 147–49, 157–66
 development of, 132, 139–208
 direct mail, *see* Lead Generating Letters; Lead Processing Letters
 establishing controls in, 147, 160
 examples of, 144, 146, 149–57, 158–66
 fallback sections of, 152–54, 182
 first-call, 124, 149–66, 183–92
 gender and salutations in, 147–49, 150
 inclusion of offers in, 44, 140–42, 145–46, 149, 150–51, 162
 introductions in, 147–50
 messages of, 45, 133, 135
 mixing and matching parts of, 182
 pros and cons of, 133–39, 252
 qualification, 154–57
 recording and practicing of, 136, 241, 247, 249
 rules of, 146–47
 sample, 163–66
 second-call, 124, 149, 169–83, 192–96, 211
 standard wrap-up in, 156–57
 telephone, 111–14, 124, 125–26, 127, 143–208
 testing of, 277–78
 writing and rewriting of, 27, 53, 143–208, 277
 see also Lead Generation Scripts; Lead Processing Scripts
Search.com, 71
Second-Call Appointment Script, 187
Second-Call Appointment Script Development Form, 182–83
securities industry, 11, 29, 34, 60, 81, 82, 89, 90, 140–41, 151, 298
Securities Industry Association, 11, 149
Select Phone, 62, 65, 69–70, 80, 83
services, 140–41
 see also products
shopper newspapers, 81
SIC (Standard Industrial Classification), 62, 64, 70
software products, 69
Sony, 78
Southern California Retailer, 78
Southwest Publishing Company, 11
stage fright, 11, 242
Standard Industrial Classification (SIC), 62, 64, 70
Standard Rate and Data: Direct Mail Lists, 70
sticky notes, 35, 211
stockbrokers, 9, 18, 60, 62, 69, 81, 87–88, 242, 275–76
street address directories, 57, 62, 65, 66, 67, 96, 303
superstars, 10–11, 19, 121, 305

Targeting Transitions: Marketing to Consumers During Life Changes (Mergenhagen), 79, 80
tax assessor's office, 65, 66–67
taxes, 66
 homeowners onetime capital gains exclusion and, 84
tax-free bonds scripts, 151, 153, 163–64
Telephone Marketing Association, 291
telephone numbers:
 dialing speed and, 254–56, 279, 284–85
 gender and listings of, 147–48
 "important," 270
 requesting of, 35
 unlisted, 67, 68–69, 83
telephone-prospecting campaigns:
 business to business, 81–82, 192–94
 business to residence, 194–96
 connections and, 90–91

delegating portions of, 124–25
designing of, 12
focus in, 252
follow up calls in, 20, 23, 26, 35, 36, 38, 41, 72, 90, 125
frequency principles in, 111, 112, 113, 114
geometric vs. arithmetic progression in, 250–51, 252
humor in, 68, 136
in-coming calls in, 7, 23, 43, 89
keeping track of calls in, 268–72
leaving messages in, 258–60, 265–66; *see also* voice mail
maintaining contact in, *see* dripping, telephone
markets suitable for, 8–10
negative responses to, 15, 16, 19–20, 22, 24–25, 30, 37
objectives of, 111, 112, 113
recording of calls in, 299, 303, 305
scripts for, 111–14, 124, 125–26, 127, 143–208
testing of, 27–28
timing of, 60, 72, 73, 123
using optimum time for, 57–58
volume of calls in, 12, 20–21, 45, 56, 60–61, 62, 72–73, 250–73, 277, 282
see also cold calls; *specific telephone campaigns*
telephones:
allowing four rings on, 257
headsets for, 253
holding on, 12, 68, 257
inline taps on, 299
new connections of, 80
refusal to take or return calls on, *see* No Calls
sound and skills on, *see* vocal delivery
television, 11, 29
Tested Advertising Methods (Capples), 221, 223
time management studies, 116
title insurance, 82
trade associations, 64, 69, 78, 88
trade publications, 11, 77, 78, 81, 82

training seminars, 66, 125, 138–39
author's, 23–24, 25–26, 31, 35, 36, 56–57, 64, 86, 133–34, 145, 172
in-house, 31, 56–57, 145
public, 25–26
recycling of prospect lists for, 29
selling of, 25–29, 31, 125, 142, 172
telephone sessions in, 56–57

unlisted phone numbers, 67, 68–69, 83
Usenet, 71

variables, 43–45, 49, 50–51
changing of, 43, 46, 48, 122, 280–83
control of, 43, 45, 46, 48, 280
definitions of, 43, 46, 122, 280
reevaluation of, 280–83
videotapes, 20, 126
vocal delivery, 45, 241–49
"canned pitch" in, 134, 242, 285
emphasis in, 242, 246–47
enthusiasm in, 242, 247–49, 285
first impressions and, 242, 282–83
inflections in, 242–45, 285
pacing of, 242, 245–46, 285
speed of, 242, 247, 285
voice mail, 12, 59, 158
drip techniques and, 202–8
greetings on, 206
informative, 206–7
leaving messages on, 161–62, 193, 196, 201–8
persuasive, 162, 206, 207–8
rules with, 161, 270–73

Wall Street Journal, 11
White Pages, 278
on CD, 69–70
wills, probate of, 82, 84
Word-of-Mouth Principle, 31, 61, 63, 64, 65, 71
Working Press of the Nation, volume 5, 78
World Wide Web, 241

Yellow Pages, 58, 69, 78, 280–81
online, 71–72

zip codes, 80